Other Books by Ruth A. Tucker

HOW TO SET UP YOUR OWN NEIGHBORHOOD PRESCHOOL
(with Kit Bernthal)

FROM JERUSALEM TO IRIAN JAYA: *A Biographical History of Christian Missions*

DAUGHTERS OF THE CHURCH: *A History of Women and Ministry from New Testament Times to the Present*
(with Walter Liefeld)

FIRST LADIES OF THE PARISH: *Historical Portraits of Pastors' Wives*
(reprinted as *Private Lives of Pastors' Wives*)

GUARDIANS OF THE GREAT COMMISSION:
The Story of Women in Modern Missions

CHRISTIAN SPEAKERS TREASURY

ANOTHER GOSPEL: *Cults, Alternative Religions and the New Age Movement*

STORIES OF FAITH:
Inspirational Episodes from the Lives of Christians

WOMEN IN THE MAZE: *Questions and Answers on Biblical Equality*

MULTIPLE CHOICES: *Making Wise Decisions in a Complicated World*

THE FAMILY ALBUM: *Portraits of Family Life Through the Centuries*

SEASONS OF MOTHERHOOD

NOT ASHAMED: *The Story of Jews for Jesus*

WALKING AWAY
from Faith

UNRAVELING

THE MYSTERY

OF BELIEF

& UNBELIEF

Ruth
A. Tucker

InterVarsity Press

Downers Grove, Illinois

To
Alan and Virginia Neely
for friendship and love and laughter
and for making so enjoyable
our unending quest
to unravel the mysteries of life

InterVarsity Press
P.O. Box 1400, Downers Grove, IL 60515-1426
World Wide Web: www.ivpress.com
E-mail: mail@ivpress.com

Scripture quotations, unless otherwise noted, are from the New Revised Standard Version of the Bible,
*copyright 1989 by the Division of Christian Education of the National Council of the Churches of
Christ in the USA. Used by permission. All rights reserved.*

Cover photograph: Alan Ross/Stone

ISBN 0-8308-2332-8

Printed in the United States of America ∞

Library of Congress Cataloging-in-Publication Data

Tucker, Ruth, 1945-
    Walking away from faith: unraveling the mystery of belief and unbelief / Ruth A. Tucker.
        p. cm.
    Includes bibliographical references.
    ISBN 0-8308-2332-8 (cloth: alk. paper)
        1. Faith. 2. Belief and doubt. 3. Ex-church members. I. Title
    BV4637 .T83 2002
234'.23—dc21

                                                                                    2001051942

P	17	16	15	14	13	12	11	10	9	8	7	6	5	4	3	2	1
Y	15	14	13	12	11	10	09	08	07	06	05	04	03	02			

Contents

Preface 7

PART ONE ———————————————————————————————

1 "Lord, I Believe; Help My Unbelief"........................... 15

2 A Tale of Two Evangelists 29
   Billy Graham & Chuck Templeton

3 The Smith Family 43
   A Case Study in Doubt & Unbelief

4 Knowing God... 54
   Mystery or Matter of Fact?

5 The Dark Night of the Soul.................................. 67
   The Fine Line Between Belief & Unbelief

PART TWO ———————————————————————————————

6 Biblical & Historical Reflections of Doubt & Unbelief.............. 81

7 The Challenge of Science & Philosophy......................... 98

8 The Challenge of Theological Complexities
   & Biblical Criticism... 117

9 The Challenge of Psychology & Social Issues. *134*

10 Disappointment with God & with Fellow Christians *151*

PART THREE ———————————————————————

11 The New Life of Unbelief *169*
   Seeking Happiness Outside the Family of Faith

12 Missionaries of Unbelief *183*
   The Appeal of the Message & the Messenger

13 Answering Doubt & Unbelief *196*
   Confronting the Serious Issues

14 Real Stories of Returning to Faith *209*

Postscript. *223*

Notes. *225*

Selected Bibliography. *236*

Index. *239*

Preface

"Lord, I believe; help my unbelief." These familiar words are from Mark 9:24, spoken by a man who brought his son to Jesus, asking for him to be healed from epileptic seizures. Jesus told the man that all things are possible—if he believed. The man could have simply responded with a declaration of belief, but he knew his own heart all too well. Jesus rewarded him, despite his confession of unbelief. He healed his son.

My introductory chapter is titled "I Believe; Help My Unbelief." A friend who read that chapter in its first draft indignantly asked, "What's your point? Are you trying to shock people?" I told him I wasn't—that I was being honest. But as I thought of his comments and read the draft again, I realized what I have always known: that what a writer means is not always what the reader understands. I trust that the reader will understand my struggles with faith and, at the same time, understand my sincere and honest search for God.

Where is the line that divides religious belief from unbelief? I'm not sure. All of us in our faith fall somewhere on the vast, subjective spectrum that ranges from absolute certainty to unrestrained skepticism. Some profess a confident belief in God that is never questioned; others cling to a belief riddled with doubts, only a millimeter shy of unbelief. Some are insecure in their unbelief, while others appear to be content in their confident belief that there is no God. No matter where we find ourselves on this spectrum, we need to listen to the voices of others and refrain from hasty judgment.

Mary Kingsley, a journalist who explored Africa in 1893 and later wrote of her findings in *Travels in West Africa,* spent time with Mary Slessor, the great pioneering Presbyterian missionary to Calabar. Of Slessor, Kingsley writes, "She gave me some of the pleasantest days of my life." They talked for hours about spiritual matters, but they were speaking from two very different realms. As the visitor confessed to her missionary hostess, "I would give anything to possess your beliefs, but I can't, I can't; when God made me He must have left out the part that one believes with."[1]

I resonate with this woman, and my heart goes out to her and to all the Mary Kingsleys of this world. For them I have no condemnation. Why is it that she and so many others like her cannot seem to believe? And why is it that others cannot seem to retain their beliefs, despite valiant efforts? I have pondered these questions for decades, and I now seek to offer some tentative responses—primarily through the voices of those who have, so to speak, *been there, done that.*

The theological issues related to belief and unbelief, and to whether an individual can walk away from faith, fill many volumes. These doctrinal riddles, however, are not the focus of this book. Rather, I seek to grapple with belief and unbelief from a human perspective, operating on the premise that there is surely the *appearance* of losing faith. This then is the paradox for those of us in the Reformed tradition who believe that a Christian's salvation is secure and cannot simply be lost or denied or abandoned. We are left in a quandary. How do we explain the one who faithfully ministers in the church for many years and then walks away from the faith? The answer, I think, is that there simply is no explanation—none that solves the problem, none that satisfies. So we tend to avoid the issue as we watch our brothers and sisters in the Lord *appear* to walk away from faith. We avoid the issue rather than *living* in the paradox.

It is through the lens of human perspective that I will deal with this topic. I cannot see through God's eyes and distinguish those who are truly sincere from those who are insincere. Nor can I know those who will in God's time kneel before the throne and confess the name of

Jesus. These matters are all in the hands of a sovereign God. But these individuals ought to have an honest hearing. As a Christian, I need to listen to their stories to better understand them and to more faithfully reach out to them in dialogue and love. Frequently, the Christian's response is characterized by anger and accusations. We are threatened by the very presence of those who have abandoned the truths that we hold dear, and I sometimes wonder whether our own insecurity is a cause for the breakdown in communication between those who believe and those who once believed.

So how do we regard those who have walked away from the faith? I was challenged with this enigma tonight as I talked with Rob and Kim in their home in Grand Rapids, fifteen minutes from where I live. I had been given Rob's name as someone I should contact—someone who had abandoned the faith. He invited me over, and I spent the evening talking with him and Kim in their living room. Both had been raised Catholic, but as young adults became "born again" believers and joined the Reformed Baptist church, where they were actively involved for more than a dozen years.

"I would have given my life for the faith," Rob recalls. "Fifteen years ago, I couldn't have imagined in my wildest dreams that I could be sitting here tonight telling you I am an atheist." But that is what he was doing. His story is like so many others I have heard and read over and over again. First there were questions—relatively minor questions—regarding apparent biblical inconsistencies. Then major questions and unresolved issues. And finally the whole system seemed to crash and crumble. The journey from fundamentalism to liberalism to agnosticism took several years. "I could never go back," says Rob. "Never."

The one thing that most impressed me during the visit was how likable and good-spirited Rob and Kim are. They are intelligent and well-read—the parents of four children, aged seven to seventeen. They communicated easily with each other and with me, and there was no reason to doubt that they had found a measure of happiness in life—happiness that Rob insisted did not characterize their life of faith. They seemed to be living an incredibly normal life. This is not the picture of a happy family life that we allow ourselves to imagine as evangelicals. What's going on here? This is the basic question I seek to answer in this book. How do we unravel this mystery of belief and unbelief?

The focus of this volume as it relates to the profile of those who walk away from faith is narrow in many respects. The most common "walk-away" is the one who is raised in a Christian home and makes a profession of faith as a young person but drifts away during adolescence or young adulthood—or perhaps later in life. There is more apathy than anger and rarely any profession of atheism or agnosticism. Indeed, when polled, such people may even say they are Christians and profess to believe in God and heaven and the importance of the Bible, but for all practical purposes, the Christian faith is not practiced in private or in community. As interesting as their stories may be, this book is not about them. Neither is this book about the youthful rebel who expounds atheistic philosophies without ever having given the Christian faith serious consideration; nor is it about the one who walks away to another denomination or cult or religion.

Rob and Kim are more representative of those featured in this volume—once strong professing Christians, now agnostics. And the focus is primarily on the North American scene, and more specifically, on those of European descent—though not by design. If there are significant testimonies of African or African American or Hispanic "walk-aways" who now profess atheism, I have inadvertently missed them.

One thing that I have discovered as I have been working on this project is that for many people, this issue touches a raw nerve. For some the very idea of someone's walking away from faith is highly offensive and threatening. For others it is bewildering and sad. Recently I was with a friend as he met his daughter at the airport. After we were introduced, he told her about a lecture we had just attended on this very subject of walking away from faith. Her comment was "I can't understand how anyone could ever do that." I do understand. In fact, apart from God's sovereign grace, I sometimes cannot imagine how anyone could keep on believing. As for myself, despite the ever-present unbelief, I have a sense of security that utterly assures me that I could never walk away. I cannot explain it. It is a mystery to me that belief and unbelief exist in ever-present tension in my life—an affliction, perhaps, but an affliction that spurs me on and never lets me relax in my spiritual pilgrimage.

Most of the time I do not delve deep inside myself to try to unlock this mystery. But I was pushed to do so recently when I read a publisher-solicited review of this manuscript in its nearly finished form. The reviewer had some thoughtful and penetrating observations:

> Reading between the lines, I came to the conclusion that Tucker held herself back to a significant degree. And my sense was that in her heart she was inclined to more fully explore these kinds of questions. . . . Tucker is in a sense taking issue with Evangelical theology at a profound and deep level. . . . There were moments when I wondered if Tucker was simply too restrained in her effort because of the extreme amount of energy it took to be subtle and cautious. . . . Tucker has a deep awareness that what she is exploring is in fact a powder keg issue. . . . However, I believe that she is so conscious of the "shocking" nature of her material that she does not go far enough in her explorations. Her honesty is a highly cautious honesty, and I wonder if being so cautious got in the way at times.

I was amused when I read that. My first thought was, *He's got me wrong. This man does not know me and, as such, does not realize that the person he is pushing to explore the depths of understanding is a person who has always and only been comfortable in the shallow waters.* Deep thinkers tend to believe they must go to the depths to find profound truths. That may be true, but I stay in the shallow waters and skim the surface for insights and truths that are often passed over by the deep thinkers. If I come across as inconsistent and superficial and less than precise, I accept that assessment, but I do not think I am seeking to disguise my true thoughts and feelings. If I am expending an extreme amount of energy being subtle and cautious it may be due to uncertainty more than any fear of being fully honest—though I must take this reviewer's intuition to heart for my own benefit, if not for the benefit of others.

In part one I introduce the topic of losing faith first by seeking to honestly disclose my own pilgrimage and then by offering two other "case studies": one that follows the path of two evangelists and another that profiles a family's struggle to hang onto faith. This section also considers the mystery of the "main character" in this drama, God, and the mysterious search for God often spoken of as the "dark way" or "the dark night of the soul."

Part two focuses on historical and contemporary challenges to the Christian faith. This section features the stories of once-professing believers who have abandoned the faith. It also explores the various "reasons" for walking away from faith—such as those that arise when one studies certain aspects of science and philosophy, when one grapples with theological complexities and biblical criticism, when one seeks answers to psychological and sociological issues, and when one faces disappointment with God and with fellow believers.

Part three seeks to present both sides of the story: on the one side, depicting the new life of unbelief (positive and negative) and featuring missionaries of unbelief, and on the other side, answering serious questions of unbelief and telling stories of returning to faith.

This book is for those who believe and those who do not. My challenge to believers is that you seek a better understanding of those who do not believe—particularly those who have walked away from the faith—and that you listen carefully to their stories and respond with honesty and sensitivity. To believers who are struggling with faith-threatening doubts, this book offers no easy answers. But it does offer an opportunity to wrap yourself around the issues of mystery and paradox—to follow the advice of Parker Palmer, who challenges his students to love the questions and to "live the tensions" of life. "There is only one alternative: an unlived life."[2]

My challenge to unbelievers is that you reflect very seriously on what you are missing in your life of unbelief and to ask yourself whether you are denying faith for all the wrong reasons—such as demanding proofs for a faith that is not founded on proof. The journey of faith is not for the faint of heart. It can sometimes seem like running an obstacle course through quicksand and swamps. Yet the rewards along the way—intangible though they may be—make the journey infinitely worthwhile.

Part One

To understand the phenomenon of walking away from faith, one must listen to the stories with an open and understanding heart and mind. Faith is a gift from God, but it is also a human "endeavor." As such, faith is never static. It is always moving toward or away from God. So I begin, in chapter one, with my own faltering journey of walking toward and away from God. I offer my story not because I view it as typical or as particularly interesting, but because readers may wonder about the faith journey of the one who writes about the topic of walking away from faith.

Chapter two features, from a different slant, the story of Billy Graham and Chuck Templeton. It is the story of one man's determined walk toward God and another man's tortuous walk away from God. This chapter, among other things, dispels the myth that people who walk away from God are angry and rebellious. For Templeton and for many others, the process is full of sorrow and a sense of loss. Chapter three features the story of Robert Pearsall Smith and Hannah Whitehall Smith, a celebrated ministry couple in the nineteenth century. It powerfully illustrates how nature and nurture enter the picture. This family seems almost to possess an *unbelief gene*, but the family also lived in an environment of unbelief. It is a story that offers important lessons for today.

The chapter that follows asks the question, Who is the One at the focal point of this discussion? God is that One, the known and the unknown, the One who so consumes the individual who is walking away. This One is the sovereign God who holds onto me, despite my shaky faith. The fifth and final chapter in this section pushes the definition of faith to the limits. The primary means of finding God through the Bible—as in "Thy word is a lamp unto my feet and a light onto my path" (Ps 119:105)—is turned on its head in the testimonies of "the dark way." From my vantage point of growing up in the fundamentalist and evangelical world, this way is strange and scary, but it is prominent in the literature of spiritual formation, especially in works written from a Roman

Catholic perspective. Thus it is critical to understand this "way" not as a "walking away" but as an alternative to finding God amidst the darkness of distance and silence and the unknown. It is a way that Christians who are struggling with doubt and unbelief should ponder in their own spiritual pilgrimage.

1

"Lord, I Believe; Help My Unbelief"

When we write about what matters to us most,
words will take us places we don't want to go.
You begin to see that you will have to say
things you don't want to say,
that may even be dangerous to say,
but are absolutely necessary.

— KATHLEEN NORRIS

Where is God in the vastness of this universe? Where is God among the billions of stars and billions of light years and billions of people on this planet? Easy answers ring hollow. The unruffled, childlike faith of bygone years seems insufficient in the face of scientific discoveries that all too easily engulf God in a black hole. When I look into the night sky, I sometimes wonder whether my faith is a figment of my imagination. Where is God—not the God of the big bang, not the unmoved mover, not the ground of being, but *God*—this very personal God of the Bible who knows me and who knows my every thought?

As we begin this new millennium we hear much about renewal, revival and mission outreach. People are seeking God. There is a heightened sense of spirituality in the air. The sale of spirituality is everywhere—almost like the sale of indulgences in Martin Luther's day. As the year 2000 approached, the religious hype was everywhere. I came across one full-color, twenty-eight-page advertising brochure titled "Everything You Need to Set Off the Greatest Celebration in 2,000 Years." One page offered readers a volume titled *Men's Ministry Manual* for $25 and, farther down the page, the answer to "How to Know God Personally" for a quarter—a real deal.

But there is another side, a dark side, of this millennial consciousness—an aspect of faith that is not new to this generation. Indeed, it has been with us from time immemorial: it is that aspect of faith we rarely talk about—simply stated, losing it. Nobody wants to throw a bucket of ice water on the celebration, so losing faith is not a topic typically discussed in nice religious gatherings. But it is a reality that Christians must seriously confront in this era of praying and fasting and raising hands to God.

Postmodernism has provided an environment that is more accepting of supernatural belief. But this environment has not stopped the leaky pipe of Christianity—the leak that resists the Teflon paste and waterproof tape and just keeps dripping. Even as the reservoirs of the faithful keep rising, the seepage continues—a steady dribble that no postmodern plumbers' compound can remedy. Indeed, in this era of postmodern spirituality, which ranges from New Age fuzziness to charismatic fervor, old-fashioned orthodoxy might almost appear reasonable. But skeptics of the humanistic bent are not impressed by a *reasonable* religious belief. And despite all the eulogies to "secular humanism" and scientific naturalism, modernism is not dead and postmodernism has not taken its place. Humanism is alive and well. And this philosophical creed continues to be, I would argue, the underlying reason for walking away from faith.

My interest in the phenomenon of losing faith has persisted for decades. I remember the debates of my college days about whether a person who was saved could lose salvation. The doctrine taught in my theology courses denied such a possibility, but I was not restrained by a doctrinal formula. I looked around—and reasoned in my heart—that a person could be a Christian, only to later renounce that religious commitment through an apparent act of the will. The eternal security so taken for granted by most of the Christians I knew then, and know today, has not always been so secure with me.

How am I supposed to interpret the testimonies past and present of individuals who have lost their faith? What do I do with Dan Barker, who—after his long ministry as an evangelist and a writer and publisher of Christian music—not only no longer believes but now professes atheism. Was he never a Christian? I can claim that, if it is the only way his story fits my theological system, but this means my not taking him at his word. Or I could say that although he claims he is no longer a Christian, he really is, but that would also be dismissing him. For I have no reason to assume that he will come back to faith during his lifetime.

Theological formulas are valuable, but they ought not bind us with precise language and metaphysical terminology so much that we fail to comprehend the reality of living—and dying—faith.

Like the people discussed in this book, I have a story—a story interwoven with belief and unbelief. This book is based largely on stories; indeed, narrative is a key element in unraveling the mystery of belief and unbelief. My story begins in a farming community in northern Wisconsin, and my religious pilgrimage begins as a small child. For a childhood conversion, mine is actually rather interesting. It was the last day of vacation Bible school. I was six. The invitation was given, and my nine-year-old sister raised her hand. I reasoned that if she could do it so could I, so I also raised my hand. I was then led to the back of the church where I waited at the end of a short line to get saved.

As I waited, a boy came running into the back of the church announcing that my mother had arrived to take us home. At the moment, my concern that I would miss my ride home took precedence over missing heaven, and I hurried out to the car. That is when my real search for faith began. My family was not considered religious. We regularly attended that little country church, but my folks were not part of the "in" crowd. My father flirted too much with Seventh-Day Adventism and any other religious belief that was presented to him; and Mom had an *attitude*. I'm not sure why, but from hints she gave during my growing up-years, I think hers was a rebellion against the hell-fire and brimstone sermons she had heard as a child and continued to hear as an adult.

The lack of encouragement on the home front, however, did not stifle my search for faith—or, more accurately, my fear of going to hell. I wanted to be saved even though my six-year-old mind told me I had missed my opportunity. But, as sure as the mayflowers would bloom in spring, we would have vacation Bible school next June. So I waited—for one whole year. I made it through the first morning session, but after my teacher, Miss Buck (a Bible college student), dismissed us for lunch, I caught up with her on the way over to the parsonage. I had one very simple question: "Can I get saved?" She was floored. In fact, she started to cry. I didn't know how to react, and was sure I had said the wrong thing. But that fear was quickly assuaged as she bent down, put her arms around me and suggested we go back into the church.

We went into the basement of that little country church, and there we knelt together on that cold concrete floor. It was at that moment that I "invited Jesus into my heart." It didn't take long. And when the prayer was over, Miss Buck assured me that my name was written in the Lamb's book of life. The key word for me was *written*. I took that to mean written in cursive, having recently learned to write my name in longhand. I could visualize Jesus *writing* my name, Ruth Anne Stellrecht, in the Lamb's book of life.

That is an experience I will never forget—one that I will cherish the rest of my life. My two brothers and two sisters also made confessions of faith at VBS, but they no longer walk in that faith. As for me, doubts emerged within weeks of my conversion experience. I remember wondering how the biblical account of creation fit in with what I had been learning about dinosaurs. But alongside my doubts was a childlike faith with which I could look up into the puffy clouds on a warm summer day and know for certain that, in the words of my favorite chorus as a youngster, "Somewhere beyond the blue, there's a mansion for me."

My faith far surpassed my doubts as a youth, and at thirteen, I made a commitment at a summer Bible camp to be a missionary. The featured speaker, a missionary on furlough from Africa, gave a stirring message. I stood up at the invitation he gave, signifying my response to God. It was a "call" as real as any teenager can have in the midst of high emotion; and it had a formative influence on my life. A footnote to this story recently appeared in a news item. The report told of sexual abuse at a missionary boarding school in Africa, and the name of that very missionary popped off the page at me. I was numb. Two years before he came to the Bible camp where I heard him speak, he was a dorm parent molesting little girls. Is it any wonder, I sometimes ask myself, that people lose their faith?

My "call" to be a foreign missionary both inspired and burdened me through my high school, college and young adult years, and eventually died a slow death, only to be resurrected later as I became involved in missions through writing, teaching, preaching and short-term overseas missionary assignments. All the while my doubts continued to fester. In college, while taking a Bible minor, I struggled with the issue of the canon. Who decided which books would be in the canon? Even if the Bible is God's inspired word (or more than that—if the original manuscripts are inerrant), the determination of which books made it and which did not remains a very human decision. No one was claiming inspiration for that. Of course I know there is good church tradition behind the canon—I have seen all the lists that prove a certain degree of uniformity among the church fathers (no church mothers were in on it)—but there is still room for error. And if certain books made it in that should not have, and others should have made it in and did not, then we have a problem. That was the issue of my college days, and to some extent it is still an issue for me today.

Apart from my problems with the canon, I had no particular doctrinal doubts. Some people doubt the deity of Christ or the virgin birth or the resurrection or the reality of heaven. I have never been troubled specifically with things like that, probably because my doubts went directly to the biggest issue of all—the very existence of God. And that is precisely where my doubts lie today. When I look up into the night sky and know that there are billions of stars and galaxies and light years of space beyond what I see, I too easily wonder where in this vastness of space is God. Indeed, most of my doubts are of the "night sky" version. The very scientific discoveries that make so many Christians worship God in awe leave me feeling cold. In fact, I have thought to myself many times that I would be better off with some sort of medieval Christianity, in which the earth was the center of God's universe and the stars were put in place on the fourth day of creation. But unfortunately for me, I am hit every day with new scientific discoveries that put God further and further out of my reach.

And it is not just the night sky that troubles me. Years ago I taught a history of philosophy course. The first time through was not bad. The subject matter was so over my head that I had little time for contemplation. My only goal was understanding the material well enough to somehow teach the subject to my students. But the second time through was an entirely different matter. I contemplated what those philosophers were saying, and what they were saying did not strengthen my faith. A few years after that, I had occasion to read some books on the sociology of religion for a project I was working on. For the first time I was faced with arguments that sharply challenged the supernatural foundations of religious beliefs and practices. When I was finished with my project, I determined that I would simply stay away from the topic.

There is an incident in my life that also has an effect on my belief and unbelief. The day was September 23, 1969. A phone call from my brother broke the news that Mom had been killed in an auto accident. My world caved in. It was bad enough to have a mother—a vibrant, outspoken woman who could not contain her pride in her five children—dead, but worse than that was to contemplate that she might not have gone to heaven. My fundamentalism (albeit riddled with doubts) did not allow for someone of my mother's ilk to go to heaven. She regularly attended that tiny country Christian and Missionary Alliance church where I was saved—but she had never "played the game." If she had a "testimony," she never gave it in public, and she never prayed aloud. And that alone was enough to make her suspect. It did not matter that "In the Garden" was her favorite hymn and that she was delighted that I had decided to go to Bible college. I know now she believed and that her faith was in many ways stronger than mine. But I pray so well in public, I have such a good testimony, and I even preach a good sermon now and then—and that, in the eyes of many people, is what counts.

But Mom's death was something I could not easily reconcile with my perception of God. The accident was not a twenty-car pileup in a northern Wisconsin blizzard. It happened on a clear afternoon in early autumn at a remote intersection of a country road. And to add insult to injury (and to death), it occurred a stone's throw from my mother's childhood home (her brother, then living on the farm, was the first at the scene) and three miles away from the farm on which I grew up. I had crossed that intersection (which had no stop sign) hundreds of times, and *never* had there been an approaching car. But on this day there were two cars approaching the same intersection, and neither driver saw the other one in time to stop.

Already struggling with abstract doubts, I now had very personal doubts about the God I worshiped and how this incident, this accident, fit into my faith. "All things work together for good"—I know the verse (Rom 8:28) by heart. *But no, no, no!* I screamed, *all things don't work together for good. And in this case, if there truly is a God out there who is all powerful, why, O God, why,* I asked, *did you not prevent this terrible accident?* I asked myself that question in the days and months and years following the accident, but never with any real righteous indignation. After all, I had my own guilt to deal with—for not getting my mother saved before she died.

There is a poem, a prayer, by Meredith Gray that speaks the words of my heart at that time in my life—words that leave unresolved one's struggle with God in times of sorrow:

Dear God!
How can you walk serenely
Through the starry meadows of eternity,
Swinging your moonlit lantern,
Calling the long night watches:
"All's well! All's well"
When my heart's only heaven
Is black with grief. . . .
My life's great lamp is broken and dark,
And I falter . . . unmothered![1]

Many years later, while teaching a large team-taught course at
Calvin College, I viewed for the first time a filmed portrayal of Elie
Wiesel's play *The Trial of God*. God was being tried for the Holocaust. It was a powerful experience, and I went back to my discussion group and, with no premeditation, put God on trial. I told my
students that while none of us have a holocaust to deal with, we all,
no doubt, have a case against God. I told them I wanted them to
contemplate their own situation, as I brought my case against God.
This was spontaneous. It had never before crossed my mind to put
God on trial, but I did it then and there right in front of twenty-
three students.

I told them about Mom and how desperately I loved her. I told
them how she was in the prime of her life at fifty-seven—how she had
emerged from being just a farmer's wife to having her own "career" as
a nurse's aid at the hospital, how she loved to go to auctions and estate
sales with her newfound women friends at work. She was losing weight
and her blood pressure was down. She had twenty-five years ahead of
her. And then on that awful day she was killed. I've never been able to
say she "passed away." Even "died" is not the way it happened. She
was *killed*, and the harder that word sounds the more it fits what happened. She never lived to see me become a mom. I had married one
year earlier, and my son Carlton didn't come along for another five
years. She would have adored him.

This is how I described her to my students as I choked back the tears. Now, I'm not saying—and was not saying back then—that anyone purposefully *killed* her. But if there is an all-powerful God who sees every sparrow that falls, why did this happen? What is going on here? If God did not *will* it to happen, I have to believe God could have at least prevented it. And that, in a court of law—in my court, with God on trial—means, at minimum, a verdict of manslaughter.

With my story finished, the students opened up more than I ever could have imagined. One by one they told their stories—and there were tears in that class that January afternoon. When it was over I prayed a prayer of commitment and I asked forgiveness if the Lord thought what we had done was wrong and needed forgiveness. I wasn't sure. That interim course continued on every day for two more weeks; and I noticed, if anything, a deeper consciousness of God among the students and a deeper sense of their own vulnerabilities.

For me, putting God on trial released some deep-seated anger of which I had not even been aware, and it helped me to move beyond these feelings. But a more serious problem persisted: Putting God on trial is surely not a sign of unbelief. Indeed, it is the ultimate sign of belief. Why would anyone go through such a sacrilegious exercise if one didn't believe in God? My problem was more threatening to my faith than anger. My problem was God's silence.

I don't hear the voice of God like other people do. My friend Marcia in Evergreen, Colorado, hears the voice of God. She has this pipeline of sorts that I've never known to exist anywhere other than with some of the Old Testament prophets. And God comes to her in living color. She's an artist, and she puts her visions on canvas. I love to hang out with Marcia. She has more than enough faith for both of us, and she loves and accepts me for who I am.

But I simply cannot connect with God as she does. God's voice is too often silent—except when I'm singing an old hymn or when I'm lifting my hands in the midst of an enthusiastic crowd, singing "Shine Jesus Shine." It is here where sometimes I think I hear the voice of God—and I sense the presence of God as sure as my vocal vibrations are penetrating the universe. But those times are not the times that characterize my life. I've come to terms with this, in part through the poetry of Emily Dickinson.

I know that He exists.
Somewhere—in Silence—
He has hid his rare life
From our gross eyes.

'Tis an instant's play.
'Tis a fond Ambush—
Just to make Bliss
Earn her own surprise!

But—should the play
Prove piercing earnest—
Should the glee—glaze—
In Death's—stiff—stare—

Would not the fun
Look too expensive!
Would not the jest—
Have crawled too far![2]

"I know that He exists." This was the most confident confession of faith Dickinson could muster. I confess that too. I will put it in print. Yes, God exists. But like Dickinson and like the psalmist, I often feel as though God is hiding—somewhere beyond the galaxies. Fortunately for me, I am part of the Reformed tradition—more specifically, the Christian Reformed tradition—which takes the psalms very seriously. The Psalter is our pew hymnbook, and many contemporary praise choruses are drawn from the psalms. "The silence of God is a recurring theme in the so-called lament Psalms," writes Kelly Clark, who teaches at Calvin College. "Nearly half of the Psalms are lamentations of God's apparent abandonment of his people. They are cries of complaint to a God who seems indifferent to Israel's wretched plight."[3] Psalm 13:1–2 is an example:

How long, O LORD? Will you forget me forever?
How long will you hide your face from me?

How long must I bear pain in my soul,
  and have sorrow in my heart all day long?

In recent years, as I have contemplated doubt and as I have read books on the subject, it has concerned me that few writers take the negative side of doubt as seriously as I think they ought to. Doubt—no matter who writes about it—is not properly respected for the power it wields. So much of the writing on doubt is to assure us doubters, that bottom line, doubt is good, that our faith is strengthened through doubt, that to be a good thinking Christian one must experience doubt. The title of Alister McGrath's book says it all: *The Sunnier Side of Doubt*. In *Living Faith While Holding Doubts*, Martin Copenhaver assures the reader that "belief in God is a gift" and "doubt is also a gift." Lesslie Newbigin titled a chapter in one of his books "Doubt as the Way to Certainty." But little is said of the dark, fierce, hoary side of doubt and of the next logical step—unbelief.

That, indeed, is the subject of this book. The stories in this volume are the testimonies of once-professing Christians—many of them involved in long-time Christian ministry—who have abandoned the faith. This is not, then, a book that speaks to the joys of doubt. These accounts are real. They are not joyful—except in the instances where the individuals testify of the greater happiness they have found outside Christian belief. The stories behind these testimonies include some of the most fascinating literature ever written within the Christian context. Who are these people who fight a valiant battle to believe and often—though not always—end up the loser? The opening line of Father Michael Paul Gallagher's book, *Help My Unbelief*, is no less than spellbinding: "It was Thursday evening at Mass that I entered into my atheism in a deeper way than ever before."

It is my interpretation of these stories that makes this book unique. This is a volume that takes the progression from belief to unbelief seriously and that does so with understanding. I understand the unbelief. I read the stories, and I say, "Me too." But unlike these who have abandoned the faith, I will not—if for no other reason than the mysterious fact that God has a grip on me. Besides, this is my culture, my tradition. I love the Bible stories and the old hymns of the faith. I can close my eyes and see Jesus "on a hill far away on that old rugged cross." I love to sit at the piano and sing "Softly and Tenderly Jesus Is Calling" and the other invitation hymns in the pages that follow in that tattered hymnbook. I teach my darling little granddaughter Kayla songs and Bible verses. This is my faith, and I will never abandon it—nor will God abandon me.

But do I believe it? If everything depended on my belief, there are some days when, I think, I would be doomed. But my salvation does not depend on the strength of my faith; it depends only on God's grace. Even when my faith is weak, I have confidence in God's hold on my life. I sometimes envy those who have an unwavering faith—people who, in many cases, are a lot smarter than I am. I desperately wish I did not have to fight and struggle for every little bit of faith I have. I wish the big question was not, at least unconsciously, ever before me: Is there really a God out there, or is my faith tradition a concoction of men, as the sociologists of religion would say? But I accept the conflicts and questions as part of my psychological and spiritual makeup, which allows me to humbly reach out to those with similar struggles.

The lines of Friedrich Heinrich Jacobi, which are printed on a card above my desk, express my struggle:

> I . . . am a heathen in my reason and a Christian with my whole heart. I swim between two bodies of water which will not unite so that together they can hold me up, but while one continuously holds me, the other is constantly letting me sink.

I have often reflected on why belief in God seems more difficult for me than for most of my Christian friends and colleagues. As I ponder the Jacobi quote, I think of my own religious background, which allowed for very little merging of *reason* and *heart*. Through the altar calls and revivals at the country church of my childhood, I was introduced to a *heart* religion that was connected to God through experience. People often testified to how God spoke to them and answered their prayers in very personal ways and sometimes of how he even broke through in miracles and visions and voices. These experiences were not mine. If God was using such means to get through to me, I was missing the signals. Yet I reached out to God the only way I knew how—through my emotions, my heart.

Then during my young adult years, which were spent in a more strictly fundamentalist setting, the emphasis on experience was replaced by an emphasis on a rational biblical literalism. But this brought me no closer to God. Once again I seemed to be missing any real signals that God might be sending my way. The rational apologetics seemed only to raise more questions and doubts. And my *secular* life became more and more separated from my *spiritual* life. This dualism of *reason* and *heart* continues for me today. I sometimes think it would be better if my faith were weighted to one side or the other. But such imbalance lacks the stability needed to navigate the storms in the turbulent seas of uncertainty. Whether the deluge of doubt erupts from swells of sorrow and pain or from undercurrents of metaphysical arguments, there is no stability when the vessel of faith is bobbing back and forth or listing with all the weight on one side or the other. Equilibrium comes when the cargo of heart and reason are merged together and firmly anchored in God's grace.

In the present environment, it is easier to affirm both heart and reason than it was for those who lived a generation ago. Rationalism no longer reigns as it once did, and most Christians do not struggle to stay afloat as Jacobi did—and as I do. I have come to terms with this spiritual adversity, as I sometimes think of it—an adversity that prevents reason and heart from uniting in the sea of uncertainty. Flannery O'Connor used a similar watery metaphor: "Faith comes and goes. It rises and falls like the tides of an invisible ocean."[4] So while the *heart* continuously holds me, *reason* is constantly letting me sink. But ever conscious of this pull of the undertow, I cling all the more to the life preservers of the heart—especially the old hymns of the faith.

Jesus, Savior pilot me
Over life's tempestuous sea;

Unknown waves before me roll,
Hiding rocks and treach'rous shoal. . . .

As a mother stills her child,
Thou canst hush the ocean wild. . . .
Wondrous Sov'reign of the sea,
Jesus, Savior, pilot me.

When at last I near the shore,
And the fearful breakers roar. . . .
May I hear Thee say to me,
"Fear not—I will pilot thee!"

One thing I know for certain is that the reality—the existence—of God does not depend on me and on my belief or unbelief. God knows and understands my often-wavering faith. God can handle the honest confession of my heart. God surely hears my prayer, "Out of my bondage, sorrow and night, Jesus, I come, Jesus I come," even if sometimes I cannot go on to the next lines with confidence: "Into thy freedom, gladness and light, Jesus I come to thee."[6] And God knows, far better than I do, why I have such a struggle believing. Maybe it's in my family's genes. Maybe none of us five kids are able to truly believe, but unlike my siblings, I give my unbelief to God.

"Wondrous Sov'reign of the sea, Jesus, Savior, pilot me."

2

A Tale of
Two Evangelists

Billy Graham &
Chuck Templeton

When you have Him you have all,
but you have also lost all when you lose Him.
Stay with Christ, although your eyes do not see Him
and your reason does not grasp Him.

— MARTIN LUTHER

The Billy Graham Center in Wheaton, Illinois, features a Rotunda of
Witnesses—a circular room with large fabric banners hanging from the
wall, depicting nine great saints of Christian history. Each banner features a quote. One of those banners particularly caught my attention—
the one depicting Martin Luther, with the above quote imprinted on
the bottom.

I recently visited the Billy Graham Center. As I browsed through
the museum, I was conscious of that quote from Luther as I glanced
over many of the thousands of photos and newspaper clippings of Graham and his developing ministry over the past half century. One particular photo caught my eye. It is a picture of Graham and three other
young men in front of an airplane, taken as they were about to leave

O'Hare airport for London. One of the men in the picture is Charles "Chuck" Templeton. To the museum's casual visitor, this photo would not have stood out. But I had just finished reading Templeton's autobiography, *Farewell to God.* I felt the irony of the situation: I see Templeton and his fellow evangelists saying farewell to their supporters and homeland on their way to proclaim the word of God; and I read of Templeton's bidding farewell to God in his book. I wondered whether the book was in the museum library or whether the museum curator had any plans to include an update on Templeton.

The stories of Billy and Chuck illustrate the mystery of belief and unbelief. From a human perspective, no logical explanations for this mystery can be discerned, although the disciplines of psychology and sociology offer us theories. There are no easy answers to the question of why one person finds believing as natural as breathing and another person finds belief an intellectual and emotional struggle that in the end is not worth the effort. There has been speculation by some that there may be a gene that gives a person a predisposition to believe, that belief is shaped by *nature.* Others would suggest that *nurture* plays a key role, that environment and family influences are the most important elements. I thought of this nature-nurture dichotomy as I watched *Larry King Live* on CNN. Franklin Graham and Ann Graham Lotz were featured. They share a strong family resemblance to their father—in their looks, their mannerisms, their tone of voice, and even their respective callings. Both spoke of their unflagging belief in Jesus as "the way, the truth and the life," a belief tied to a fervent commitment to spread that message, reminiscent of their father's zeal for evangelism. Is there something in the Graham family's genes? Is it home environment and upbringing? Is it a combination of both?

Whether dependent on nature or nurture, the capacity to believe appears to be greater in some individuals than in others, and sometimes one individual is judgmental of the other: the one who easily believes often sees rebellion and obstinacy as the obstacles to belief, while the one who has difficulty believing often sees superficial thinking and "intellectual suicide" as the easy road to belief. The fact is that both judgments can be right. But for the purpose of this study, neither accusation is helpful—though the burden of fairness lies with the believer who is obligated to reach out with concern and understanding to the one who has walked away.

That people who struggle with doubts or walk away from faith are rebellious or dishonest simply does not correspond with the testimonies. Yet these charges persist. A typical response was offered in a student paper recently submitted in one of my classes. The student wrote, "I believe that the intellectual struggles are not the basis for their loss of faith. They are simply the masks or excuses that they need to rationalize their unbelief. . . . As long as they have these excuses, they have a crutch to keep them from dealing with the real issue of having to come before a holy God."

Most people who are walking away from faith are not put in the position of making excuses. The process often spans years, and by the time they disclose their so-called excuses, they already consider themselves unbelievers. Coming "before a holy God" is not an easily defined concept, and it lends itself to subjectivity. So it is of little help to insist that the one who has intellectual struggles is really masking an unwillingness to "come before a holy God." Who can judge that but God alone?

The story of Chuck Templeton speaks to these issues. In his book, he identifies himself as "an agnostic—not an atheist, not a theist, not a skeptic, and certainly not indifferent."[1] The book, besides being personal, offers a standard catalog of arguments against the Bible, Christianity and religious belief in general. The first section is titled "The God Myth." The section on Jesus is titled "The God Men Created." His positions are not subtle or disguised, and they are radically different than they were the night he met Billy.

It was in the spring of 1945. They were backstage in a jam-packed stadium in Chicago. The war was over. The nation was eager to move on and leave the past behind. The focus was on the future—the youthful generation on whom the mantle of this military-industrial giant would fall. Two men in their late twenties met for the first time as

they talked and prayed and planned for the big event of the evening.
When the moment arrived, they walked onto the stage. The vast sea of
young faces awaiting them was full of electricity and expectancy. It was
a Youth for Christ rally. As Billy was being introduced to speak, he
leaned over and whispered, "Pray for me, Chuck, I'm scared to death."[2]

Chuck was a pastor and evangelist from Toronto; he became
involved in youth ministry and then began working with Graham in
Youth for Christ. They continued to work together even as their lives
and ministries took them in different directions. Some months after
that Chicago rally, they met with other Christian leaders to form Youth
for Christ International. Chuck was selected to be one of the three vice
presidents, and Graham was appointed evangelist-at-large. The new
movement grew quickly, and when the team left from Chicago for
Europe and the British Isles, reporters and photographers watched
their every move. For three weeks they conducted nightly rallies. "No
building was large enough to house the youngsters who flocked to the
meetings."[3]

A Difference in Upbringing

Apart from their both having economically distressed backgrounds,
the circumstances in which Billy and Chuck grew up were very different. Billy, a southern boy from Charlotte, North Carolina, was raised in
a Christian home. Here God held the place of honor from the first day
of his parents' marriage. His father, Franklin Graham, proposed to his
sweetheart, Morrow, in 1912, but it was not until the fall of 1916 that
she was ready to tie the knot.

> Before setting out for their five-day honeymoon in the mountains, she
> carefully tucked her Bible into her suitcase—"I just wouldn't have felt
> like a clean person without my Bible with me." On their wedding night,
> at last standing alone together in a bleak and sallow-lit hotel room,
> Franklin immediately had his bride kneel beside him on the worn lino-
> leum and proceeded to conduct the two of them in an extended and
> slightly wavery prayer there by the side of the bed, "dedicating our mar-
> riage and our family to the Lord."[4]

Billy's father had sensed God's call to the ministry, though he did not follow that call in the public realm. But in the home, he took his Christian responsibilities very seriously. From the earliest Billy can remember, Bible study, prayer and family devotions were a central part of the Graham home:

> He grew up . . . in a regimen of diligent pieties in his household; by the time he was ten, he had memorized all the 107 articles in the Shorter Catechism. "We had Bible reading and prayer right after supper, even before I cleaned up the kitchen," says Mrs. Graham. "We all got down on our knees and prayed, yes we did, sometimes from twenty to thirty minutes. That was the main event of the day in our house." . . . On Sundays, Billy was forbidden to read the comics in the newspaper, to play ball, to venture into the woods—the only diversions during that day being the perusal of Scripture and religious tracts, with Mrs. Graham collecting the children into the front room in the afternoon to sit together listening, on their radio console, to Charles Fuller's *Old-Fashioned Revival Hour.*[5]

Chuck's family life was very different. He grew up in Toronto, with his parents and four siblings—until his father left, never to return, leaving the family impoverished and with no choice but to go "on relief." These were difficult years, as he recalls:

> There was one unforgettable twenty-four-hour period when there was nothing—not a morsel of food—in the house to eat. How often the six of us poised hushed and motionless, like animals freezing when a predator is near, until the bill-collector had gone from the front door. I can still see Mother at the kitchen table counting the coins kept in a china teapot, dabbing at her eyes with a handkerchief.[6]

When we consider these two lives, we must consider the issue of fatherhood. In a recent book titled *Faith of the Fatherless: The Psychology of Atheism,* Paul Vitz argues that the father's role in the child's upbringing is closely tied to the child's belief in God. After studying the lives of prominent atheists and theists, he concluded that such an individual's "disappointment in and resentment of his own father unconsciously justifies his rejection of God." This is a reverse of Sigmund Freud's concept of wish fulfillment—that belief in God is an illusion, "a projection of our own intense, unconscious desires." Vitz uses Freud to explain atheism: "The irony is that he [Freud] inadvertently provides a powerful new way to understand an illusion as the psychological basis for rejecting God—that is, a projection theory of atheism."[7] Vitz's theory, like Freud's, is certainly not foolproof; but when comparing the experiences of Billy and Chuck, Vitz's theory fits, offering a possible interpretation of their spiritual journeys.

Apart from the obvious difference in their relationships with their fathers, the two young men had many things in common. They were both passionate about sports. Billy dreamed of being a baseball player—and was actually paid token amounts to play for a local team. Chuck's first important job was that of a sports cartoonist for the Toronto *Globe:* "My weekly salary in dollars matched my age in years—eighteen."[8] But in other ways, their lives had gone in opposite directions. Billy, the "nonsmoking, nondrinking, churchgoing son of devout parents," was converted at a revival meeting at the age of seventeen. After high school he enrolled at Bob Jones University and then transferred to Florida Bible Institute, where he trained to be a preacher.[9]

Chuck had only a ninth-grade education, though he was wise to the world and lived a worldly life. But that all changed in a moment. He was transformed one night after he returned at 3:00 a.m. from a strip show that he describes as "a sleezy affair." His mother was still awake, and she called to him.

> She began to talk to me about God, and about how she longed to see me with the other children in church. . . . I felt shoddy, unclean. . . . As I went down the hall, I was forming the first fumbling words of a prayer in my mind. I knelt by my bed in the darkness. . . . I found myself—I don't know how much later—my head in my hands, crouched small on the floor at the center of a vast, dark emptiness. Slowly, a weight began to lift. . . . I hardly dared breathe, fearing that I might alter or end the moment. And I heard myself whispering softly over and over again, "Thank you, Lord. Thank you. Thank you. Thank you."[10]

A Ministry Riddled with Doubt

At age nineteen, Chuck left his job at the *Globe* to enter the ministry. After reading some books and meeting with local pastors, he was ordained as a minister in the Church of the Nazarene. For the next three years he served as an itinerant evangelist, traveling across the continent from Ontario to California. While in Michigan, he spent some free time in a pastor's library where, for the first time, he confronted books that challenged the Christian faith—books by Thomas Paine, François Marie Voltaire, Bertrand Russell and Robert Ingersoll. Their arguments so jolted his faith that he stopped preaching for several weeks. "The way back," he writes, "was tortuous and slow." Some time later, while preaching in an evangelistic campaign in Grand Rapids, he met Constance Orosco. "She was the singer and I was the evangelist. We were married six weeks later."[11]

After their marriage the Templetons made their home in Toronto, where they rented a twelve-hundred-seat church building and began holding services. There were twelve people—mostly relatives—present at the first Sunday service. Within six months, however, the church could no longer accommodate the crowds that turned out for the Sunday evening meetings. After a fire destroyed the church building, a larger facility was built, and the church's growth continued in the years that followed. It was during this time that Chuck began working with Billy in Youth for Christ. But the doubts that haunted him earlier resurfaced. "Slowly, and much against my will for I could perceive the jeopardy in it, my reason had begun to challenge and sometimes to rebut the central beliefs of the Christian faith."[12]

Finally, after "frequent bouts of despair," Chuck concluded that his doubts might be aggravated by his lack of theological education, so he decided to seek formal training. He applied to Princeton Seminary and, with his stellar Canadian connections, was admitted as a "special" student in a non-degree program. He resigned from his church in Toronto and began preparation for the fall term. Twice during that summer he spent time with Billy—once flying to be with him at his home in Montreat, North Carolina, and on a second occasion, meeting with him in New York City, where they "spent the better part of two days closeted in a room in the Taft Hotel." It was during this time, according to Chuck, that their "differences came to a head."

> In the course of the conversation I said, "But, Billy, it's simply not possible any longer to believe, for instance, the biblical account of creation. The world wasn't created over a period of days a few thousand years ago; it has evolved over millions of years. It's not a matter of speculation; it's demonstrable fact."
>
> "I don't accept that," Billy said. "And there are reputable scholars who don't."
>
> "Who are these scholars?" I said. "Men in conservative Christian colleges."
>
> "Most of them, yes," he said. "But that's not the point. I believe the Genesis account of creation because it's in the Bible. I've discovered something in my ministry: when I take the Bible literally, when I proclaim it as the Word of God, my preaching has power. When I stand on the platform and say, 'God says,' or 'the Bible says,' the Holy Spirit uses me. There are results. Wiser men than you and I have been arguing questions like this for centuries. I don't have the time or the intellect to examine all sides of each theological dispute, so I've decided, once and for all, to stop questioning and accept the Bible as God's Word."
>
> "But, Billy," I protested, "you can't do that. You don't dare stop thinking about the most important question in life. Do it and you begin to die. It's intellectual suicide."
>
> "I don't know about anyone else," he said, "but I've decided that that's the path for me."[13]

It was not long after that encounter that Billy flew to Los Angeles to conduct an evangelistic campaign—just another campaign—but one that would make him a household name. Chuck was just another student—a "special student"—at Princeton Seminary.

Just prior to that campaign, "everything came to a climax" for Billy. It was a moonlit night, and he was at a retreat in the San Bernardino Mountains. He got down on his knees and prayed a prayer that would set the stage for his future ministry. Gripping a Bible, he prayed, "Father, I am going to accept this as Thy Word—by *faith*. I'm going to allow faith to go beyond my intellectual questions and doubts, and I will believe this to be Your inspired Word."[14]

Education for Further Ministry

While studying at Princeton, Chuck sought to resolve some of the doubts that he had been struggling with—not only through his studies, but also through spiritual disciplines. He fasted one day a week, and he spent time praying and meditating, especially at night when he would walk alone on a golf course near the seminary. He was seeking an experience of God that would somehow confirm his faith in the face of his intellectual doubts. Then it came without warning:

> I was caught up in a transport. It seemed that the whole of creation, the trees, the skies, the very heavens, all of time and space and God Himself was weeping. I knew somehow that they were weeping for mankind: for our obduracy, our hatreds, our ten thousand cruelties, our love of war and violence. And at the heart of this eternal sorrow I saw the shadow of a cross, with a silhouetted figure on it . . . weeping.[15]

After completing his studies at Princeton, Chuck was ordained by the Philadelphia Presbytery of the Presbyterian Church, U.S.A. He then accepted a position with the National Council of Churches to conduct "preaching missions"—campaigns that appealed primarily to youth. *Time* magazine reported this appointment and compared Chuck and his modest salary to Billy and his bulging sacks of "love offerings." To his credit, writes Chuck, Billy "immediately put himself on a salary."[16]

Chuck's success as an evangelist did not by any means rival Billy's. But his ministry was noteworthy enough to be covered by major newspapers and magazines. In a television series he was presented as a "young Canadian" who was "passing up the old hellfire-and-damnation oratorical fireworks" and replacing it with a contemporary "persuasive approach that presents religion as a commodity as necessary to life as salt," setting "a new standard for mass evangelism." During a two-week campaign in Evansville, Indiana, more than ninety thousand people were in attendance. In Harrisburg, Pennsylvania, the local paper described the final meeting as "the greatest crowd ever to gather in the history of Harrisburg."[17]

It might have been a heady time for him as he climbed in popularity and name recognition. But on his drive from Harrisburg to his home in New York, he told his wife that he had decided to leave the ministry. His old doubts would not go away. "I would cover them over with prayer and activity but soon there would be a wisp of smoke and a flicker of flame and then a firestorm of doubt." He struggled with depression and with chest pain, which he believed was a result of the spiritual turmoil he was enduring. His departure from Christian ministry, however, was a slower process than he had anticipated. He was invited to head the Department of Evangelism for the Presbyterian Church, U.S.A., and for the next three years he trained ministers, hosted a television program, wrote books and occasionally preached on Sundays.[18]

Yet, his doubts continued and intensified, especially following an appointment with the captain of the Yale debating team. They discussed—and debated—the merits of Christianity, and after it was over Chuck was elated: "I'd beaten the captain of the Yale debating team." But that experience finalized his decision to leave the ministry. He could no longer pretend to believe something that he did not: "There was no real choice. I could stay in the ministry and live a lie or I could make the break. My wife and I packed our few possessions in a rental trailer and started on the road back to Toronto where, nineteen years earlier, I had begun."[19]

No single issue had led Chuck to his gradual loss of faith, but the problem of pain and evil troubled him more than any other. If there was a moment that separated the time of his belief from the time of his unbelief, it was when he saw a photo in *Life* magazine of an African woman with a dead baby in her arms, "looking up to heaven with the most forlorn expression." As he saw the desperation in her eyes, he asked himself, "Is it possible to believe that there is a loving or caring Creator when all this woman needed was *rain*?"[20]

As Chuck's ministry ended, Billy's celebrity status grew. Millions attended his crusades each year, and tens of thousands came forward when the invitation was given. Through the years they kept in touch, and in the early 1970s, when Billy was in Toronto, he spent an evening in the Templeton home. "The evening ended earlier than planned," Chuck recalls. "We simply ran out of subjects of mutual interest." After driving Billy back to his hotel, Chuck remembers feeling "a profound sense of sorrow." Billy may have picked up on that feeling. Some years later when he was being interviewed for a book, Graham reflected on his friendship with Chuck:

> I love Chuck to this very day. He's one of the few men I have ever loved in my life. He and I had been so close. But then, all of a sudden, our paths were parting. He began to be a little cool to me then. I think . . . that Chuck felt sorry for me.[21]

After Chuck published *Farewell to God* in 1996, his health deteriorated. He disclosed to Lee Strobel in an interview that he had been suffering from Alzheimer's disease for three years. Yet his mind was clear enough for him to discuss matters of belief and unbelief. He responded to Strobel's concern that he might be worried about being wrong about God, especially considering his terminal illness. Chuck insisted that he was not. Why?

> Because I have spent a lifetime thinking about it. If this were a simplistic conclusion reached on a whim, that would be different. But it's impossible for me—*impossible*—to believe that there is anything that could be described as a loving God who could allow what happens in our world daily.[22]

When Strobel asked whether he would like to believe, Chuck responded, "Of course! If I could, I would. I'm eighty-three years old. I've got Alzheimer's. I'm dying, for goodness sake!"[23]

Reflections on a Friendship
Looking back over his friendship with Billy, Chuck made some interesting and telling observations:

I occasionally watch Billy in his televised campaigns. Forty years after our working together he is saying the same things, using the same phrases, following the same pattern. When he gives the invitation to come forward, the sequence, even the words, are the same. I turn off the set and am sometimes overtaken by sadness.

I think Billy is what he has to be. I disagree with him at almost every point in his views on God and Christianity and think that much of what he says in the pulpit is puerile, archaic nonsense. But there is no feigning in Billy Graham: he believes what he believes with an invincible innocence. He is the only mass-evangelist I would trust.

And I miss him.[24]

An Alternative Altar Call

Chuck's response to Billy's televised messages is not surprising. Most people who have walked away from their Christian beliefs would have a similar response—if, indeed, it were that charitable. But Billy's message and invitation did not stir Chuck to return to his earlier faith. Is there a message, I ask myself, that might more directly resonate with those who struggle with doubts or those who have walked away? Billy is unquestionably America's—and the world's—premier evangelist, but his words are not always in a language that communicates effectively to the ones most troubled by unbelief.

There are other individuals, however, who call people back to faith—those whose words are easier for some to hear than are Billy's words, those whose voices we need to hear at the beginning of this millennium. One such voice is that of the widely recognized sociologist of religion, Peter Berger. He, like Billy, challenges us with the words of Scripture—with the message of the cross that is as relevant today as it was in ancient times. But he also speaks to the one who is struggling with unbelief and the silence of God.

It was the message, the "word of the cross" preached by Paul, which struck both Jews and Gentiles as scandalous foolishness. . . . Paul's "word of the cross," of course, is the core of the Gospel: That God came into the world in the improbable figure of a small-town carpenter turned itinerant preacher, who was executed as a criminal, despised and

abandoned, dead and buried—and who then, in a moment that transformed the whole structure of reality, rose from the dead to become the
mightiest power in the universe and the lord of all human destinies. . . .
Paul's scandalous proposition is that the *weakness* of God reveals His
true power, including the power to triumph over sin and death.[25]

Berger goes on to suggest that through modern technology—and
modernism generally—"precious" things have been lost. Here he is
referring particularly to the wonder of the supernatural that is lost
when science seeks to explain all phenomena in natural terms. He
speaks of angels, reminding me of Graham's book on the same subject
that I read years ago:

Our ancestors didn't know about particle physics, but they spoke with
angels. . . . Are we, *can* we be so sure that the truths of modern physics
necessarily imply the untruth of angels? I'm not sure at all; indeed, I'm
strongly inclined to believe the opposite. In that case the Christian
churches (and other religious institutions) would be paying a very high
price for the "updating" of their tradition—the price being some precious truths that they were the last to hold onto.[26]

In his book *A Far Glory*, Berger titles his epilogue "The Burden of
Silence," drawing from Isaiah 21:11–12:

The oracle concerning Dumah [meaning "silence"]. One is calling to
me from Se'ir, [where God appeared to Moses in flaming fire before his
death (Deut. 33)] "Watchman, what of the night? Watchman, what of
the night?" The watchman says: "Morning comes, and also the night. If
you will inquire, inquire; come back again."

Berger sets this scene in our contemporary situation:

We too have our "watchmen" today. Some pretend to know what time it
is in our night of waiting; but it invariably turns out to be the wrong
time. Others, even worse, try to convince us that there is nothing to wait
for, that the night in which we find ourselves is all there is, that in effect
God's morning will never come. We also have honest watchmen, like the
one who made his rounds in long-ago Se'ir, who tell us that they do not
know. Now as then, this is a discouraging reply. Our short text, though,

ends on a note of hope: come back and ask again, for the morning *will* come. The burden of God's silence will be lifted and He will return once more in the dawn, "with flaming fire at his right hand," in the "fullness of His glory."[27]

Berger's invitation to believe is extended to those who, like Chuck, are troubled by the silence of God. The invitation is for those who struggle with unbelief and doubt, and the response is in the words of the predictable invitation hymn of the Billy Graham Crusades, "Just As I Am":

Just as I am, tho tossed about
With many a conflict, many a doubt,
Fightings and fears within, without,
O Lamb of God, I come! I come![28]

3

The
Smith Family

A Case Study in
Doubt & Unbelief

At this low period in my life I noticed the
dusty paperback books by Hannah Whitall Smith
that had been sitting on my bookcase since 1967.
I opened the first volume, called *God of All Comfort*, and began to read.
Though she wrote this book at a time when she was
beset with all manner of difficulties,
Mrs. Smith had a message of God's tender love and care
that fell like life-giving rain on the parched ground of my thirsty soul.

— M A R I E   H E N R Y

The story of Hannah Whitall Smith and of her husband, Robert Pearsall Smith, is a fascinating family history and case study in doubt and unbelief. Here we see psychological and lifestyle issues converging in their effect on religious belief. And as was true with the story of Billy Graham and Charles Templeton, this story is closely tied to the age-old debate of nature versus nurture. Is this family story determined more by genes or by environment? Hannah Smith compared her psychological makeup to that of her husband's, noting their different emotional response to experiential faith. She viewed him as the emotional one, but it was *emotion*—the death of little ones—that strengthened her own faith. When Robert denied the faith, his emotional nature was again a factor, but equally important were matters of morality and lifestyle. In the end Hannah drew her own theological conclusions to cope with unbelief. Some might suggest that she created God in her own image—an image of a mother whose love for her children is ultimately unfailing.

Hannah is better known than her husband, largely because of her bestselling Christian classic, *The Christian's Secret of a Happy Life* (which by 1984 had sold some ten million copies worldwide). Hannah was probably the most widely read Christian writer of her day, but according to her biographer, Marie Henry, the "triumphant faith" she wrote about, "would be challenged mightily in a Job-like series of personal tragedies." Her lifelong motto, a verse she often quoted (Job 13:15 KJV), summed up her determination to follow God: "Though he slay me yet I will trust him."[1]

Both she and her husband were Bible teachers and evangelists with close ties to the Keswick, or "Higher Life," movement, which had perfectionist leanings. They had seven children, only three of whom survived to adulthood; but Hannah's grandchildren, who were abandoned by her daughter Mary, became her own after their father's death. Of this large family so immersed in the Christian faith, only Hannah's faith survived to the end—and even hers was often riddled by doubts.

I have "known" Hannah for many years. Hers is one of those voices that rise out of the grave and speak to me. I resonate with her in so many ways. I understand her doubts, and I admire her for being a strong woman who heralded women's rights long before it was popular to do so. And she spoke forcefully for equality in marriage: "My ideal of marriage is an *equal partnership*, neither one assuming control over the other. . . . Any marriage other than this is to my mind tyranny on the one hand and slavery on the other." But even more I resonate with her as a mother and a grandmother. She was convinced that she was more committed to the responsibilities of motherhood than most women were, and after her first grandchild was born she described herself as "a perfectly idiot grandmother."[2] All I can say is, *Yes, Hannah, I know that feeling; your sentiment is mine.*

A Struggle to Find God

Hannah was raised in a very religious Quaker home, but she began to experience religious doubts early in her adult life. In 1855, four years after her marriage to Robert, she went through a difficult time of questioning God, as she later recalled: "I began to wonder if God could be all-powerful since the creatures He created seem to have so little power to resist evil." The following year she reflected back on that time: "At least I am not now in such a totally hopeless spiritual state as I was last year. . . . There must be a good and merciful and loving spirit somewhere in the universe." It was the inconsolable grief of losing her little five-year-old Nellie that brought Hannah out of her spiritual darkness.[3]

> For the first time in the two years since Hannah had openly questioned her faith, she felt a sense of God's presence. Nellie's spirit seemed near, encouraging her to strive earnestly after holiness. Once she called out to her daughter, "My precious child, my angel child, thou shalt indeed be, I trust, a link to draw me up to heaven."[4]

Another traumatic time for Hannah came when she decided to depart from her Quaker heritage. Her Bible reading, which had not been encouraged among the Quakers, had begun to transform her life, and she was convinced of her need to be baptized and to partake in the Lord's Supper with other believers. As a result of this choice, she was ostracized from her family "like an outcast from my earthly father's house." As time passed, however, the anger and hurt subsided, and family ties were reestablished.[5]

From the time of their initial contacts with Baptists, the Smiths eagerly sought spiritual counsel from Christians in other faith traditions—particularly those in Methodist holiness groups. And it was during a holiness camp meeting that Robert experienced the "second blessing," also referred to as the baptism of the Holy Spirit: "Suddenly from head to foot, Robert was shaken with what seemed like a magnetic thrill of heavenly delight," Hannah later wrote, "and floods of glory seemed to pour through him, soul and body."[6]

Hannah longed for what her husband had experienced, but she simply could not get it. She went down to the altar, armed with handkerchiefs, thinking she would be overcome with weeping, but nothing happened. The following year, she fasted and prayed for two weeks prior to a Bible conference. Other people, including Robert, were praying for her as well. Finally the night of the conference arrived, and hours passed as the lamps grew dimmer, but Hannah had no wonderful experience to report. She concluded that she had a consciousness of God's presence and that there was "nothing more needed, no manifestation of His presence or His love, no melting of heart, no fullness of joy."[7]

She later concluded, no doubt using Robert as her prime example, that "emotional blessings" were not as stable and permanent as were the spiritual truths that sprang from Scripture.

In 1872, Hannah mourned the death of her oldest child Frank, stricken at eighteen by typhoid fever. The indescribable sorrow only exacerbated problems that had already surfaced in the marriage. Robert was a very emotional person—not infrequently mentally unstable—and he wanted Hannah to be more loving and responsive to him. From Hannah's letters and diaries, her biographer concluded that she was probably "not a sexually responsive woman."[8]

Trials of Married Life

In 1873, Robert took for a trip abroad, hoping to find a cure for his depression and physical ailments. Hannah was pregnant when he left, and later that year she gave birth to a stillborn baby. Some weeks earlier, she had written her cousin Carrie, saying, "Life with its failures has pressed upon me of late with the most unspeakable sadness." After the birth, she wrote again: "Oh, Carrie, I did long for my baby so inexpressibly. No one knows the need I have of just the comfort a baby always brings to me."[9]

Hannah's trials came in many forms. In 1874, she sailed to England and joined Robert, who had recovered from his depression. Together they preached effectively at Higher Life conferences—though there were many who opposed the idea of a woman preacher. Yet Hannah preached on every opportunity that was offered her—even onboard ship as they returned to America, though "she was somewhat hampered by the fact that she had lost her false teeth during the course of the Oxford convention." After that she took with her a "spare set of false teeth."[10]

Robert returned to Europe alone in 1875 and soon became "an international figure, mesmerizing large audiences with his preaching," which often took place before thousands of people packed in auditoriums. He reported to his son that "all Europe is at my feet." When Hannah joined him, she, too, was hailed as a great Bible teacher. Their styles were very different, however: the emotional Robert brought his audience to tears, whereas Hannah taught the Bible in a "plain, vigorous manner."[11]

In the summer of 1875, Hannah left England for Switzerland for a short rest. For nearly two years, her life had been good. "Robert's nervousness was entirely gone. He had become a world-famous preacher. There was sweet accord once again between husband and wife."[12] They had four healthy children, and Hannah's bestselling book, *The Christian's Secret of a Happy Life*, had been released.

But storm clouds loomed on the horizon. Before her trip to Switzerland was over, Hannah received a telegram informing her that Robert was ill in Paris and that she should go there immediately. When she arrived she learned from her husband that he had been dismissed from his preaching at the Brighton conference because a young woman had reported that he had come to her room and made improper advances toward her and "explained to her the physical thrills that a man and a woman can experience together while holding each other and praying" (a "doctrine" Robert had come to believe some years earlier). Now the famous evangelist was making headlines again: "Famous Evangelist Found in Bedroom of Adoring Female Follower."[13]

From Saving Souls to Losing Faith

The Smiths returned to Philadelphia, where Robert's mental condition deteriorated. Hannah reported to a friend, "I have not the faintest hope that he will ever recover from it." Yet, by the summer of 1876, Robert had recovered sufficiently to preach again, this time in America at the Framingham conference. But when those meetings were over, Robert concluded he would never speak again—and with good reason. He was seriously doubting his beliefs, and by 1877, "he was in the process of losing his faith altogether."[14]

Virtually every *reason* for doubting and losing faith can be found in the experiences of this family, including depression and mental illness, immorality, philosophical reasoning, biblical criticism and disappointment with God. There is no doubt that depression and mental illness contributed to Robert's loss of faith and perhaps influenced other family members in their struggle to believe. "In his bouts of depression," writes Henry, "Robert had a habit of reciting off a list of family mental disorders."[15]

Hannah struggled with doubts herself. She had sought the baptism of the Holy Spirit on several occasions and again in 1876 and 1877, following Robert's scandal. Friends had felt "floods of blessings" from the experience, but she, by her own account, remained "a dry old stick" and was convinced that she had not received the baptism because of her unbelief.

> Questions about God continued to plague her. In her letters of 1876 to 1878, she expressed her anxiety and doubt. Since her faith in God was the most important thing in her life, her anguish of spirit must have been beyond belief as she feared that she was losing it.[16]

But death again intervened. "Little Ray, our youngest, our perfect little girl, was only eleven and her life was full of promise," Hannah wrote in her diary. "For her loss there was no comfort, but simply and only the sweet will of God. As I sorrowed, I began at once to say, 'Thy will be done,' and that blessed will has surrounded me like a fortress from that moment to this."[17] She now had one more link to heaven.

Hannah was heartbroken by Robert's loss of faith. And his loss of faith corresponded with a loss of moral grounding. In 1882, she discovered his secret relationship with another woman. In the years that followed, all she could do was look the other way in "disgust watching Robert sneaking out of the house to go to his mistress." There is no direct connection between Robert's loss of faith and his extramarital relationship with his "polished female friend," as he referred to her. But even if he had been able to fool the public, he could not have pretended to his wife that he was a man of faith. His "blatantly immoral behavior angered her," but there was little she could do.[18]

Sins of the Father Visited on the Children

There would be more heartache in Hannah's life in her later years—especially as it related to her daughter Mary, who abandoned her husband and two young girls for another man. Hannah often struggled with an angry son-in-law to maintain a close relationship with her granddaughters, and when he died prematurely, she went to court to gain custody of them. She won the battle against his appointed guardians, and she loved her granddaughters as her own children.

Hannah, unlike her husband and children, clung to the faith to the very end. She defended her faith to her daughter in very practical terms. In one particular instance she spoke not of her certainty of the existence of a personal God but of her certainty of her *belief* in God: "All in me that is good comes directly from my belief in a personal God. And my *greatest* strength has come from my persistent holding on to this belief through days and months of fierce temptation to the contrary. Thy father gave place to doubt, . . . the growth and development of agnosticism in [him]." She begged her children not to talk with their father about issues of faith, because she believed "his unbelief is contagious."[19]

But there were others besides her husband who influenced her children. The Smith family almost seemed to be a magnet for unbelievers—some of whom were well-known celebrities of the day. Walt Whitman, for example, who lived nearby, visited in 1882, at Mary's invitation. He stayed in the Smith home, occasionally for days at a time, and "formed a lifelong friendship with all of them except Hannah."[20] Whitman's religious beliefs were secular, embracing self and individualism. "I celebrate myself, and sing to myself," he penned in his most celebrated work, *Leaves of Grass.* "Divine am I inside and out, and I make holy."[21] He contemplated starting a new religion, with its own Bible, *Leaves of Grass*—a work many regarded obscene because of its overt sexual references. Poet John Greenleaf Whittier referred to it as a "phallic frenzy."[22]

If his celebrated sexuality was not enough to alarm Hannah, Whitman's testimony was. "I have never had any particular religious experiences," he boasted, "never felt that I needed to be saved—never felt the need of spiritual regeneration—never had any fear of hell or distrust of the scheme of the universe. I always felt that it was perfectly right and for the best."[23] This was not the message Hannah wanted propagated in her home—even if the preacher was one of the century's most famous poets.

Her efforts to prevent her three children from losing their faith was "like trying to stop an avalanche with two bare hands," writes Henry. "Unbelief dominated the intellectual, literary and artistic circles with whom Mary, Logan and Alys traveled." Logan later testified that he lost his faith as an eleven-year old boy. Mary began to turn away from the faith while reading Herbert Spencer at Radcliffe College, and her failed marriage to a Roman Catholic and subsequent affair with a freethinking artist sealed her unbelief. Alys married Bertrand Russell, five years her junior, a "brilliant and articulate atheist. Her faith did not last more than a month after their marriage."[24]

A Theology of Heaven and Unbelief

When Robert died in 1898, Hannah grieved. All of her bottled-up resentment seemed to dissipate. Soon after he died, she wrote to a friend that in death, her "dear husband was permitted to escape from the earthly tabernacle" and "that his long time of darkness is over and that God's light has shown upon him at last." She did not blame him: "I have always felt sure his clouded spiritual life was the result of physical causes and I believe it was truly the 'binding of Satan' from which deliverance has come."[25]

Hannah's response to his death—and her ability to thoroughly enjoy her children and extended family, despite their massive defections from the faith—is best explained by her theological perspective. In death, Robert had been "safely gathered," just as she believed all God's children would one day be "safely gathered"—including her own unbelieving children and grandchildren.[26]

Indeed, Hannah was considered suspect by many ministers and conference organizers of her day because of what some people defined as universalism. She was convinced that in the end God would bring all people to himself. She strongly opposed the doctrine of election: that God would chose only certain ones for eternal life. Her focus was on the love of God—more specifically the mother-love of God. She was convinced that all people—even the most wretched ones she met on the streets—were God's creatures and that God would not abandon them in the end.

> As a mother, I will never cease to love my children, no matter what they do. God, our loving God, has a heart of mother-love infinitely greater than mine. He never withholds his love from any sinner, no matter how black-hearted or unrepentant the person may be. His love is completely unconditional. Oh, it is too much. I cannot bear to hear a preacher of the gospel say such limited and untruthful things about the Love of God.[27]

Her belief that in the end God would restore all people to himself was termed the doctrine of "restitution," and it was strongly opposed by virtually all ministers of her day who preached on the torments of hell for unbelievers. But she insisted that theirs was the unbiblical position. Henry sums up her biblical arguments:

> Hannah's message was basically this: "God is the Creator of every human being; therefore He is the Father of each one and they are all His children. Furthermore, Christ died for *everyone*, and is declared to be the 'propitiation' not for our sins only, but also for the sins of the

whole world (1 John 2:2). However great the ignorance or grievous the sin, the promise of salvation is without limitation, whether it happens in this world or the next."[28]

That final restitution comes when "at the name of Jesus every knee should bow, of things in heaven, and things in earth and things under the earth; and that every tongue should confess that Jesus Christ is Lord, to the glory of God the Father" (Phil 2:10–11).

Hannah's effort to present an alternative to the Christian doctrine of condemnation is understandable. Hell, when viewed as a place of eternal punishment—whether for those who have never heard the gospel message or whether for family members who have had every opportunity to hear and yet turned away—is a stumbling block. Christians through the centuries have struggled with the doctrine of hell. The matter was recently discussed in straightforward terms when the president of a fundamentalist Southern Baptist seminary told Larry King that any Jewish person who does not profess faith in Jesus will go to hell. It was this kind of "playing God" that Hannah was confronting.

Many people do not believe the matter is solved by the Calvinist perspective, which insists that God has elected people for salvation before the foundations of the earth. But the typical Reformed Christian would quickly insist that God alone knows who is among the elect. Such a view denies to any mere mortal the authority of telling a talk-show host who is in and who is out. Indeed, from a Reformed perspective, election from a human level is most clearly understood as a call to service. This concept comes through powerfully in the writings of the late missionary and Anglican bishop Lesslie Newbigin, who argues that election is "not a special privilege but special responsibility."[29]

But Newbigin does not solve the problem of hell. Nor is there any way to *solve* the problem of eternal punishment. Indeed, apart from some form of universalism like the doctrine of restitution, there is no easy consolation for the one who watches a loved one walk away from the faith. The Christian's consolation must rest in the boundless grace of God, to whom all judgment belongs.

Marjorie Holmes addresses this issue from a very personal perspective. In "My Child Has Lost Faith," Holmes gives words of comfort and hope to all Christians who are heartbroken, as Hannah was, by loved ones who have walked away from faith.

> My child has lost faith in you, God, and my heart is sad.
>
> I hear him using all the familiar, well-worn arguments that deny your very existence. And I want to laugh and I want to scold and I want to cry.
>
> For I remember far too well my own young voice of arrogance and inflated learning, dismissing you. And I see my mother gazing at me with the same expression I must be wearing now.
>
> Only more hurt, more deeply disturbed, saying "I can't answer your logic. I can only say I *know*."
>
> I remember all the years I kept her waiting, hurt her, rejected her, condescended to her as I stormed and stumbled along all the enticing, argument-cluttered paths to find a faith that she had never questioned.
>
> Waiting for a time when I would exclaim, "Why, it's true! I know."
>
> And now I see my child kicking aside the foundations, setting off on the identical stormy journey. And I can only ask you not to lose sight of him. Not to let go of him altogether. And wish him a safe return.
>
> Wish for the time when (I hope it won't take him so long) he too will say, with an air of discovery and relief: "I know."[30]

4

Knowing God

Mystery or
Matter of Fact?

We must be aware of the depth
of the mystery that confronts us.
Man must hesitate when he is about to
say something about God's being.

— J. H. BAVINCK

"God vs. God." This was the title of a two-page editorial in *Christianity Today*. I was familiar with the debate, but I plunged into the editorial eager to read what new light might be shed on the issues. I knew also that this kind of controversy would stir up my seminary students.

I love paradox and mystery and tension in life—and in my classes. Indeed, on the first day of class as I am introducing a course, I often quote from Parker Palmer's book *The Courage to Teach*. He challenges teachers to allow for differences and tensions in the classroom as well as in their own lives: "Be patient toward all that is unresolved in your heart. . . . Try to love the contradictions themselves. . . . Do not now seek the resolutions, which cannot be given because you would not be able to live them. . . . Live the contradictions now."[1] Theologically, the mystery and paradox and unknowability of God are balanced by God's self-revelation in the Scriptures. And that is essentially what "God vs. God" is all about.

At the very heart of this debate is the question of God's nature: who is this One that we as Christians worship? The editorial's opening paragraph grabs the readers' attention:

> There is no more boring concept of God than that traditionally presented by philosophical theism. Besides which, who wants to pray to an abstract and uninvolved deity? Certainly, the classic philosophical arguments tend to yield a "maximal Being" rather than the God of the Bible who loves his creatures passionately and hates corruption and oppression. The biblical God is not boring, but is, as Pascal wrote: "Fire! God of Abraham, God of Isaac, God of Jacob, not of the philosophers and scholars. Certitude. Certitude. Feeling. Joy. Peace. God of Jesus Christ."[2]

The debate pits classical theists against the proponents of the "openness of God," including Clark Pinnock, John Sanders and Gregory Boyd. These theologians depict God as one who has a very personal, give-and-take relationship with his creatures—one who takes "risks by engaging his lost creatures in truly mutual relationships that have no guaranteed outcomes." As such, "God does not genuinely know the future, and he actually changes his mind when shifting situations demand it."[3]

Classical theists, on the other hand, insist that when God is depicted in Scripture as having limitations or moral deficiencies, the biblical writer is using human analogy: "At the heart of the idea of anthropomorphism is the idea that though we speak of God by means of human analogy, we do not have access to the inner works of his mind."[4]

Five years before this "God vs. God" editorial appeared, *Christianity Today* presented a forum on the same topic, focusing on *The Openness of God*, a collection of essays authored by Clark Pinnock and others.[5] In response to these authors' hope that good will triumph over evil, Timothy George writes:

But the "open God" cannot guarantee that it will. He can only struggle with us against the chaos and keep on trying harder. One might feel sorry for such a God, even sympathize with him in his cosmic battle against the power of darkness. But one would hardly be moved to fall down and worship such an attenuated, transcendence-starved deity. The "open God" is a long way from the awesome, holy, unsurprisable (yet ever-surprising) God of the Bible, the God who "is a consuming fire."[6]

George goes on to suggest that "in their desire to defend 'God's reputation,' " these authors "have devised a user-friendly God who bears an uncanny resemblance to a late-twentieth-century seeker. They need not be so concerned about 'God's reputation.' They only need to let God be God."[7]

The "God vs. God" debate is certainly not the first controversy over the nature of God, nor will it be the last. Indeed, it is interesting that theologians—who should be in the know—seem to struggle as much as philosophers do in an effort to understand or define God. Since all Christian theologians depend on the Bible as their primary source of revelation, one might think there would be more agreement among them.

The fact is that they approach the Bible and theological understandings from very different perspectives. In his argument against the openness of God, featured in a cover story in *Christianity Today*, Christopher Hall makes reference to theologian J. I. Packer: "Packer has warned me," Hall writes, "to beware of draining the mystery out of the Scripture in a misplaced desire for rational consistency. . . . Hence I have learned to live with incompleteness, paradox, incomprehensibility, and deep mystery in my relationship with God and as I think theologically."[8]

The current debate between classical theists and open theists is primarily an in-house controversy among evangelicals in which both sides view the Bible as the authoritative word of God. More often the theological debates about the nature of God pit liberals against evangelicals—though in many instances, evangelicals do not seriously enter the debate because they regard the authority of Scripture as a foundational tenet without which the discussions are essentially useless.

Process Theology and the Limited Power of God

The "openness of God" theology, some argue, draws from process theology, which also sees limits to God's power and knowledge; process theology, however, significantly limits the authority of Scripture. One might define process theology simply as a view that perceives God as a verb more than as a noun, a view in which God is a being or essence who is ever moving and ever changing. A popular book that shows the influence of process theology is *God: A Biography* by Jack Miles, a former Jesuit who has his training in religious studies and Near Eastern languages. The issues in the book are described on the back cover: "What sort of a 'person' is God? What is his 'life story'? Is it possible to approach him not as an object of religious reverence, but as the protagonist of the world's greatest book—as a character who possesses all the depths, contradictions, and ambiguities of a Hamlet?" In the first chapter, "Can God's Life Be Written?" Miles lays out some of the difficulties with doing just that:

> The plot begins with God's desire for a self-image. It thickens when God's self-image becomes a maker of self-images, and God resents it. From this initial conflict, others emerge. . . . Why did God create the world? Why on flimsy grounds, did he destroy it so soon after creating it? Why, having so long shown no interest whatsoever in the wars of mankind, did he suddenly become a warrior? Why, having attended slightly if at all to morality, did he become a moralist? As his covenant with Israel seemed to break down, what consequences loomed for him? What kind of life awaited him after that impending breakup? How did he adjust to his failure to keep the promises he made through the prophets? What is his experienced life as a being without parents, spouse, or children?[9]

How should we respond to Jack Miles—or for that matter to Clark Pinnock or John Sanders? It is easy for those who have abandoned the Bible as the word of God to dismiss such musings as inconsequential; but for those who take the Bible very seriously, these are difficult questions. In his critique of the arguments made by "openness of God" proponents, Douglas Kelly argues that they "have failed to think through the profound difference between created (finite) being and uncreated (infinite) being." (The same could be said for process theologians and for Miles.) "They seem to work on the assumption," continues Kelly, "of the univocal validity of language for both God and man. That is, a word must mean for God the exact same thing it does for human. For instance, 'before and after' impose on God's experience the same limitations they do on that of humankind."[10]

The Hiddenness of God

Who is God? This is the most fundamental question related to belief and unbelief. *Who* is God? *Where* is God? *What* affinity does God have with humans? These questions and issues challenge theologians, philosophers, sociologists, psychologists and a host of other specialists. For many Christians, these questions are superfluous. The God depicted in children's Sunday school lessons is sufficient for a lifetime. For many unbelievers, an "unknown God" is surely no God at all.

Indeed, there are many who easily confuse the issue of God's existence with the issue of his "unknowability." The difference between belief and unbelief is usually cast in terms of those who not only *believe* in God but *know* who God is, and those who do not believe and thus cannot know who God is. And perhaps that generalization is valid. But there is a subcategory of those in the former group who believe in God but who concede they cannot grasp the essence of God. From the psalmist to Martin Luther to Karl Barth, many speak of the distance, the hiddenness, the otherness of God.

The unknowability of God is a concept not often raised in evangelical circles. Evangelicals tend to speak very freely of their personal relationship with God; and from their music and prayers to their Bible-centered devotions, they are on very familiar terms with God. The more "charismatic" they are, the more they tend to testify to *knowing* God and to God's speaking to them and interacting with them as though they shared a two-way relationship between friends of equal standing—almost between best buddies.

With an allusion to Aristotle's "unmoved mover," Pinnock speaks of new understandings of God in his article "God as Most Moved Mover: How the Pentecostal Theology of Experience Is Changing Our Understanding of God." Here Pinnock censures two of the most influential theologians in Christian history, Augustine and Aquinas, suggesting that it was through them that "the pagan/Christian synthesis" was "concocted," resulting in a one-sided view of God that favored "distance over nearness." Pinnock and others who insist that "God has been held hostage by philosophy" emphasize their knowledge of God through personal experience and speak of being in dialogue and partnership with God.[11]

The confession and experience of *knowing* God is something that should not be dismissed, although in most evangelical churches that is where the sole emphasis is placed. "The hiddenness of God is a topic seldom discussed by Christians," writes Kelly Clark, "but it is a prime source of our anxiety. In it are rooted the problems of religious doubt, human suffering, and the meaning of life."[12] This hiddenness should not be exaggerated, but the *known* and the *unknown* dimensions of God ought to be viewed in one sense as complementary and in another sense as paradox. In his *Dictionary of Latin and Greek Theological Terms*, Richard Muller gives the following entry, which is helpful to our understanding:

> Deus absconditus/Deus revelatus: the *hidden God/the revealed God*; the paradox of God's unknowability and self-manifestation as stated by Luther. The issue is not that God has been hidden and has now revealed himself, but rather that the revelation that has been given to man defies the wisdom of the world because it is the revelation of the hidden God. God is revealed in hiddenness and hidden in his revelation. He reveals himself paradoxically to thwart the proud, and *sub contrario*, under the opposite, omnipotence manifest on the cross.[13]

In Reformed circles, this paradox is more readily accepted. The majesty and sovereignty of God are emphasized, and Reformed folks (at least, historically) have tended to see their status before God as one of utter submission. Almighty God has spoken for all times through his Word, and our response in the presence of God is to fall—albeit, figuratively—prostrate before him. God's sovereign will is sometimes confused with determinism, but whatever that will is, it does not suggest the give-and-take relationship that is implied by the theological construct known as relational theism or the "openness of God."

John Calvin, who is often regarded a master of theological details, readily acknowledged that he himself was often stumped by the unknowability of God. One of his biographers writes:

> In the absence of divine revelation, therefore, Calvin recommended, on religious matters, a deliberate agnosticism, a *docta ignorantia* that allows God to be wiser than we are. "To be ignorant of things which it is neither possible nor lawful to know," he argued, "is to be learned." He retold with approval Cicero's anecdote about Simonides who, when asked by Hiero the Tyrant what God is, requested a day to consider, asked for further delays as the question was repeated, and finally concluded that the question only became more baffling the longer the thought about it. "He wisely suspended judgment," Calvin concluded, "on a subject so obscure."[14]

J. H. Bavinck and the "Unknown God"

"The Unknown God"—this is the title of a chapter in J. H. Bavinck's book *Faith and Its Difficulties.* I have only recently come to know the late Reverend Dr. Johan H. Bavinck (1895–1964), and I am still barely an acquaintance—having read only two books by him and some articles about him. But he intrigues me. He was a Dutch Reformed missionary to Indonesia whose "radical surrender to Jesus," according to one source, "was the deep well from which flowed his ecumenical inclinations."[15]

Many Reformed believers tend to shun ecumenical activity, but for Bavinck, ecumenicalism grew naturally from his faith. "He was ecumenical, not because he felt forced to be showy or stylish, but simply because with childlike simplicity he thankfully and joyously recognized the Spirit of Jesus Christ in whichever human beings and church communions He was revealing Himself."[16]

Some of the descriptions of Bavinck by J. Verkuyl, a fellow Dutch missionary and scholar, seem more fitting of a contemporary charismatic than of a highly trained Dutch scholar whose studies and writings were focused on issues of theology, philosophy, psychology and missiology:

> The genius of his [Bavinck's] transparent Christian devotion lay in his act of repeatedly and radically surrendering himself to Christ. . . . His radical devotion to Jesus was also the source of his deep sensitivity toward the needs of his fellow human beings. He had utmost respect for human beings and loved them all—people of every race and station in life, children, and young people. His extraordinary courtesy and friendliness toward everyone were not for him mere acquired rules of social intercourse; they flowed from the sensitivity to people which he ever and again was learning through union with Jesus.[17]

But there was another side to Bavinck of which his colleague only hints: "He had been brought out of the power of darkness. . . . And how keenly did he know of the powers of darkness, even in his very own life!"[18] Whatever this darkness may have been, Bavinck was able to speak about the difficulties of faith like few others can. Unlike other missionaries who speak of God with the confidence of evangelists, he spoke of being "constrained by fear and dread when we venture to talk about God, whose thoughts we cannot think after Him, and whose motives we cannot fathom or understand." No matter what language we use, we "come far short in doing justice to His greatness and holiness." Indeed, Bavinck feared he would "run the danger of pulling Him down to the *niveau* of my own life and thought."[19]

Although Bavinck goes on to say that the *Unknown* can become *Known* through nature, through leading and guidance, and through "His revelation in Jesus Christ," yet the mystery, awe and uncertainty remain:

> In all the voices that reach my ear, in all the books I open, I recognize and see Him, the mighty Unknown, the Regent of life, the Ruler of all nations. And with every step I take, I have difficulty understanding that the Unknown God is the same as the God who spoke to me in Jesus Christ. And sometimes I am oppressed with fear and anguish that I can

see no confluence of these two, that I cannot see them proceeding in
one direction, and that everything will be demolished and destroyed.
That is our tension and our strain. And we shudder![20]

The honesty of this missionary, a man who devoted his life to proclaiming the Christian message, is encouraging to anyone who has difficulty finding God in the contemporary world of global pluralism and
infinite cosmic distance. His words are as profound today as they were
decades ago when he wrote them—and they speak to those who struggle with the hiddenness and absence of God.

God's Hiddenness and Absence

Most people who struggle with doubt and unbelief experience an
absence of God's presence. They may feel a sense of loss—or they may
not care at all—about having little or no sense of God's nearness. They
typically make no pretense of "running" or "hiding" from God, for
they have no sense of God's searching for them. It is true that Adam
and Eve, Jonah and others sought to hide from God, but their particular problems related to their conscious disobedience, not to their
doubt. Today many people testify of their conscious disobedience, of
their anger and of shaking their fist in the face of God because they
resent God's interference in—not his absence from—their lives.

Yet others feel God's absence profoundly. Here again Bavinck offers
understanding:

> According to the Bible the world in which we now live is an absolutely
> abnormal world. Our aeon is a misty, nebulous age in which things are
> not what they are in reality. One of the consequences of this is that it
> often seems as if God is absent. God hides Himself: "Verily thou are a
> God that hidest thyself," Isaiah says (Is 45:15). It is moving to read the
> many complaints in the Bible about the secrecy of God. Again and again
> we read that He hides His countenance, that He does not stretch out
> His arm, that He does not show His helping hand. Even in the very
> heart of the gospel we find the touching cry: "Why hast thou forsaken
> me?" . . .
>
> God often remains hidden so that one would think He does not exist,

but He executes His plans in spite of the manifold events of History. Even though it seems at times as if things take their own course, God has a hand in them more than we think. Even in this misty age, He is far more actually King than we suppose, although we can see practically nothing of His Kingdom.[21]

Bavinck was able to find God's presence most profoundly in the incarnate, living Son of God, Jesus Christ. But those who have abandoned faith in God often regard the deity of Christ—and his imminent return—as little more than a myth or a cosmic joke. We have made God in our own image, many sociologists of religion insist, and Jesus is our key to understanding this god with whom we can identify. The story of the incarnation, they would argue, has been told one way or another in ancient traditions.

God and Myth and C. S. Lewis

C. S. Lewis spoke to this issue of God and myth. In fact, his abiding love for ancient mythology gave him insights into the Christian faith that have helped remove a major stumbling block for believers and unbelievers alike. In his essay "Myth Became Fact," he took the very objections often hurled at Christianity and turned them into supporting evidence.

> The heart of Christianity is a myth which is also a fact. The old myth of the Dying God, *without ceasing to be myth*, comes down from the heaven of legend and imagination to the earth of history. It *happens*— at a particular date, in a particular place, followed by definable historical consequences. We pass from a Balder or an Osiris, dying nobody knows when or where, to a historical Person crucified . . . *under Pontius Pilate*. By becoming fact it does not cease to be myth: that is the miracle. . . . God is more than god, not less: Christ is more than Balder, not less. We must not be ashamed of the mythical radiance resting on our theology. We must not be nervous about "parallels" and "pagan Christs": they *ought* to be there—it would be a stumbling block if they weren't.[22]

Lewis is a powerful example of one who found a middle ground between the impersonal theology of what is often termed classical theism and the open theology that some charge turns God into a god. "Yes, Lewis will provide us with the scholastic proof," writes Louis Markos, "but he will not let us rest until we acknowledge and feel the overwhelming reality and presence of that God whom Lewis describes, variously, as the hunter, the lover, and the bridegroom."[23] The image of God as hunter is probably the most familiar, particularly as it relates to Lewis's own conversion story.

Belief in God was something that Lewis had taken for granted as a child—at least until the death of his mother. Why, he wondered, had not God, if there was a God, answered his prayers for her recovery? During Lewis's young adult years, God was no longer in the picture; and for all practical purposes, Lewis was an atheist. Following World War I, he went to Oxford University and then began a teaching career. It was during this period of his life that he sensed "that God, if there was a God, was almost ruthlessly following him. . . . That *he* was the prey, and was being quietly remorselessly hunted, and that God was closing in on him." Finally, in 1929, he realized he could no longer escape God: "I gave in and admitted God was God, and knelt and prayed: perhaps, that night, the most dejected and reluctant convert in England."[24]

Lewis came to know and understand God through the Scriptures and ancient creeds as well as through personal experience and mythology. And permeating all these ways of knowing was the element of mystery.

Proclaiming a Mystery

Lewis helps me to comprehend God more clearly, especially during those times when I am struggling with a profound sense of God's absence. It is *mystery* that allows us to live at peace with absence. I cannot imagine faith apart from mystery. Mystery permeates every particle of the truths I hold so dear, and writers who proclaim that mystery grab and hold my attention.

Frederick Buechner, a minister and prolific writer, is one such

writer. He speaks of mystery in his book *Telling Secrets*. Indeed, he is a
preacher of mystery—what every preacher ought to be.

> I had never understood so clearly before what preaching is to me. Basi-
> cally, it is to proclaim a Mystery before which, before whom, even our
> most exalted ideas turn to straw. It is also to proclaim this Mystery with
> a passion that ideas alone have little to do with. It is to try to put the
> gospel into words not the way you would compose an essay but the way
> you would write a poem or a love letter—putting your heart into it, your
> own excitement, most of all your own life. It is to speak words that you
> hope may, by grace, be bearers not simply of new understanding but of
> new life both for the ones you are speaking to and also for you.[25]

Recognizing and appreciating God as mystery—as opposed to God
as defined by facts and proofs—can be an important step in coming to
terms with doubt and unbelief. God's hiddenness and absence make
sense only in the context of mystery. But emphasizing *mystery* is a
dangerous path, a well-known evangelical apologist recently warned
me; in his mind it smacked of Eastern mysticism. Perhaps so. But in
contemplating mystery, I stand with a long tradition of Christian thinkers—including J. H. Bavinck, a great missionary and evangelist who
honestly confessed his fear and anguish and difficulty in melding
together the Unknown God with the One who spoke to him in Jesus
Christ.

Coming to terms with mystery is a key element in retaining faith—at
least for me. And as I contemplate the stories of so many who have
walked away from faith, it occurs to me that they have walked away not
so much from *God*, but rather from a mistaken perception of God.
Recently I was jolted in my pew as I listened to a prayer that concluded the children's message in a Sunday morning worship service.
The pastor prayed, "Hi, God. It's me again." This kind of conversa-
tional familiarity, which is often heard in evangelical churches, is, it
seems to me, less than helpful in our comprehension of God and in
our efforts to make God known to our children. If God is greeted as we
would greet a friend on the phone, we may easily wonder if there is
anyone on the other end of the line. Many of those who lose their faith

are walking away from a "chatty daddy," not the Ultimate One who is truly *God*.

This God is not just my God of disaster. This God is my God of everyday living. From that perspective, yesterday's worship service was redeemed for me through the singing of the well-known hymn, "How Great Thou Art." It is a prayer that recognizes God as *God*—powerfully pondering God's creation in "awesome wonder."

> O Lord my God, when I in awesome wonder
> Consider all the worlds Thy hands have made. . . .

> And when I think that God, His son not sparing,
> Sent him to die, I scarce can take it in. . . .

> How great Thou art![26]

5

The Dark Night of the Soul

The Fine Line Between Belief & Unbelief

I battled to know my God real in the dark
while living in his silence, in the sense of his absence.
Now and then lightning forked from the sky, like a mystical sword,
or a watery sun gleamed from the earth's edge.
Sometimes I felt a glimmering of spirit like a clear night in the country,
away from the artificial city brightness. . . .
But mostly it was a long darkness, like a sentence of death.

—LUCI SHAW, *GOD IN THE DARK*

There is a particular kind of doubt of which I know nothing about—except through my reading. It is the doubt and darkness that often comes to mystics and meditators, those whose lives are devoted to a search for God and who, in the process of their search, dig so deep or reach so high only to come to a place where they find emptiness and darkness. There are also those Christians who encounter a spiritual darkness that is accompanied by psychological depression. These experiences are often described as *the dark night* or simply *the darkness* of the soul. This *dark night of the soul,* according to Georgia Harkness, is one that has troubled the hearts of fervent seekers in every age.

This experience of the dark night of the soul is a common theme in mystical literature. Not only St. John of the Cross but his teacher and comrade in spiritual reform, St. Teresa of Avila, describes with great vividness the soul's bereftness during periods of struggle to recapture the lost sense of God's nearness. . . . The most characteristic note in all descriptions of this unhappy state is that of a frustrated quest for the divine Presence. One who has found in God precious companionship desires to go on to more intimate spiritual fellowship and finds, to his great dismay, that he seems to be further from God than ever before.[1]

My understanding of the darkness of the soul, limited though it may be, comes primarily through the stories of those who have experienced this condition in their own spiritual pilgrimage. As I reflect on their testimonies, one of the most obvious and yet puzzling inferences I come away with is that there is often a very close relationship between seeking God and losing faith—though not necessarily losing faith altogether. It is perhaps a detail of more than passing interest that the majority of those who speak of this darkness are Roman Catholics. What do these Catholics have to say, I ask myself, to the fundamentalists and pentecostals and evangelicals whose stories are so prominent in the "losing faith" genre? In this chapter I offer a series of condensed stories that I hope will shed light on spiritual darkness and remind those who are encountering such darkness that they are not alone and that such darkness is not a sign of loss of faith.

One of the first accounts of this condition is *The Dark Night of the Soul*, written by John of the Cross, a sixteenth-century mystic. It was his belief that going through the dark night was part of the pilgrim's journey toward perfection. Thus this night was entrusted only to those who could endure it.

Dangers on the Journey of Darkness

John of the Cross (1542–1591) was part of the Spanish Carmelite tradition and a friend of the well-known mystic Teresa of Ávila. When describing the "dark night of the soul," he speaks of various levels, beginning with the first night and then continuing on into deeper progressions, with many references to darkness. In this vein, he writes:

> The spiritual night is the portion of very few; and they are those who
> have made some progress, exercised therein, of whom I shall speak
> hereafter. . . . God thus leaves them in darkness so great that they know
> not whither to betake themselves with their imaginations and reflec-
> tions of sense. They cannot advance a single step in meditation, as
> before, the inward sense now being overwhelmed in this night, and
> abandoned to dryness so great that they have no more any joy or sweet-
> ness in their spiritual exercises, as they had before, and in their place
> they find nothing but insipidity and bitterness.[2]

John warned spiritual pilgrims that they would face dangers on this
journey of darkness—dangers so severe that the one seeking God might
end up falling away:

> During the aridities, then, of the night of sense . . . spiritual persons
> have to endure great afflictions . . . because they are afraid that they will
> be lost on this road; thinking that they are spiritually ruined, and that
> God has forsaken them, because they find no help or consolation in
> holy things. . . . Under these circumstances, if they meet with no one
> who understands the matter, these persons fall away, and abandon the
> right road.[3]

John of the Cross offers practical counsel for the contemporary
spiritual seeker. He warns us that deep meditation is not without its
risks and that increasing the intensity of one's search for God does not
necessarily ensure one will *find* God. In fact, one might abandon the
faith in the process. To avoid such an outcome, the spiritual seeker
must be in contact with someone who knows how to navigate this dark
path. A fundamental question remains, however, as to the value of
intentionally pursuing the dark way—a question is properly raised as
we look at the testimony of Meister Eckhart and others who sought
this path.

Knowing God Through the Darkness of the Soul
It is important to realize that although the darkness of the soul often

includes a period of doubt and unbelief, the seeker's goal is to end on a higher spiritual plane. Indeed, many seekers have celebrated the concept of darkness as a way to light. Roman Catholic mystics have demonstrated this in their lives and in their writings. Meister Eckhart, a medieval German mystic, was an "enthusiastic exponent of the dark way." He insisted that a Christian who truly begins to find God realizes that the One who is found is not at all the One who was sought for. "Seek God," he wrote, "so as never to find him." It is this sense of *not finding* and *not knowing* that sets apart many of the pilgrims on the dark path.[4]

For Eckhart, seeking God was the closest one could get to knowing God, but his perspective on this unknowable God was characterized by disinterest:

> Bear in mind also that God has been immovably disinterested from the beginning and still is and that his creation of the heavens and the earth affected him as little as if he had not made a single creature. But I go further. All the prayers a man may offer and the good works he may do will affect the disinterested God as little as if there were neither prayers nor works.

Yet Eckhart was consumed with God, convinced that "my blessing in eternity depends on my being identified with God."[5]

Following a Dark Path

Thomas Merton (1915–1968), a widely recognized Catholic mystic, also followed a "dark path" in his pilgrimage of faith. Merton is a fascinating character who has almost gained a "cult" following in the decades since his untimely death. He was born in France; his parents were artists and essentially nonreligious. In his early twenties, after studying at Cambridge, he moved to America to live with relatives—both of his parents having died years earlier. He completed undergraduate and graduate studies in literature at Columbia University, during which time he lived a self-indulgent lifestyle and was involved in radical groups including the Communist Party. But while still in his early twenties, he became a religious seeker; and in 1938 he was baptized and joined the Roman Catholic Church.

Three years later he turned his back on the world and entered the Trappist Abbey of Our Lady of Gethsemani in Kentucky. It was here that he devoted much of his time to writing and spiritual seeking. His autobiography, *The Seven Story Mountain*, tells the story of his spiritual transformation and his quest for God.

During the last few years of his life, Merton abandoned the communal lifestyle of the monastery in order to live a solitary life in an isolated dwelling on the abbey grounds. This time of intense meditation and study led him more deeply into the mysticism of darkness. The end came suddenly: "In 1968, on a tour of Asia to confer and exchange ideas with religious leaders and to address a conference on Asian Christian contemplation, which included Buddhist monks, Merton died by electrocution while bathing in Bangkok, Thailand."[6]

Merton saw himself in a tradition of Christian contemplatives, whose concepts of God were understood within the framework of apophatic theology: "the God who has revealed Himself to us in His World has revealed himself as unknown in His ultimate essence." The Christian contemplative "is called mainly to penetrate the wordless darkness and apophatic light of an experience beyond concepts, and here he gradually becomes familiar with a God who is 'absent' and as if he were 'non-existent' to all human experience." God is experienced often as "a dazzling darkness" or as "the brightness of a most lucid darkness." God is "known in darkness . . . by not knowing him."[7]

Merton's seeking after God took him to such depths of darkness and emptiness that he lost all sense of God's presence. William Shannon powerfully captures this sense of void:

> The God we thought we had known is taken away from us and the mind is no longer able to think of Him. The joy of His presence is gone, because we no longer know Him who is present. We are not even sure that Anyone is present at all. The will that once loved God so ardently seems unable to love, because the object of love seems to have disap-

peared into impenetrable darkness. We no longer have Anyone even to
pray to; hence "gone is the sweetness of prayer. Meditation becomes
impossible, even hateful." . . . Then one day there is an illumination.
The soul comes to realize that in this darkness it has truly found the living God.[8]

As I contemplate Merton and his "wordless darkness," I again see
the fine line between the dark way and unbelief, as well as the difficulty
of distinguishing between the two. I am also reminded that this dark
way arises out of Roman Catholic tradition, where tradition itself is
given a much higher place than in Protestant circles. Protestants who
see the Scriptures alone as their authority will search in vain to find a
precedent for pursuing this dark path. Thus most Protestants (and
Catholics as well) balance a portrayal of God as *unknown* with God as
known—known particularly through the special revelation of Scripture.

The Absent God

The mystic who perhaps more than any other encountered the darkness of the soul was Simone Weil (1909–1943). She was born in Paris
into an assimilated Jewish family and later identified most closely with
Catholicism. At the age of fourteen, she writes that she "fell into one of
those fits of bottomless despair that come with adolescence." She felt
inferior to her brother, and she feared she would never understand the
truth of life. "After months of inward darkness," she writes, "I suddenly had the everlasting conviction that any human being . . . can
penetrate to the truth . . . if only he longs for truth and perpetually
concentrates all his attention upon its attainment." So began her
search for truth.[9]

In some respects, Weil followed the path of other spiritual pilgrims and mystics. For example, she recalled a time in 1937, writing,
"I had two marvelous days at Assisi. There alone in the little twelfth-
century Romanesque chapel . . . where Saint Francis used to pray,
something stronger than I was compelling me for the first time in my
life to go down on my knees."[10] She had other such experiences that
might be described as typical or ordinary for a mystic, but Weil was

far from the garden-variety Christian mystic.

Weil carries the concept of darkness to an extreme—though the term *darkness* itself is not one that she frequently uses to describe the state of the soul. She spoke of the "emptiness" and "void." "God is absent from the world," she writes, "except through the existence of those in this world in whom his love lives." Not only was God absent, but for all practical purposes, he was nonexistent: "we have to believe in a God who is like the true God in everything except that he does not exist." Then, we must ask, who is God? "This world, in so far as it is completely empty of God, is God himself." For Weil, one could know God through suffering, following the model of Jesus in his death on the cross. Her focus on suffering was formed through real observations of suffering in the lives of the working poor and the meaningless anguish of the Nazi death camps.[11]

To the average spiritual seeker, Weil's concept of God makes no sense. Most helpful in this regard is Susan Taubes's article on Weil, titled "The Absent God." Here Taubes distinguishes between religious atheism and secular atheism, and she sees Weil as the foremost proponent of a religious atheism that is characterized by "a mystical atheism, a theology of divine absence and nonbeing, of divine impotence, divine nonintervention, and divine indifference." Weil believed that "the existence of God may be denied without denying God's reality."[12]

A major difference between Weil and other mystics is that her mysticism is fused with intellectual skepticism rather than ecstatic reverie. She testified to no special revelation, visions or voices; indeed, she was skeptical of those who had such experiences. "Voices and visions, she writes, result from an illegitimate admixture of imagination in supernatural love; and the lives of the saints would have been still more wonderful without them."[13]

Is Weil's religious atheism preferable to secular atheism? For me this is not an easy question to answer. I would not want to disparage hers or anyone else's honest search for God. If her mystical atheism represents the most confident confession of faith she can muster, who am I to judge? But it seems to me that one's confession must include belief in the existence of God—a component that seems missing in Weil's confession.

A Sunless Tunnel and a Heavy Cross

Almost a polar opposite of Simone Weil is St. Thérèse of Lisieux (1873–1896), known as the "Little Flower," who has become a favorite saint of Christian seekers—both Catholic and Protestant. She died at age twenty-four—still almost a girl. Yet her effect on the Christian world has been enormous, especially since the publication of her autobiography in English. She was regarded "the greatest saint of modern times" by Pope Pius X.

Born in France as the youngest of five daughters of a wealthy merchant, St. Thérèse followed her sisters in entering a local Carmelite convent after her mother died. She had one goal: "I want to be a Saint." The story of her childhood was initially written "in obedience to her Superior"—and then it expanded as a spiritual pilgrimage of her life. What is perhaps most interesting about this pious saint is that during the eighteen months before her death in which she suffered from tuberculosis, she struggled with doubt and loss of faith. When she first sensed she was going to die, "the hope of going to heaven," she writes, "transported me with joy." But then came the dark night of the soul, of which she speaks in a very straightforward manner:

> On the evening of that happy day I went back joyfully to my cell and was going to fall quietly asleep when my dear Jesus gave me, as on the night before, the same sign that I should soon be entering eternal life. In those days my faith was so clear and vigorous that I found perfect happiness in the thought of heaven. I could not believe that there were people without faith. . . . But during those radiant days of Easter Jesus . . . allowed pitch-black darkness to sweep over my soul and let the thought of heaven, so sweet to me from my infancy, destroy all my peace and torture me. This trial was not something lasting a few days or weeks. I suffered it for months and am still waiting for it to end. I wish that I could express what I feel, but it is impossible. One must have traveled through the same sunless tunnel to understand how dark it is. . . . The voice of unbelievers came to mock me in the darkness. . . . May God forgive me!

He knows very well that although I had not the consolation of faith, I forced myself to act as if I had. I have made more acts of faith in the last year than in the whole of my life.[14]

For St. Thérèse, the story does not end with black darkness. "God sent me this heavy cross," she emphasized, "just at the time when I was strong enough to bear it." Although she did not seek such darkness, she was convinced that it was a necessary restraint of her natural desires on her pilgrimage to perfection—"all natural satisfaction from my longing for heaven." Even the desire to be with Jesus was motivated by selfishness, which she believed had to be eradicated. "By letting my faith be tempted, God has greatly increased my *spirit of faith*."[15]

It is difficult to separate one's spiritual experiences from one's emotions. Indeed, even as there is often a fine line between belief and unbelief, so also is there a fine line between the spiritual and the psychological. A psychologist might have a very different evaluation of the experiences described by Merton or Weil or St. Thérèse than would a spiritual counselor. What are the underlying causes of the darkness? Is depression a factor? In some instances, the darkness of the soul does not appear to be directly related to depression, but in other cases there is a very close connection, as was true with Henri Nouwen.

Henri Nouwen's "Depression of the Soul"

During the 1980s, after a remarkable tenure of teaching at Harvard University, Henri Nouwen (1932–1996), a Roman Catholic priest, gave up the prestige and camaraderie of his faculty position and moved to the L'Arche Daybreak community in Toronto. This was not a monastery, remote from the world. It was a "family"—six mentally handicapped people and four who were not. Of this group, the one who had the most lasting effect on Nouwen was Adam, a profoundly retarded twenty-five year old man—a man who could not walk, speak, laugh or cry. "As my fears gradually lessened," Nouwen confessed, "a love emerged in me so full of tender affection that most of my other tasks seemed boring and superficial compared with the hours spent with Adam. Out of his broken body and broken mind emerged a most beautiful human being offering me a greater gift than I would ever offer him."[16]

Many people who have been inspired by Nouwen's writings are entirely unaware of the deep depression he endured—a depression that combined the spiritual and emotional into a dark night of the soul. The worst episode of this darkness came soon after he began his ministry at Daybreak. It was precipitated in part by the severing of a close friendship with a young man who was also ministering at Daybreak.

Bart Gavigan, a counselor, who worked closely with Nouwen during his deepest period of depression, feared that he might not emerge from the darkness. Nouwen himself entertained those fears. Of this time, Gavigan writes:

> Henri was courageous and I admired him—but it was very, very dark indeed. He couldn't work out the despair in his life. This was not just a dark night of the soul, it was a dark night of everything, of the spirit, at the point of faith, at the point of his own being, desires, longings, and sexuality. It was a dark night at the point of his own calling, work, and writing. But he did not lose his faith.[17]

He did not lose his faith—at least in any sort of permanent sense—but according to his biographer, he "began to feel homeless, devoid of faith, and abandoned. He could no longer sleep, [and] cried uncontrollably for hours." Interestingly, the only source of consolation during this time was his study of Rembrandt, "the tormented . . . Dutch painter whose own agonizing inner journey had ultimately enabled him to paint *The Return of the Prodigal Son.*"[18] Nouwen's darkness was not a pilgrimage that he purposefully sought. He emerged with the strength of his faith intact, and the testimony he has left has encouraged others who endure what might be termed a "depression of the soul"—a terrible psychological and spiritual depression combined into one.

When I seek to compare the darkness that Nouwen experienced to the dark path of Merton or other *proponents* of the dark way, I see some significant differences. The darkness Nouwen encountered parallels the experience of other Christians from biblical times to the present. His dark night of the soul was far more an affliction than a path to follow. And out of this affliction came a life and testimony that has a powerful message of God's grace in a hurting world. As I reflect on Nouwen's dark night, I am inclined to think it truly is an *affliction* that many Christians are called upon to bear. But it is not something that should be sought as a path to God. The risks and dangers along the way are too high, and the benefits are tenuous at best.

God in the Dark

Luci Shaw writes powerfully of the curse of this affliction. "If doubt is a sin, I am a great sinner. I am cursed with questions, damned by doubts." So writes Shaw in *God in the Dark*. "I wonder," she continues, "whether I have any right, in this state, to teach in a Christian college, minister in church, or write." For Shaw, a widely acclaimed poet and writer, God remains in the dark—even at the end of her book. To a friend she confessed, "I'd relaxed my clutching for God, and am waiting in the dark night of doubt for God to make *his* move." The main body of the book focuses on the terminal illness of her husband, Harold, and on his subsequent death. But her doubts extend far beyond issues of grief. The book opens with her story of "one of her longest, darkest cycles," which lasted seven years.[19]

> I remember. I remember the dark clouds moving across the years of my life, stretched like a field of prairie wheat in the sun, dulled by the sudden shadows. Like the wandering weather, my seasons of doubts and questioning have often come and then moved on. . . . I battled to know my God real in the dark while living in his silence, in the sense of his absence. Now and then lightning forked from the sky, like a mystical sword, or a watery sun gleamed from the earth's edge. Sometimes I felt a glimmering of spirit like a clear night in the country, away from the artificial city brightness. . . . But mostly it was a long darkness, like a sentence of death.[20]

For some like St. Thérèse, the resolution to the darkness, the tunnel of darkness, is in a real sense light at the end of the tunnel. For others, there is never any real resolution—except to live one's life in the misty fog of uncertainty. For still others, there is acceptance of the condition. In the last paragraph of her book, Shaw writes:

> So I am waiting. And letting go. And have quit striving. I am allowing the community of Christians in the church to carry me along with them. At this moment I feel Jesus coming closer in a subjective but fulfilling way. It is not a rational proof of his reality, but it feels enough for now, as if something is clicking, snapping into place like the buttons on my Lay Readers cassock as I vested this morning to read about Abraham whose faith, flawed as it was, seamed with doubt, was enough.[21]

In my own spiritual pilgrimage, which began in childhood, doubt and faith have coexisted. This is not a condition I have chosen for myself, and it is not something that I can eliminate—nor would I necessarily want to. Doubt brings tension and vitality to my faith; it is ever challenging me to dig deeper, to mine for the gold nuggets of God's reality in my own life, and ever challenging me to soar higher and to discover the reality of God in the universe. Though I dig to the depths and soar to the heights, I am always grounded in the Bible, the very Word of God. But the Scripture does not limit (nor should it) my search elsewhere for that which can help unravel for me the mysteries of God. Thus I look to these spiritual pilgrims for insights that, at minimum, show me I am not alone in my struggle to find God.

In the end, though, the most important aspect of my spiritual pilgrimage is connecting with God in a way that is authentic to my own personality and being. To some that may seem terribly egocentric. God is God. How dare I identify my self as the starting point? But I know that any concept I have of God is filtered through the whole essence of who I am. Thus, as I pause in introspection, it does not surprise me that I find God neither in darkness nor in bright ecstasies. Once again an old hymn speaks the prayer of my heart in my search for God:

> I ask no dream, no prophet ecstasies,
> No sudden rending of the veil of clay,
> No angel visitant, no opening the skies,
> But take the dimness of my soul away. Amen.[22]

Part Two

This section explores major challenges to the Christian faith. The first of these chapters presents an overview from biblical times to the present, demonstrating that doubt and unbelief have been present in every era. It also identifies various challenges to faith that have arisen over the centuries. These challenges and obstacles to faith—both intellectual and emotive—are addressed more specifically in the chapters that follow.

Chapter seven focuses on the most prominent disciplines associated with unbelief, science and philosophy, which often function as a deterrent to Christian faith. From the time of the Enlightenment, many assumed that these disciplines counteracted a biblical form of Christianity, though for the most part intellectuals associated with the disciplines ignored the specifics of Christian teachings.

Certain other disciplines speak very directly to issues of religious faith and doubt, sometimes profoundly influencing Western culture and the rise of unbelief since the Enlightenment. In fact, some of the very academic disciplines that are presumed to strengthen Christian belief have had the opposite effect. Prime examples of these are the areas of theological and biblical studies, the challenges of which are featured in chapter eight. Other disciplines are so infused with unbelief that they obliterate any conception of God. Indeed, at times it was assumed that no credible philosopher, scientist, psychologist or sociologist could believe in the God of the Bible. Chapter nine addresses the fields of psychology and sociology as well as the social and lifestyle issues that frequently deter faith.

Other practical, nontheoretical matters serve as stumbling blocks to faith—problems that involve disappointment with God and disappointment with God's people. These issues form the subject matter of chapter ten, which deals with pain and evil in this world and in our personal lives; it deals also with the problem of sin and hypocrisy among Christians. All of these *objections* to the Christian faith, identified in this section, should be taken seriously. To dismiss them is to dismiss the experience of ones who are walking away from beliefs they once held dear.

6

Biblical & Historical Reflections of Doubt & Unbelief

*It is a common modern fallacy that the development of
scientific knowledge has made Christianity harder to accept. . . .
Only if we have the skill and patience to discover
why the gospel was a shock to man of the first century,
shall we be able to use it to shatter the complacency
and lift the vision of our own generation.*

— G . B . C A I R D

As a church and missions historian, I have always been curious about the numerous accounts of doubt and unbelief that I have encountered in my studies. We often presume that the history of Christianity is a story of belief that follows a sequence from the age of martyrdom, to the age of faith, to the age of reform, to the age of revivals, to the age of modern missions and evangelistic campaigns. Of course, every era has its share of infamous heretics, and we can clearly distinguish the unfaithful from the faithful. Beneath the surface, however, the history of Christianity is far more complex. It forms a tapestry in which threads of doubt are woven among the threads of certainty. Indeed the threads of belief and unbelief are often so closely shaded and well blended that they are difficult to differentiate.

The origins of unbelief are unmistakable. The Bible opens in paradise, with unbelief only a temptation away. From the Fall onward, God's people have an inclination toward unbelief. Martin Marty, the premier historian of American church history, writes of this phenomenon:

> What is original in today's unbelief? It is misleading or fruitless to ask this question as if unbelief itself were a new phenomenon. . . . The Bible gives no license for its readers to draw the conclusion that belief came without struggle to man or that faithfulness prevailed in its time. Even the most casual reading of medieval history reveals the extent of ignorance, faithlessness, apathy, and rebellion in "the Age of Faith." The Reformers, by their own admission, left the world and the church in many ways as they had found them, and faith did not prevail. As a modern process, secularization is now centuries old.[1]

Doubt and Unbelief in Biblical Narratives

We should not be surprised that problems related to unbelief arise in the very opening pages of the biblical narrative. The creation of human beings with capabilities of thinking and acting independently seems almost to lead naturally to a difficulty of believing in God. That is not to suggest that Adam and Eve were atheists or agnostics in the modern sense of the terms. They were not. But they were—as was Cain, their son—practical atheists: that is, they acted as though they did not believe in God or at least in God's omniscience or omnipresence. They conversed with the serpent as though God were not present. They disobeyed God's command not to eat the fruit as though God would not know. They hid themselves as though God could not find them.

The difficulties that Adam and Eve had in fully believing in God are the same difficulties that have been common to humankind ever since. Even among those who would most fervently affirm their absolute belief in God, there remains that tendency toward what I would term *practical* atheism—living as though one does not believe in a personal, omnipotent, omnipresent, omniscient God.

This scenario is played out again and again in the Old Testament record of Israel: the Israelites serve other gods; God punishes them; they turn back to "the Lord their God." But in many ways, these are narratives of unfaithfulness more than stories of Israel's disbelief in God. Indeed, strange as it may seem, with all its stories of carnage and crime and immorality and intrigue, the Old Testament includes no explicit stories of people's denying the existence of God. It comprises stories of disobedience, defiance and deception, but none of its narratives turn on the theme of doubting God's existence.

Narratives of doubt and unbelief are found in the New Testament, however, in the stories about Jesus. Here the issue is not whether God exists but rather who Jesus is: Is he truly the Messiah, the Son of God? Or is he just another rabbi, a carpenter's son? Many people doubted his claims, including Jesus' mother and his brothers; but the most conspicuous doubters are John the Baptist and some of the disciples.

Judas, Odd Man Out

When I think of the issue of "losing faith" from a biblical perspective, the first person who comes to my mind is Judas, the thief and traitor who walked away from the faith and betrayed our Lord for thirty pieces of silver. Unlike your garden-variety loss of faith, Judas *betrayed* Jesus—with a kiss, no less. There he was at this time of crisis. The days and hours were numbered. The single most unjust crime in history was soon to occur: "On a hill far away stood an old rugged cross, the emblem of suffering and shame." And in this crime, Judas would play a significant role.

Judas has been a controversial figure since biblical times, in part because the gospel accounts of his life, his betrayal of Jesus and his death are difficult to unravel. Indeed, some scholars deny that Judas actually betrayed Jesus. William Klassan, for example, insists that scholars have translated the Greek word incorrectly. In his book *Judas: Betrayer or Friend of Jesus?* he summarizes his findings: "It has been shown that there is no linguistic basis . . . for a translation of 'betray' to describe what Judas did." Besides disputing the word translated "betray," Klassan argues that the evidence proves Judas was neither a "small-time informer" nor an "arch traitor." He maintains that "our earliest sources say . . . that Judas did nothing until Jesus told him to do it." Indeed, he argues that Judas did not know that the chief priests would turn Jesus over to the Romans.[2]

Professor Klassan's conclusions are derived in part from his selective use of New Testament sources. It is true that there are difficulties in meshing the gospel accounts of Judas, but Klassan seems to discount the narrative in the Gospel of John altogether. Yet John's account is essential to a full understanding of Judas's actions. In John 6:70–71 we read: "Jesus answered them, 'Did I not choose you, the twelve? Yet one of you is a devil.' He was speaking of Judas son of Simon Iscariot, for he, though one of the twelve, was going to betray him."

As speculative as Klassan's work is, he does raise some interesting questions related to the issue of walking away from the faith. "What lesson is there to be learned," he asks, "from Judas, his deed, and his end? Must we not take heed that if Judas, who lived so close to Jesus, could turn defector or even traitor, does not a similar possibility exist for each one of his followers?"[3]

It is in John's Gospel that the nature of "losing faith" is most clearly explained in terms of God's providence, and Judas is not the only one who walks away from the faith. There were many followers of Jesus who were having difficulty understanding and heeding his message, as we read in John 6:64–66:

> For Jesus knew from the first who were the ones that did not believe, and who were the ones that would betray him. And he said, "For this reason I have told you that no one can come to me unless it is granted by the Father." Because of this many of his disciples turned back and no longer went about with him.

Though the story of Judas seems to show that some who appear to be disciples are not among the elect, we also find narratives which show that neither a hasty denial nor serious doubt would merit the charge of losing faith. The narratives of John the Baptist, Peter and Thomas are examples of this.

John the Baptist

Whenever my faith is weak and I am doubting whether the gospel message is true, I take comfort in knowing I am not alone. I have company even among the biblical "greats," including John the Baptist.

> When John heard in prison what the Messiah was doing, he sent word by his disciples and said to him, "Are you the one who is come, or are we to wait for another?" (Mt 11:2–3)

"On the surface at least, doesn't this seem like an unnerving question to ask the Son of God?" asks Gary Habermas. "It's not just the question itself that's so staggering. If it had come from someone in the crowd, it would probably be dismissed by many readers as being from someone who lacked faith. What turns it into such a bombshell is that it comes from John the Baptist, God's chosen forerunner for Jesus."[4] While it is true that John, indeed, was the forerunner of the Messiah who baptized him, his confusion about Jesus' divinity is understandable when viewed in the context of a depression, which could easily engulf someone imprisoned and facing execution.

The theology of a major cult, the Unification Church founded by Sun Myung Moon, is rooted in this incident. The *Divine Principle*, the Unification scripture that was allegedly given to Moon by divine inspiration, opens the door for a new messiah (now identified as Moon himself) on the basis of John's "betrayal."

> Nevertheless, John the Baptist later became gradually more skeptical about Jesus and at last betrayed him. Naturally, the Jewish people, who believed and followed John the Baptist . . . were forced to stand in the position of disbelieving Jesus. . . . Accordingly, the foundation of faith that John the Baptist had set up for the first worldwide course of the restoration of Canaan was, in the end, invaded by Satan.[5]

The problem with Unification theology is that the Bible never states that John betrayed Jesus. At most, it presents a man in prison struggling with doubt and unbelief. But more importantly, the Scripture goes on to present what Jesus did and said. First Jesus sent his disci-

ples back to John with a report of the miracles that he had performed,
and then he spoke to the crowd:

> What did you go out into the wilderness to look at? A reed shaken by
> the wind? What then did you go out to see? Someone dressed in soft
> robes? Look, those who wear soft robes are in royal palaces. What then
> did you go out to see? A prophet? Yes, I tell you, and more than a
> prophet. This is the one about whom it is written,
>   "See, I am sending my messenger ahead of you,
>   Who will prepare your way before you."
>   Truly I tell you, among those born of women no one has arisen
> greater than John the Baptist. (Mt 11:7–11)

Peter, the Apostle

> While Peter was below in the courtyard, one of the servant-girls of the
> high priest came by. When she saw Peter warming himself, she stared at
> him and said, "You also were with Jesus, the man from Nazareth." But
> he denied it, saying, "I do not know or understand what you are talking
> about." And he went out into the forecourt. Then the cock crowed. And
> the servant girl, on seeing him, began again to say to the bystanders,
> "This man is one of them." But again he denied it. Then after a little
> while the bystanders again said to Peter, "Certainly you are one of them;
> for you are a Galilean." But he began to curse, and he swore an oath, "I
> do not know this man you are talking about." At that moment the cock
> crowed for the second time. Then Peter remembered that Jesus had said
> to him, "Before the cock crows twice, you will deny me three times."
> And he broke down and wept. (Mk 14:66–72)

Peter's denial of Jesus is of a different nature than is John's uncertainty. Both Peter and John were facing the cruel arm of religious persecution the likes of which is not known in the contemporary Western
world. But John's uncertainty arises out of despair, whereas Peter's
denial is a defensive and dishonest cover-up. It is not difficult to imagine that Peter, like John, may have had his own uncertainties about
who Jesus was; but at the moment that he was confronted, he was far
more concerned about self-preservation than confessing his doubts.
Yet he shows regret and immediately repents of his denial—though his

repentance comes, some suggest, once he is out of imminent danger. The significance of his denial is indicated by its being recorded in all four Gospels.

As was true with Judas' betrayal of Jesus, Peter's denial did not take Jesus by surprise. In fact, we know that Jesus predicted Peter's betrayal several hours before it happened. And as surely as John's Gospel presents Judas as a tool of the devil, the Gospels present Peter as repentant. After the resurrection he was included among the eleven disciples, all of whom were "upbraided . . . for their lack of faith and stubbornness because they had not believed those who saw him after he had risen" (Mk 16:14).

Doubting Thomas

The biblical figure most often associated with doubt is the apostle Thomas. For Thomas, the issue was not greed, as with Judas; nor confusion and depression, as with John the Baptist; nor fear, as with Peter. Thomas stood face to face with either the greatest miracle or the greatest hoax the world has ever encountered, and his future was at stake. For him, as for every woman and man since, believing in the resurrection was a life-and-death issue. I wrote about this incident in an article for *The Church Herald* in 1991, pointing out that one of the most profound aspects of the Easter story is that it speaks so powerfully of both faith and doubt. On the one hand, we see the faith of women disciples—last at the cross, first at the tomb. And on the other hand, we see the doubt of some of the men disciples, especially Judas, Peter and Thomas. Thomas is the one I single out:

> But Thomas played a crucial role. He stood in for me and all the other followers of Jesus throughout history who are prone to doubt. He asked the questions and demanded the proof that my weak faith often requires. He deserves no praise for this, but I will ever be grateful to him for his refusal to accept the testimony of the other disciples. He was a doubter and he needed proof for himself, and that proof has often reassured me.
>
> I have a hunch that Thomas was a skeptic by nature, and that his

powerful confession, "My Lord and my God," did little or nothing to change his basic personality. . . . Nevertheless, it was Thomas who, tradition tells us, had the most far-reaching ministry of the twelve apostles. He went to India, where he planted churches that continue today.[6]

Thomas was the disciple who was absent when Jesus made his postresurrection appearance to the other disciples, who were locked together in a house. He heard about this visit from the other disciples, but found their account just too hard to believe: "Unless I see the mark of the nails in his hands, and put my finger in the mark of the nails and my hand in his side, I will not believe" (Jn 20:25). When Jesus appeared again to the disciples a week later, Thomas was among them—Jesus spoke directly to him, inviting him do what he said he wanted to do. Thomas responded with words that ring through the centuries: "My Lord and My God!" (Jn 20:28). That says it all.

Yet Jesus would have the last word: "Have you believed because you have seen me? Blessed are those who have not seen and yet have come to believe" (Jn 20:29).

From a cursory glance at New Testament figures we seen an embodiment of faith that is not always unwavering and tidy. There is tension, uncertainty and messiness. The good is mixed with the bad, pride is mixed with humility, and the true is mixed with the false. Judas appears to have abandoned whatever faith he may have had. John the Baptist faltered in his faith. Peter denied and cursed. Thomas demanded proof. And they were all insiders, so to speak. Indeed, doubt and unbelief, as presented in the Scriptures, by no means constitute the so-called unforgivable sin. Time and again there is a sense of understanding and forgiveness. The message of Scripture is unmistakable. God is sovereign, and he knows our doubts and denials before they even occur. Yet we are solely responsible, deserving rebuke for our lack of faith. "Take heed," the apostle Paul warns, "lest you fall" (1 Cor 10:12 KJV).

Post-Apostolic Persecution and Denial
As we move out of the biblical era and into what is often designated

"church history," the context of doubt and unbelief does not significantly change. Belief in the supernatural is assumed. Though the specific character of supernatural belief might be debated and God's silence may be felt, the world of the supernatural was almost universally taken for granted in the history of the church.

Much has been written about the great faith of early Christians in the face of persecution. Perhaps the most noted martyr of the post-apostolic era was the aged Bishop Polycarp. He hid in a hayloft to escape capture but was found and brought to trial. When the proconsul demanded he take an oath by the divinity of Caesar and curse Christ, Polycarp made his now-famous declaration, "For eighty-six years I have served him, and he never did me wrong, and how can I now blaspheme my King that has saved me?"[7] The rest of the story is history. Polycarp was burned at the stake.

But not all professing Christians responded as Polycarp did, as we learn from the writings of the early church historian Eusebius. Many denied the faith in the face of torture and persecution. He writes of the indescribable torture of women and men—Quinta, Apollonia, Metra, Serapion and others—who endured to the end. But there is another story as well. The emperor's cruelty put Christians to the ultimate test. So horrific was the torture, writes Eusebius, that were it "possible, the very elect would stumble." The following account tells of the terror in Alexandria in the third century:

> The decree had arrived, very much like that which was foretold by our Lord, exhibiting the most dreadful aspect; so that, if it were possible, the very elect would stumble. All, indeed, were greatly alarmed. . . . But some advanced with greater readiness to the altars, and boldly asserted that they had never before been Christians. . . . Some, also, after enduring the torture for a time, at last renounced. Others, however, firm and blessed pillars of the Lord . . . became admirable witnesses of his kingdom.[8]

Unbelief in an Age of Faith

The medieval period of history has often been referred to as the Age of

Faith, but it was an age of unbelief as well. During much of the period the Roman Catholic Church reigned in both ecclesiastical and political realms, but the level of spirituality was often very low—especially in the highest echelon of leadership, including the pope himself.

Philosophers in the Age of Faith strongly defended the Christian faith, drawing from classical philosophy. Anselm (1033–1109) stands out for his ontological proof for the existence of God: that God's nonexistence is inconceivable. Another brilliant philosopher of the eleventh century was Peter Abelard, who wrote *Sic et Non* ("Yes and No"), which created an uproar in ecclesiastical circles. Here he laid out his philosophical method: the key to wisdom is doubting—a precursor to Enlightenment thinking that would come centuries later.

Thomas Aquinas (1224–1272), the most celebrated philosopher and theologian of the medieval period, confessed that "the most man can know is that he does not know God." Yet his claim to fame was, perhaps more than anything else, his formulation of the famous "Five Ways" that sought to establish the existence of God through natural theology. It is noteworthy that in this supposed Age of Faith, Aquinas expended so much effort on proving the existence of God— though he did so perhaps more for his own benefit than for the benefit of others. These "ways" were philosophical arguments, drawn largely from Aristotle, and they were a means of bringing faith and reason together.

In this Age of Faith it was natural that serious questions about God were debated; and in the midst of the debate, some struggled to believe. One such personal testimony comes from Otloh of St. Emmeram (1010–1070): "For a long time, I found myself tormented by a compulsion to doubt altogether the reliability of Holy Scripture and even the existence of God himself." Otloh later found his way back to secure faith, but his confession illustrates the struggles confronted by thinkers long before the Enlightenment.[9]

Reformation and Puritan Doubt and Unbelief
Even as we do not associate doubt and unbelief with the Age of Faith,

neither do we associate this skeptical mindset with the Reformation. Yet the most celebrated Reformers found their faith severely tested on occasion.

In 1527, only a decade after he nailed his celebrated Ninety-five Theses to the church door in Wittenberg, Martin Luther was paralyzed by depression and doubt. "For more than a week," he writes, "I was close to the gates of death and hell. I trembled in all my members. Christ was wholly lost. I was shaken by desperation and blasphemy of God." Luther spoke on other occasions of God's hiddenness, but he always was drawn back to the Scriptures—the Word of God on which he had risked his very life. But the Scriptures themselves were often troublesome to Luther. This is illustrated by his comments on the Gospel passage about the Canaanite woman, whose place, Jesus seemed to be saying, was not at the table but rather with the dogs (Mt 15). Luther had only one explanation: "All this is written for our comfort that we should see how deeply God hides his face and how we must not go by our feeling but only by his Word."[10]

To those who struggled with doubt and unbelief, Luther offered pastoral words of counsel and comfort:

> If God hides himself in the storm clouds which brood over the brow of Sinai, then gather about the manger, look upon the infant Jesus as he leaps in the lap of his mother, and know that the hope of the world is here. Or again, if Christ and God alike are unapproachable, then look upon the firmament of the heavens and marvel at the work of God, who sustains them without pillars. Or take the meanest flower and see in the smallest petal the handiwork of God.[11]

John Calvin also struggled with doubt and, like Luther, viewed it as a serious affliction. In summarizing Calvin's view, William Bouwsma writes that "sinfulness, as long as the Christian opposes it, is not fatal" since "salvation is by faith alone." But potentially fatal is a far worse adversary—"not sin but doubt, of which anxiety is the immediate consequence." Indeed, for Calvin, "doubt and anxiety are thus the most terrible adversaries of every Christian, even the most faithful," and in discussing the matter, he seems to include himself:

"Every one of us knows only too well, from his own experiences," Calvin insisted, "our difficulty in believing." "Everyone's weakness certainly witnesses to many the doubts that steal upon us." The saints "frequently stagger in unbelief." "Faith is never without its combats," for the devil constantly suggests "many occasions for incredulity." Calvin bore witness to the terrors of doubt.[12]

As we move along in history we encounter the Puritans, who, more than many religious groups, were very conscious of their relationship with God. God was simply taken for granted in every aspect of life. Thus, questioning the existence of God would seem utterly out of place. Yet one of the most profound confessions of unbelief comes from among the ranks of the Puritans, and from a woman, no less. Anne Bradstreet was Colonial New England's most noted female poet. Her father and husband were both prominent Massachusetts Bay Colony governors, and she was the mother of eight children. In the following letter to her children, she confesses her struggle with doubt and unbelief. Yet, despite her doubts, she remained true to the faith of her childhood.

> Many times hath Satan troubled me concerning the verity of the Scriptures, many times by Atheisme how I could know whether there was a God; I never saw any miracles to confirm me, and those which I read of how did I know but they were feigned. That there is a God my Reason would soon tell me by the wondrous workes that I see. . . .
>
> But how should I know he is such a God as I worship in Trinity, and such a Saviour as I rely upon?[13]

Enlightenment Skepticism

The Enlightenment took a toll on the Christian faith. The eighteenth century was the one that produced Voltaire and Hume and Kant and other philosophers who challenged the very foundations of Christian belief. Their philosophical treatises had a trickle-down effect, so that within a matter of generations the whole of Western society was affected. But the eighteenth century also saw the spread of pietism and evangelical revivals, especially through the ministries of John Wesley, George Whitefield and Jonathan Edwards.

Both the Enlightenment and the evangelical revivals would have profound lasting effects—and very often they would be competing for the
souls of men and women. This tension is illustrated in the story of Robert Taylor (1784–1844), a child of the eighteenth century who came to
adulthood in the century that followed. As a young man, Taylor, having
been "converted by a Calvinist preacher," abandoned his medical prac-
tice and prepared for the ministry. He had a gift for preaching and was
on his way toward a promising Anglican ministry, but after only four
years, "the drama of his life" began. One of his own parishioners had
loaned him books by Edward Gibbon and Thomas Paine, books that
challenged the supernatural foundations of the Christian faith and the
Christian church. So drastically were his beliefs shaken that he, by his
own testimony, became "convinced . . . that the Christian religion . . . is
the greatest curse that ever befell the human race."[14]

After this "drama," Taylor left his parish ministry—but not for long.
He recanted his unbelief and continued on in ministry, though not
without opposition. Another Anglican cleric published a tract accusing
him of disguising his unbelief in his return to the ministry. Taylor
briefly held posts at other parishes, but due to rumors of his infidelity,
they were short lived. "In his last parish," according to author Jim
Herrick "he decided to deliver sermons of the utmost irony so that he
could heave 'the anchor of religious convictions' of the whole parish
and set 'em all afloat. Crowds came to hear the infidel priest, and he
was barred from ever again entering a pulpit."[15]

For the remainder of his life, Taylor was consumed with spreading
his skepticism through books and through his founding of the Christian Evidence Society, the purpose of which was to promote evidence
for unbelief. He was rewarded for his efforts by arrests and two prison
terms. But he nevertheless made his mark on British society. In 1834
a textile employer published a petition that set forth the need for more
Christian teaching. It included the following lines:

> Infidelity is growing amazingly. . . . The writings of Carlile and Taylor
> and other infidels are more read than the Bible or any other book. . . . I
> have seen weeks after weeks the weavers assembled in a room, that

would contain 400 people, to applaud the people who asserted and argued that there was no God. . . . I have gone into cottages around the chapel where I worship, I have found 20 men assembled reading infidel publications.[16]

The Great Century—of Unbelief

The nineteenth century was designated by historian Kenneth Scott Latourette as "the Great Century" of missions. Christianity spread out worldwide as the result of the sacrifice of Western missionaries who zealously desired to bring the gospel to every tribe and tongue and nation. There was also a strong humanitarian impulse permeating foreign missions and home missions as well. It was the era of volunteer societies in Victorian England and in North America: people united together to minister to prisoners, orphans, "fallen" women and countless others who had fallen between the cracks of industrialized society.

The Great Century was also a century of much-publicized revival campaigns led by such charismatic figures as Charles G. Finney and Dwight L. Moody and of celebrated preachers such as Charles Hadden Spurgeon and Henry Ward Beecher. But at the very time that Christianity seemed to be on the rise, there were ominous threats to the historic faith. The Darwinian revolution profoundly affected the Victorian mind, resulting in a collective loss of faith. Matthew Arnold, one of the most provocative poets of Victorian England, captures this mood in his poem "Dover Beach: The Eternal Note of Sadness," which encapsulates the decline of faith and the increase of skepticism in his generation:

> The Sea of Faith
> Was once, too, at the full, and toward earth's shore
> Lay like the folds of a bright girdle furled.
> But now I only hear
> Its melancholy, long, withdrawing tear,
> Retreating to the breath.
> On the night wind, down the vast edges drear
> And naked shingles of the world.

"For Arnold this lack of faith is no cause for celebration," writes Kelly Clark. "The world now lacks a loving and redeeming center to reconcile all things. . . . Where people once heard the voice of God crashing in on the waves, now Arnold hears only silence."[17]

The Twentieth-Century Crisis of Faith

Perhaps the greatest threat to faith in the twentieth century has been the progress of modern technology and the unconscious (though sometimes conscious) sense that the world will either solve all its problems or destroy itself without any help from God. There was a time, especially in the 1950s and 1960s, when there was a sense of optimism set against this sense of despair, neither of which required any interference from God. I remember that era so well. I was going through my teenage years, and it was a time when my faith in God was of utmost importance to me. Yet I had fallen into the myth of unending progress on the one hand and the potential destruction of the world on the other—the latter having a theological twist.

I recall a trip I made from Texas to Wisconsin during my college years and how I took full advantage of a highway span that had an 80-mile-an-hour speed limit; and I remember thinking to myself, *In a few years the speed limit will be 100 miles an hour, then 125 miles an hour, and then 150.* So much progress had unfolded already in my lifetime that I could not imagine the "progress" ever slowing down. And unconsciously, that progress seemed to have very little to do with God.

So it is that the double-headed god of technology and progress has challenged the biblical God for most of a century. But another god reared its head during the twentieth century to challenge God—the god of social revolution and Marxism that fueled the rapid spread of communism. By midcentury the Cold War had pitted these gods against each other in colossal magnitude. But decades earlier, this god of social revolution had begun capturing the hearts of individuals whose disbelief infected a whole nation. This saga is illustrated by the testimony of a young man in Russia, a man whose story depicts the negative effect atheistic communism had on a generation of Russians.

Sergei Bulgakov (1871–1944) was born into a family of Russian Orthodox priests, and as a youth he was sent to seminary to train for this same profession. In seminary he experienced a profound religious crisis that, he later confessed, "ended in my losing religious faith for many, many years." His family was deeply troubled not only by his loss of faith but also by his new credo: "In losing religious faith I naturally and, as it were, automatically adopted the revolutionary mood then prevalent among the intelligentsia." He enrolled in Moscow University, where he later became a lecturer. But he had no real sense of contentment: "My mind developed along the lines of social and socialistic thought . . . until finally I appeared enslaved by Marxism, which suited me about as well as a saddle fits a cow."[18]

After a decade of living "without faith," Bulgakov sensed that "a religious emptiness reigned in my soul." Finding his way back was a slow process. "Having regained faith in a 'personal' God, instead of the impersonal idol of progress, I accepted Christ—whom I had loved and carried in my heart as a child." He then began studying Orthodox theology, and he finally returned to the church of his heritage. This reconversion to the church stirred communist authorities against him, forcing him to flee his homeland. He emigrated to Paris, where he was later appointed dean of the Orthodox Theological Academy, whose faculty have included several leading twentieth-century Orthodox theologians.[19]

Reflections of the Past and on the Future

What can we conclude about the prevalence of doubt when we look back over church history? Certainly there has always been doubt and unbelief among Christians, but never before have Christians who live in what might be termed "Christian cultures" been faced with belief systems suffused with philosophical and practical atheism. British psychologist Eugene Rolfe has reflected on our modern culture of unbelief, saying, "Almost all of us nowadays conduct our lives for all practical purposes as if God did not exist."[20] What Rolfe is speaking of is a prevalent, unconscious atheism. In centuries gone by, daily life was hard and God's role was critical. Whether experiencing travel or illness or childbirth or farming, Christians looked first and foremost to God. Today we Christians, myself included, pay lip service (at best) to our dependence on God while in actuality, we *depend* on the airlines, the doctors, the weather forecasters and the irrigation systems. God becomes an afterthought. There is an optimism, however, as we look to the future, especially as we perceive a loosening in modernism's stranglehold on Western culture.

Yet, many Christians are unaware that they are no longer shackled by the tenets of modernism as they might have been even a decade ago. This unshackling is profoundly depicted by Christopher Fry in *A Sleep of Prisoners*. Here he speaks of those frozen in a system that has already begun to thaw:

The human heart can go to the lengths of God.
Dark and cold we may be, but this
Is no winter now. The frozen misery
Of centuries breaks, cracks, begins to move;
The thunder is the thunder of the floes,
The Thaw, the flood, the upstart Spring.
Thank God our time is now when wrong,
Comes up to face us everywhere,
Never to leave us till we take
The longest stride of soul men ever took,
Affairs are now soul size.
The enterprise
Is the exploration into God.[21]

7

The Challenge of
Science & Philosophy

That man is the product of . . . accidental collocations of atoms;
that no fire, no heroism, no intensity of thought and feeling,
can preserve an individual life beyond the grave. . . .
All these things, if not quite beyond dispute,
are yet so nearly certain that
no philosophy which rejects them can hope to stand.

— BERTRAND RUSSELL

Perhaps more than any other areas of academic specialization, science
and philosophy have the potential to shake the very foundations of
faith. We see this historically as scientists and philosophers one after
another abandoned the faith in which they were nurtured. There are
Christian philosophers and Christian scientists, to be sure, but there
are many who at one time professed faith only to have their belief system taken "captive through philosophy and empty deceit," as Paul
warns in Colossians 2:8.

My own faith was shaken years ago through the study and teaching
of philosophy. But my faith was also built up through the study and
teaching of philosophy—as I recognized the capacity philosophy had
for masking evil. Using rational thinking and clever logic, one could

make wrong appear as right—through the "empty deceit" Paul warns the Colossians of, "according to human tradition, according to the elemental spirits of the universe, and not according to Christ" (Col 2:8).

"Between 1650 and 1850, in the period from Spinoza to Schleiermacher," writes William Dembski, "the rational foundations of the Christian faith were fundamentally altered." Before this time, faith and reason were generally seen as complementary to each other. Spinoza initiated this era of rationalism by making a forceful attack on miracles. Hume argued against intelligent design. Kant viewed the existence of God as a reality only in human consciousness. And Schleiermacher insisted that the Christian faith could not be supported by evidence.[1]

But the fierce attacks against Christianity did not cease in the middle of the nineteenth century. In fact, the subsequent attacks had an even greater influence on political philosophy and the thinking of people outside the academy.

Friedrich Nietzsche (1844–1900) is one example of those who continued to impugn Christianity. His philosophy, aside from becoming a basis for Nazism, had the potential to do vast harm in a modern world where the technology and the ideal of progress reigned. I remember spending a lot of time trying to comprehend Nietzsche when my son was still a preschooler, more than twenty years ago. Carlton would play with his toy cars and trucks around the dining room table while I was buried deep in books, writing out lectures. As I read Nietzsche's philosophical arguments, I realized not only that was he the ultimate "anti-Christian" in his railing against the love of Jesus and his proclaiming the death of God, but that his views were diametrically opposed to any sense of self-understanding I had as a mother. Not that he demeaned motherhood—indeed "everything in a woman has one answer," he wrote: "its name is childbearing."[2]

But childbearing, for Nietzsche, was merely a means to an end. The end was superman. His philosophy made no place for the mother's heart that reached out to her little one, whether that little one might be—or might become—sick or physically or mentally handicapped. His creed was survival of the fittest, a creed incomprehensible to a protective, compassionate mother whose child is playing at her feet.

Enlightenment rationalists long before Nietzsche had shaken the very foundations of Christian doctrine, but they did not seek to eradicate Christian morality and humanitarianism. Many of the philosophers of this era "were brave enough to reject Christian theology," writes Will Durant,

> but they did not dare to be logical, to reject the moral ideas, the worship of meekness and gentleness and altruism, which had grown out of that theology. They ceased to be Anglicans, or Catholics, or Lutherans; but they did not dare cease to be Christians—so argued Friedrich Nietzsche.[3]

Nietzsche, more than any other philosopher of the modern era, is rightly identified as the premier evangelist of unbelief. There were forerunners, to be sure, who paved the way for him, undermining belief with every painful paragraph they penned. But he proclaimed the death of God with celebration and a substitute superman. He buried belief without bereavement.

"Dead are all Gods" he proclaimed; "now we will that superman live."[4]

The "Death of God" Philosopher

Like so many other philosophers of unbelief, Nietzsche had a strong Christian background. He was born and raised in a family of Lutheran preachers and was himself referred to as "the little minister." As a young child "it was his delight to seclude himself and read the Bible, or to read it to others so feelingly as to bring tears to their eyes." But soon after he entered the University of Bonn at twenty, he abandoned his faith. "Religion had been the very marrow of his life, and now life seemed empty and meaningless."[5]

Who was this young man who, like many other young adults, would walk away from faith during their university education? Of himself he said, "I was born as an old man." He avoided social interaction, and later in life he wrote, "I hate unspeakably everyone I have ever met, especially myself. . . . A man of spiritual depth needs friends, unless he still has God as a friend. But I have neither God nor friends." He condemned Christianity as "the one great curse" and "the highest of all conceivable corruptions," while on another occasion he desperately pleaded, "Come back to me, my unknown God!" He was utterly miserable much of his life, especially during the final decade. "As venereal-disease-induced psychosis claimed his mind, he slipped in and out of lucidity during the last tormented years." When he died at age fifty-six, he was buried "with full Lutheran rites."[6]

Nietzsche's most all-encompassing concept was his building on Herbert Spencer's theory of the "survival of the fittest" and turning it into a form of religion itself. Indeed, the vision for this new doctrine grew out of an almost mystical experience. Nietzsche was on his way to the front lines in 1870, to defend his beloved Germany in its war with France. As he watched the German cavalry in all its glory passing through Frankfurt, he suddenly discovered the secret of life: "I felt for the first time that the strongest and highest Will to Life does not find expression in a miserable struggle for existence, but in a Will to War, a Will to Power, a Will to Overpower."[7]

This new philosophy fiercely attacked Christianity in its concern for the poor and weak and its critique of power. In his book *The Antichrist*, Nietzsche clearly enunciates this view:

> Christianity is called the religion of *pity*. . . . A man loses power when he pities. By means of pity the drain on strength which suffering itself already introduces into the world is multiplied a thousandfold. . . . On the whole, pity thwarts the law of development which is the law of selection. It preserved that which is ripe for death, it fights in favour of the disinherited and the condemned of life.[8]

Nietzsche railed against democracy—"this mania for counting noses"—insisting that it was an unfortunate byproduct of Christianity. The superman would rise out of aristocracy and give birth to a super race of men (women were considered subordinate)—a philosophy that offered an intellectual foundation for Hitler and Nazism.[9]

Thus Spake Zarathustra is Nietzsche's most celebrated work. A defining episode in this book occurs when Zarathustra encounters a monk—a forest hermit—who talks to him about God. Zarathustra is dumbfounded. Had not this old man heard the good news that God is dead? All the gods died long ago, not "lingering in the twilight,—although that lie is told!" No, they "laughed themselves unto death!" They died laughing when a god audaciously insisted, "There is but one God! Thou shalt have no other gods before me." This "old grim beard of a God, a jealous one, forgot himself thus. And then all Gods laughed."[10]

One of Nietzsche's most often-quoted writings, "The Madman," is viewed as an autobiographical satire and has served as a foundation block in the "death of God" movement:

> Have you ever heard of the madman who on a bright morning lighted a lantern and ran to the market-place calling out unceasingly: "I seek God! I seek God!" . . . Why! Is he lost? Said one. Has he strayed away like a child? said another. Or does he keep himself hidden? Is he afraid of us? Has he taken a sea voyage? Has he emigrated?—the people cried out laughingly, all in a hubbub. The insane man jumped into their midst and transfixed them with his glances. "Where is God gone?" he called out. "I mean to tell you! *We have killed him,*—you and I! We are all murderers! . . . Do we not hear the noise of the grave-diggers who are burying God? . . . . Is not the magnitude of this deed too great for us? Shall we not ourselves have to become Gods, merely to seem worthy of it?" . . . At last he threw his lantern on the ground, so that it broke in pieces and was extinguished. "I come too early," he then said, "I am not yet at the right time. This prodigious event is still on its way, and is traveling—it has not yet reached men's ears."[11]

Nietzsche, perhaps more than any other philosopher of modern times, merits the description of philosopher of unbelief—or disbelief. Belief was harmful—not just something that could no longer be justified—as many philosophers before him had argued. Eradicating belief was necessary for the society he envisioned. But he was only one in a long line of philosophers of unbelief.

There are hundreds—yea, thousands—of men (and some women) who played significant roles in paving the way for unbelief to become an acceptable viewpoint in modern society. Some attacked the issue with erudite philosophical tomes, while others wrote popular tracts and plays. It is impossible to rate individuals' importance with any degree of consensus, but a short list of those who had an effect on the phenomenon known as "loss of faith" would certainly include the names of Voltaire, Hume and Kant.

Voltaire, Critic of Christianity—but Not of God

In many respects, the ideas of François Marie Voltaire (1694–1778) ruled the Age of Enlightenment. "For fifty years," writes Colin Brown, Voltaire "dominated the French stage."[12] Perhaps spurred by his early Jesuit education, he bitterly criticized the Catholic Church and made use of ridicule, irony and his clever wit to destroy that institution in the minds of his readers. According to J. C. A. Gaskin, "the sheer volume of his literary work probably spread more unbelief in France than the careful philosophizing of a hundred lesser men."[13]

Yet for all the unbelief that he spread through his contagious contempt for organized religion, Voltaire was not a modern-day atheist or agnostic. He believed in God and considered himself a theist. "I shall always be convinced," he penned in a letter, "that a watch proves a watch-maker, and that a universe proves a God." But his god was not the God of the Bible, as can be seen in the definition he gave *theism* in his *Philosophical Dictionary:*

> He is a true Theist who says to God: "I adore Thee and serve Thee," and to the Turk, the Chinese, the Indian and the Russian, "I love you." . . . The Theist is firmly persuaded of the existence of a supreme Being as good as He is powerful who formed all extended beings, perpetuates their kinds, punishes crime without cruelty, and recompenses virtuous actions with bounty. The Theist does not know how God punishes, or how He favours and pardons, and is not rash enough to flatter himself that he knows how God acts, but that God acts and that He is just, this he knows. The difficulties that tell against the idea of Providence do not

shake his faith, because they are merely difficulties, and not demonstrations.[14]

Hume's Denial of Miracles

Philosopher Steven Cahn believes that there was a date in history, a watershed, when the viability of atheism overcame the viability of belief. To support this point, Cahn quotes a character in *Jumpers*, a play by Tom Stoppard: "Well, the tide is running his way, and it is a tide which has turned only once in human history. . . . There is presumably a calendar date—a moment—when the onus of proof passed from the atheist to the believer." What is this date? According to Cahn, it is the day in 1779 when David Hume published *Dialogue Concerning Natural Religion*, a book that dismisses the arguments for God.[15]

David Hume (1711–1776) the brilliant Scottish thinker, is the philosopher of skepticism. "He used reason to the limits," writes Colin Brown, "to demonstrate the limitations of reason." His skepticism had a monumental effect on his view of Christianity and religion in general. He challenged the cosmological argument for God; and he rightly argued that it is impossible "for a cause to be known only by its effect" and that it is false to assume that the cause has any other qualities than those related to causing the effect. And he insisted that it is not valid to identify the first cause (if such a cause exists) as the Christian God or to give this cause a mind or moral attributes. Regarding the biblical truth of Christianity, Hume denied the validity of miracles: "A miracle is a violation of the laws of nature," he argued, "and as a firm and unalterable experience has established these laws, the proof against a miracle from the very nature of the fact, is as entire as any argument from experience can possibly be imagined." All religions, he insisted, depend on miracles, but obviously not all these miracles can be true. Thus miracles cannot be cited as evidence for faith; they can be cited only as a claim of belief by those who already have faith.[16]

But despite all his deep philosophical contemplation, and his apparent conclusions, Hume was not able to go through life without a distrust of his own methods as well as with intellectual and emotional doubts. Unlike many of the great philosophers of the modern era, he was honest enough to confess these doubts:

> Most fortunately it happens, that since reason is incapable of dispelling these doubts, Nature herself suffices to that purpose, and cures me of this philosophical melancholy and delirium, either by relaxing this bent of mind, or by some avocation and lively impression of my senses, which obliterates all these chimeras. I dine, I play a game of backgammon, I converse, and am merry with my friends; and when, after three or four hours' amusement, I would return to these speculations, they appear so cold, and strained, and ridiculous, that I cannot find in my heart to enter into them any further.[17]

Kant and the Impossibility of Proving God

"Never has a system of thought so dominated an epoch as the philosophy of Immanuel Kant dominated the thought of the nineteenth century," writes Durant. "He did not foresee that the greatest of all metaphysical tempests was to be of his own blowing."[18]

Immanuel Kant (1724–1804) was born in Prussia into a poor family. Through the efforts of his devout mother, he was immersed in the pietistic faith during his early childhood and youth—so much so that some speculate that it may have been a factor in his turning away from the faith. As a philosopher he argued that no generation ought to be constrained by the dogmas and creeds of earlier generations. In that vein, he rejected traditional proofs for the existence of God. But he did "not close the door altogether on God," writes Brown. "He had no need of God in the capacity of either a heavenly adviser or provider of incentives. He must do what his own reason tells him is right." Yet, for Kant, morality points to God. Jesus is "the personified idea of the good principle," an example for us to follow.[19]

Before Kant, philosophers of religion sought to prove the existence of God through various lines of rational argument. "Kant swept these away," writes Brown, "or at least he thought that he had. The human mind is incapable of comprehending God. Kant made his starting point: man—not God—and the only real value of God was in the realm of morals."[20]

Scientific Discoveries and the Onslaught of Unbelief

Enlightenment philosophy was not the only dragon seeking to devour the Christian faith. Many men of faith feared science more than philosophy, and with good reason, as time would tell. Nicolaus Copernicus, a sixteenth-century contemporary of Martin Luther, argued that the sun was the center of our solar system—a theory that allowed for an infinite universe. He was not the first to make such claims, but he is generally credited for initiating a scientific revolution. His book *Concerning the Revolutions of the Celestial Spheres* was published in the year of his death, 1543, three years before Luther's death.

It was not until more than seventy years after its publication, however, that his book was widely viewed as a threat to the Christian faith—so much so that it was placed on the Catholic "Index" of banned books, where it stayed for more than a century. Many theologians argued that God could not create such a universe and that thus such a theory was atheistic. The vastness of the universe continues to cast doubt in the hearts and minds of many believers. Martin Marty has summed up the struggle this way:

> The initial shock—and still for many the most profound—was the dislocating experience of astronomy. Man was edged out of centrality and his world was replaced at an obscure and unstable corner of an expanding universe. Where was God, who had been "up there" or "out there"?[21]

Part of the problem with *man* being "edged out of centrality" of the world relates to how Christians have responded to scientific discoveries. In ancient times, natural phenomena, such as thunder and lightening, were credited to God. But today they are seen as *natural;* any contemplation of the *supernatural* comes only in emergencies. "The distinction between natural and supernatural theology," writes Richard Muller, "is untenable and, I think, fundamentally damaging to

Christianity in the modern scientific context. As science more and more completely explains the phenomena of the universe, the so-called supernatural is relegated to a smaller and smaller sphere." This diminishing sense of the supernatural occurred as the Copernican conception of an infinite universe, with a God who was "out there," replaced the Ptolemaic view of an earth-centered universe and resulted in the image of a virtually absentee deity who rarely intervenes in the natural order.[22]

Initially theologians were stumped by this Copernican universe. Some reacted harshly against science; others caved in to the point of stripping the Bible and the Christian faith of its supernatural elements.

Darwin's Dangerous Idea

The greatest scientific assault against the Christian faith came from Charles Darwin's theory of evolution in the last decades of the nineteenth century. According to Richard Dawkins, "Darwin made it possible to be an intellectually fulfilled atheist."[23] Today, the theory of evolution reigns. "To put it bluntly but fairly," writes Daniel Dennett, "anyone today who doubts that the variety of life on this planet was produced by a process of evolution is simply ignorant—inexcusably ignorant."[24] Dennett's book *Darwin's Dangerous Idea* has been critiqued by philosopher Alvin Plantinga:

> First, then, what is Darwin's Dangerous Idea and why is it dangerous. . . . Darwin's dangerous idea, says Dennett, is really the idea that the living world with all of its beauty and wonder, all of its marvelous and ingenious design, was not created by God or anything at all like God, but produced by blind, unconscious, mechanical, algorithmic processes such as natural selection—a process, he says, which creates "design out of chaos without the aid of Mind." The idea is that mind, intelligence, foresight, planning, design are all latecomers in the universe, themselves created by the mindless process of natural selection. . . . And this idea is dangerous, he thinks, because if we accept it, we are forced to reconsider all our childhood and childish ideas about God, morality, value, the meaning of life, and the like.[25]

Discussing Dennett, Plantinga goes on to say, "Note that you don't have to *reject* evolution in order to qualify as inexcusably ignorant: all you have to do is harbor a doubt or two." Here Dennett's accusations parallel those of Dawkins, who wrote in the *New York Times:* "It is absolutely safe to say that if you meet someone who claims not to believe in evolution, that person is ignorant, stupid, or insane (or wicked, but I'd rather not consider that)."[26]

It is difficult for many Christians to tolerate the charge of being ignorant or anti-intellectual, and thus it is not surprising that issues relating to science and philosophy have been significant factors in prompting people to reconsider, and in some cases walk away from, their faith. Darwin's dangerous idea has profoundly influenced religious belief since the mid-nineteenth century. This idea shook the religious atmosphere of Victorian England and America to their very core. Poet Emily Dickinson powerfully illustrates the effect that this new theory had on ordinary people in that era and since.

Dickinson's Poetry in the Age of Darwin

Emily Dickinson (1830–1886) lived in a time when Darwin's theory of evolution was beginning to disrupt the unquestioned belief in a personal God. All the previous advances in astronomy had essentially left God undiminished, as Creator of all that was so magnificent in the animal and plant kingdom. "When she was born," writes Roger Lundin, "the argument from design was securely in place on a six-thousand-year-old earth; at about the time that she began to write poetry regularly, Darwin published *The Origin of Species* and the earth had grown suddenly older." Darwin's theory challenged the very idea of God's creative activity.[27]

In referring to this scientific development, Dickinson wrote in one of her poems: "God's Right Hand . . . / is amputated now / And God cannot be found." Again she wrote that "Darwin had thrown 'the Redeemer' away."[28]

Dickinson was born into a Christian family that lived in the village of Amherst in the Connecticut River valley. She was an outstanding student at Amherst Academy, where she came under the influence of Edward Hitchcock, who taught courses in geology and theology. "He spent his life building bridges between the Christian faith and science," writes Lundin, "only to have them swept away in his final years by the Darwinian flood."

> In the two decades before Darwin—the years when Dickinson came under Hitchcock's influence—efforts at reconciling science and religion centered upon not biology but geology. Long before the publication of *The Origin of Species* in 1859, geological studies had already undercut the biblical chronology of a six-day creation and belief in a six-thousand-year-old-earth. In Sir Charles Lyell's "uniformitarian" understanding of geological processes . . . the creation of the world was not a miraculous event but an excruciatingly slow process.[29]

The effort to reconcile science and theology would haunt Dickinson for the rest of her life. With Hitchcock's mentoring and with his focus on "reading nature" as God's design, Dickinson's orthodox theology was left intact. But all that changed "with Darwin's bleak reading of the book of nature." The problem seemed almost insurmountable. "By removing the necessity of a supernatural design and agent, Darwin attacked the very heart of Hitchcock's argument."[30]

Nature as revealed through scientific discoveries provided a backdrop for Dickinson's poetry that often searched for God in the deafening silence of the universe. A sense of God's absence marked her spiritual pilgrimage, as is seen in her most often-quoted poem:

> I know that He exists.
> Somewhere—in Silence—
> He has hid his rare life
> From our gross eyes.[31]

But a poem that speaks even more directly to how her concept of God was challenged by the scientific age has a profound message for those who struggle with doubts today. Dickinson, like many believers today, was essentially alone in her doubts. Her parents and friends at church appeared to be insulated from science—and silence. Emily was not, as these lines powerfully confess. Yet she offers a way of coming to terms with the silence and hiddenness of God that she experienced. When we cannot find God in personal prayer, it need not be a trifling alternative to worship in awe.

> My period had come for Prayer—
> No other Art—would do—
> My Tactics missed a rudiment—
> Creator—Was it you?
>
> God grows above—so those who pray
> Horizons—must ascend—
> And so I stepped upon the North
> To see this Curious Friend—
>
> His House was not—no sign had He—
> By Chimney—nor by Door
> Could I infer his Residence—
> Vast Prairies of Air
>
> Unbroken by a Settler—
> Were all that I could see—
> Infinitude—Had'st Thou no Face
> That I might look on Thee
>
> The Silence condescended—
> Creation stopped—for Me
> But awed beyond my errand—
> I worshipped—did not "pray"[32]

Spoiling the Certainties of Unbelief

Dickinson was a doubter. Yet despite her struggles with Darwin's theories and other scientific discoveries, her doubts never progressed to the point of unbelief—though this position is a controversial one. Both Christians and agnostics claim her as their own, and Christian scholars are certainly not in agreement on this issue. I have personally been challenged on this matter by some who insist I give Dickinson too much slack. Perhaps. God alone knows. But I find evidence of belief in many of her poems, particularly the lines that begin with "God made a little Gentian," where she seems to confess a faith that blooms, though not with the summery radiance of a rose.

But if Dickinson remained within the realm of belief, the same cannot be said for many others who were overwhelmed by Darwinian doubts. Darwin's theory of evolution paved the way for the kind of hardened unbelief that is depicted in Graham Greene's play *The Potting Shed*. This play depicts a family under the authoritarian control of an agnostic father, who wields his power to stifle any sign of belief in his wife or children. "The family is spiritually destroyed until doubt begins to intrude, in the form of an alleged miracle that shakes their unquestioned agnostic assurances." The wife is initially upset that the son has "spoilt our certainties," but deep down she is pleased by this new doubt:

> It was all right to doubt the existence of God as your grandfather did in the time of Darwin. Doubt—that was human liberty. But my generation didn't doubt, we *knew*. I don't believe in this miracle—but I'm not sure any longer. We are none of us sure. When you aren't sure, you are alive.[33]

Greene's challenge is to those who are wholly committed to their "unquestioned agnostic assurances." Today this brand of agnosticism has become something like a religion in intellectual circles—especially in those where science and philosophy have had a significant influence.

Scientism

The dogmatism that does not allow for doubting Darwinian evolution has been fueled by *scientism*, "the belief that science provides not *a* path to truth, but the *only* path."[34] Scientism is the unquestioned philosophical position held by vast numbers of scientists today. In his book, *Why Religion Matters: The Fate of the Human Spirit in an Age of Disbelief*, Huston Smith, who taught for many years at MIT, lays out the differences between *science* and *scientism:*

> Science is on balance good, whereas nothing good can be said for scientism. . . . Scientism adds to science two corollaries: first, that the scien-

tific method is, if not the *only* reliable method of getting at truth, then at least the *most* reliable method; and second, that the things science deals with—material entities—are the most fundamental things that exist.[35]

Scientism is a philosophical approach that not only aggressively defends science as the only pathway to truth, but also vigorously opposes any corollary between science and religion or the theory of "intelligent design." These scientists would claim that what has in the past been credited to God is now easily explained by scientific data. So argues scientist Dale Kohler: "We have been scraping away at physical reality all these centuries, and now the layer of the remaining little that we don't understand is so thin that God's face is staring right out at us."[36]

Other scientists, however, would argue that the more we study the natural world around us, the more complex we realize it is: it is full of complexities that are not easily explained by the evolutionary process. Indeed, some of the most exciting scientific studies in recent years—especially in the realm of information science—show serious deficiencies in the theory of evolution. A fundamental key to understanding the origins of life, and the origin of the universe, is seeking to unravel the mystery of information. "The great myth of modern evolutionary biology," writes Dembski, "is that information can be gotten on the cheap without recourse to intelligence." This, he argues, is simply not the case.[37]

Intelligent Design

Among scientists themselves, debates over Darwin rage furiously, fueled by comments such as Fred Hoyle's now-famous assertion that the chance of natural selection's producing even an enzyme is on the order of a tornado's roaring through a junkyard and coming up with a Boeing 747. But when religion enters the picture, scientists close ranks in supporting Darwinism.[38]

For generations intelligent-design theory has been so closely tied to religion that it has been discounted by scientists. And that is still true today. Most people working in the area of intelligent-design theory are Christians, and thus their work is dismissed as being religiously biased. But in recent years the field has gained more credibility and attention because good *science* is being done that supports intelligent design. "In the past," writes Dembski, "design was a plausible but underdeveloped philosophical intuition. Now it is a robust program of scientific research."[39] It is not enough to employ classical arguments, insisting that a watch cannot be designed and produced without a watchmaker, or a 747 by a tornado swirling through a junkyard. While such obvious truisms hardly need a defense, far more is required to support intelligent design in a skeptical scientific community.

Even the most improbable mathematical ratios related to our solar system and the stars in our galaxy are discounted as design by most scientists. Smith summarizes some of these statistical improbabilites:

> Were the force of gravity the tiniest bit stronger, all stars would be blue giants, while if it were slightly weaker, all would be red dwarfs. . . . Or again, had the earth spun in an orbit 5 percent closer to the sun, it would have experienced a runaway greenhouse effect. . . . If it had been positioned just 1 percent farther out, it would have experienced runaway glaciation that locked earth's water into permanent ice. On and on. We get the point.
>
> Physicists of the stature of John Polkinghorne find it impossible to believe that such fine-tuning (and the apparent frequency with which it occurs) could have resulted from chance. They toss around improbability figures in the range of one in ten followed by forty zeros. For them, improbabilities of this order all but require us to think that the universe was designed to make human life possible, to which they add that design implies an intelligent, intentional designer.[40]

It is this area of mathematical improbability and information theory that has recently captured the attention of intelligent-design theorists, who insist that their conclusions are now supported by so-called hard science. Nevertheless, there is resistance among their colleagues. Many scientists argue that modern science has no business concerning itself with design. Why, they ask, would science take a step backward and reintroduce the theory of design? Why? William Dembski, one of the leading proponents of intelligent design (who holds a Ph.D. in mathematics from the University of Chicago and a Ph.D. in philosophy from the University of Illinois at Chicago), responds:

> To answer this question, let us turn it around and ask instead, Why shouldn't we want to reinstate design within science? What's wrong with explaining something as designed by an intelligent agent? Certainly there are many everyday occurrences which we explain by appealing to design. . . . We demand answers to such questions as, Did she fall or was she pushed? Did someone die accidentally or commit suicide? Was this song conceived independently or was it plagiarized? Did someone just get lucky on the stock market or was there insider trading? . . . Entire industries are devoted to drawing the distinction between accident and design.[41]

Information science is also crucial to such fields as archeology. When an intricate pattern is discovered on an isolated rock or on the wall of a cave, scientific methods are employed to determine whether it is the result of natural forces or whether there are indications of design.

It is important to emphasize that design theory in its most basic propositions makes no claim of pointing to a personal God, much less the trinitarian God of the Bible. Nor does it share the claims made by "creation science," which would defend a young Earth (and in some cases a literal six-day creation account). Rather, intelligent-design theory is no more than a challenge to evolutionary theory's claim that intelligence has evolved from nonintelligence.

One of the most widely reviewed studies relating to intelligent design in recent years has been *Darwin's Black Box*, by Michael Behe, a biochemist from Lehigh University, who argues that a single cell indicates powerful evidence for design.

> Central to his argument is his notion of *irreducible complexity*. A system is irreducibly complex if it consists of several interrelated parts so that removing even one part completely destroys the system's function. As an example of irreducible complexity Behe offers the mousetrap. A mouse-

trap consists of a platform, a hammer, a spring, a catch and a holding bar. Remove any one of these five components and it is impossible to construct a functional mousetrap.[42]

Without one of its five parts, a mousetrap is not simply 20 percent less effective. It does not function at all. Some things in nature are not irreducibly complex. They are *cumulatively complex;* therefore removing a part leads only to a decreased function. As such, the theory of evolution would appear more reasonable. But not so in the case of irreducible complexity, where "function is attained only when all components of the system are in place simultaneously." Thus "it follows that natural selection, if it is going to produce an irreducibly complex system, has to produce it all at once or not at all."[43] Behe identifies as an example of an irreducible complexity the bacterial flagellum—microscopic in size yet necessary in the biochemical system, the design of which appears to be as obvious as that of a mousetrap.

Design theory should not be seen as a form of Christian apologetics, as some Christians imply in their embrace of this field of study. But the theory does powerfully challenge those who, like Dennett and Dawkins, seek to stifle any doubts one might have regarding atheistic evolution. Today it is easier to doubt evolution than it was in Emily Dickinson's day, but proof for God continues to remain elusive. How then does an honest seeker live life when there is no solid proof for or against God?

Responding to Una's Doubts

Is belief in God truly "without rational warrant," as many philosophers and scientists would insist? If our *rational* minds cannot comprehend God, then faith must be abandoned—or so runs the argument. Madeleine L'Engle counters persuasively that a lack of rational proofs and doubts about God need not lessen an individual's commitment to faith and church involvement. At one point she confessed, "I might be terribly unsure about God, but I was happy working in his house." In response to a teenage girl's question about God, she answered honestly: "Oh, Una, I really and truly believe in God with all kinds of doubts." She went further than that. Not only did she believe, but she testified, "I base my life on this belief."[44]

When Una probed further, L'Engle expanded on her philosophy of faith:

> There are three ways you can live in life. You can live life as though it's all a cosmic accident; we're nothing but an irritating skin disease on the face of the earth. Maybe you can live your life as though everything's a bad joke. I can't. . . .
>
> Or you can go out at night and look at the stars and think, yes, they were created by a prime mover, and so were you, but he's aloof perfection, impassible, indifferent to his creation. He doesn't care, or, if he cares, he only cares about the ultimate end of his creation, and so what happens to any part of it on the way is really a matter of indifference. You don't matter to him, I don't matter to him, except possibly as a means to an end. I can't live that way, either. . . .
>
> Then there's a third way: to live as though you believe that the power behind the universe is a power of love, a personal power of love, a love so great that all of us really *do* matter to him. He loves us so much that every single one of our lives has meaning; he really does know about the fall of every sparrow, and the hairs of our head are really counted. That's the only way I can live.[45]

8

The Challenge of Theological Complexities & Biblical Criticism

How did I come to lose my faith? . . .
It occurred when the poetry of my childhood
was squeezed out of my life by the prose of seminary education.
I realized that I could not be satisfied with the apologetics of the textbooks.
Instead of helping me, they further undermined my faith.

— SERGEI BULGAKOV

The challenges presented by science and philosophy are closely related to the challenges presented by theological and biblical issues. This is true not only in the academic arena but also on the lay level. Indeed, most people who struggle with doubt and unbelief testify to a range of unresolved metaphysical difficulties that includes a mix of all these fields of study.

For the purposes of this book, however, there is good reason to make a distinction between science and philosophy, on the one hand, and theology and biblical studies, on the other—between that which would typically be thought of as "secular" studies appropriate for a university and "sacred" studies appropriate for a church or seminary. The issues related to science and philosophy—when resolved satisfactorily—can do little more than pave the way for belief in a transcendent intelligent designer who set the universe in motion and continues to be involved in the creative processes of nature. The issues raised by theological and biblical studies, however, speak to the core of Christian beliefs. As such, they often prove to be more difficult for the one struggling to hang on to faith. How does a wavering Christian respond to the cynicism of Oxford University professor Richard Dawkins, a well-known atheist? "The virgin birth, the Resurrection, the raising of Lazarus, even the Old Testament miracles," he scoffs, "are freely used for religious propaganda, and they are very effective with an audience of unsophisticates and children."[1]

Supernatural events, apparent textual contradictions and the problem of evil—these are difficulties raised by those who have walked away from their one-time profession of faith. From Genesis to Revelation, the Bible records supernatural events. Some are similar to the accounts of the supernatural in other religions. Why should someone believe the biblical accounts and deny those that are held dear by Muslims or Hindus? Or why should people believe biblical miracles while denying or questioning similar supernatural accounts that are claimed throughout Christian history, including today?

Another problematic area for those who struggle with doubt and unbelief is the realm of apparent biblical contradictions. Some evangelicals have gone to great extremes to *harmonize* the Scriptures, often with less than satisfactory solutions; others are more comfortable with the not-so-easily-resolved problems. But for those who consider the Scriptures infallible the issues can be very troublesome—enough to lead to doubt and loss of faith.

Issues related to the nature and goodness of God and the problem of evil (theodicy) are among the most often cited reasons for walking away from faith. How, for example, could a good God—an all-powerful God—allow Hitler to exterminate millions of Jews, or an earthquake to kill tens of thousands of people in Turkey, or terrorists to murder thousands of people in the attacks of September 11, 2001? But perhaps more troubling than these questions are the biblical accounts of

God's purposefully destroying countless people—for example, when God sent the flood to kill all the earth's inhabitants but Noah and his family. Many people argue that this was the action of a just God. But others regard this as part of the problem of evil and, thus, as a severe impediment to faith.

This book—and this chapter in particular—is not meant to serve as an apologetics text or a response to the so-called biblical difficulties. There are many other volumes that seek to do just that. What I seek to do here is show the difficulties some people confront in holding on to their faith and the inadequacies of the standard apologetics.

Christianity, more than any other religion, is a historic faith that relies on the credibility of its theological formulations and its Scriptures. Christian beliefs are founded on what is believed to be historical facts—not merely on myths or moral stories, as some other religions are. This difference is illustrated by an experience that a friend of mine related about his visit to India. During a tour of a religious site, the guide was telling about the elephant god. My friend asked, "Do you really believe there was an actual elephant god?" The guide seemed perplexed by the question and was unable to give a clear answer; his concept of religious truth was very different than my friend's.

The very nature of Christianity, therefore, makes it vulnerable to attack by those who would try to use its truth claims to prove its untruthfulness. The myth of the elephant god is not threatened by liberal theology or textual criticism. But Christianity, particularly in the modern era, is challenged by its own perceived standard of truth. Christians have tended to respond to this challenge in of two ways.

One response is to lower the truth standard, making the truth claims of Christianity little more than the truth claims for the elephant god. As such, the biblical narratives are presented as stories that offer moral values, a collection of "Sunday school" tales from childhood.

The opposite response is to dig in one's heels and *prove* the truth of Christianity—or if not *prove* it conclusively, then at least *prove* that the claims of Christianity are more reasonable than are those of any other

belief system. In recent decades popular apologetics has become a bit
of an evangelical industry, with books, articles, videos, seminars and
debates that seek to challenge contemporary unbelief on its own
terms. To the one who is overwhelmed by philosophical arguments
and scientific evidence against the supernatural, philosophy and science are employed as a response. For some, this form of apologetics is
effective, and books such as Lee Strobel's *The Case for Christ: A Journalist's Personal Investigation of the Evidence for Jesus* and Gregory
Boyd's *Letters to a Skeptic* are given high praise. Boyd makes the case
for Christianity in letters written to his agnostic father, who, by the end
of the book, makes a profession of faith.

In *The Case for Christ*, Strobel, a former atheist, offers evidence as
it might be presented in a court of law. Each chapter features an expert
who deals with such factors as eyewitnesses accounts, archeology, psychology and medicine. The book has a unique format with its reliance
on experts in theology, biblical studies and medicine who "testify" as
they might in a courtroom—though the evidence presented is not new
to those familiar with apologetics. Yet Strobel's "case" is convincing
enough to persuade some skeptics.

The opposite response to skeptics—one that would dismiss biblical
accounts of the supernatural—is also frequently presented in a popular
style. Like Strobel's apologetical response, these arguments aim is to
reach an audience not schooled in the finer points of theology and biblical studies.

Marcus Borg Finds Jesus Again

One person who has turned this kind of response into a virtual art
form is Marcus Borg, who has sought to retain his Christian faith by
redefining it. In his best-selling book *Meeting Jesus Again for the First
Time*, he testifies to being a disciple of Jesus—though not the Jesus of
his childhood faith.

Borg grew up in a Scandinavian Lutheran home in North Dakota,
where faith was taken for granted. He memorized John 3:16 as a preschooler and as a young child was thoroughly grounded in evangelical

beliefs and traditions, including the hymns. In reflecting on singing "O Zion, Haste," he writes, "It was clear to me in that moment that believing in Jesus, and telling others of the tidings of Jesus, were the most important things in the world. What was at stake was nothing less than souls perishing."[2]

As he reached adolescence, however, Borg began to question the reality of the God "out there." Then in his early teens, he began to doubt the existence of God altogether. "It was an experience filled with anxiety, guilt, and fear. I still believed enough to be afraid of going to hell because of my doubts. . . . But I couldn't stop doubting." After high school, Borg attended a church-related college where his faith continued to deteriorate—to the point that he no longer prayed or feared hell. In his third year, he took a religion course, and here "the sacred cows of inherited belief began to fall." By his senior year, he was a "closet agnostic."[3]

Borg went on to seminary and there, through his study of biblical criticism, his unbelief was solidified. "The 'closet agnostic' was becoming a 'closet atheist.' " He found the study of Scripture interesting and rewarding, but the notion of God was no longer a reality for him. Neither the classical nor the more contemporary forms of apologetics were convincing. But more than a decade after his seminary studies, he began to find faith again—through mystical experiences. This was not the faith of his childhood, nor the doctrinal orthodoxy of his Lutheran heritage, but an understanding of God through the life of Jesus—a Jesus stripped of the supernatural, a Jesus not found in the Gospel accounts.[4]

Today, after becoming a bit of a celebrity though his participation with the Jesus Seminar, Borg has found a prominent place among theologically liberal Christians. But his spiritual pilgrimage—that of moving from biblical faith to unbelief and finally to a liberal version of Christianity—is not typical. For most people the second and third steps of the sequence are reversed. The stage of denying the divinity of Jesus is the intermediate zone between belief and unbelief. The incarnation is *the* central doctrine of the Christian faith. If God did not come in the flesh, in the person of Jesus, the whole system of Christian doctrine begins to fall like a house of cards. If Jesus was only a good man or a great prophet and teacher, the foundation for the Christian faith is irreparably undermined—so much so that a *faith* commitment almost seems ludicrous.

Peter Fromm

A much more typical spiritual pilgrimage is portrayed in Martin Gardner's autobiographical novel, *The Flight of Peter Fromm*. Here we see the progression from fundamentalism to liberalism to almost no faith at all. The fictional Peter Fromm, like Gardner himself, was raised in a very religious environment in Oklahoma. Speaking of himself, Gardner writes:

> My conversion to fundamentalism was due in part to the influence of a Sunday school teacher who was also a counselor at a summer camp. . . . It wasn't long until I discovered Dwight L. Moody and was deeply moved by his sermon on the blood of Jesus. . . . My fundamentalism lasted, incredibly, through the first three years at the University of Chicago, then as now a citadel of secularism.[5]

Like Fromm, Gardner "was one of the organizers of the Chicago Christian Fellowship, a small group of fundamentalists very much out of place on campus."[6] And like Gardner, Fromm goes through a similar transition from a strong biblical faith to a loss of faith in the Bible and the God of the Bible.

The novel centers around the friendship of Fromm and his professor Homer Wilson, who makes no pretense of believing in God. Chapter six, entitled "The Mustard Seed of Doubt," begins on page 48 of the novel, and from that point on, Fromm moves further and further away from his youthful fundamentalist beliefs. Chapter seven, "Chesterton," describes Peter's discovery of G. K. Chesterton, a twentieth-century Catholic writer and Christian apologist who has been a favorite of many moderate evangelicals. Chapter ten, "Karl Barth," lays out Peter's transition into what has been termed "neo-orthodoxy" or "crisis theology." From Barth, Fromm moves on to Rudolf Bultmann, Reinhold Niebuhr and Paul Tillich, though without necessarily embracing their theological tenets.

As was the case with Borg, the central issue Fromm grapples with is Christology. Who is Jesus? Who is the Christ of the Gospels? Who is the Christ of Paul's epistles? When he entered the University of Chicago's Divinity School, he did so with the purpose of getting educated and getting ordained and going out to present a brilliant defense of his biblical faith. When he graduated from seminary—after having served an interim four-year stint in the Navy and having undergone a mental breakdown—he forsook his plans for ordination and was barely holding onto faith, though he never joined his mentor in the belief that God does not exist.

Rather, while admitting his "loss of faith in orthodox Christianity," Fromm hung on to his belief in God—a holy God, consumed in mystery. Homer, his mentor, is not impressed: "That's where . . . you and I must part. I admit that emotions of awe and fascination, of fear before the Unknown, are primitive, inescapable emotions. . . . But to attribute to that Unknown a holiness, a moral concern for human history, is to project our own personality into the darkness." Homer later reflects on their differences, saying, "Peter had leaped across the void. It was a leap I could not make now even if I wanted to."[7]

Like others who have struggled to retain some semblance of faith, Peter was confronted with the problem of evil, to which he had an interesting answer. When he confesses to Homer that "evil is another dark mystery," Homer responds, "It seems to me that you're evading all the dilemmas of theism by calling them mysteries." Here Peter stood his ground with what might be construed as a convoluted argument:

> I don't think it's evasion. It's just an honest confession of ignorance. . . .
> Faith in God doesn't explain an electron. Why should it explain evil?
> Faith doesn't solve any metaphysical problem. It just eases our anxiety.
> It makes the pain a little less painful. It makes the truth a little less sad.[8]

That Gardner's Fromm walked away from orthodox Christianity

while studying under an atheist professor at the University of Chicago should not prompt those who teach at evangelical schools to smugly shrug off his story. Many of the testimonies of losing faith parallel that of Edmund Cohen more closely than that of Peter Fromm. In Cohen's case, the setting was Westminster Theological Seminary. It was here in this bastion of Calvinist orthodoxy, where American presuppositional apologetics was born, that he walked away from his faith:

> I had been on my way to becoming a regular little Savonarola, a regular little Calvin itching to get a Servetus burned at the stake. Show me a fundamentalist who does not become like that, and I will show you one who conveniently finesses the Bible's harder teachings! . . . I had been wiser at twelve than at forty! How could I have been so damned stupid? At a moment I remember vividly, in mid-1983 early in the morning while I was praying, that imaginary Divine Other simply went and was gone, never to return. What a relief, to be rid of that obnoxious, intrusive presence, and to have my privacy and the freedom to explore my own thoughts and feelings returned to me.[9]

For Fromm, faith—as vacuous as it was—served as a comfort, and this was his main reason for seeking to retain it. For Cohen, faith in God was an "obnoxious, intrusive presence." This attitude differentiates between those who would seek to preserve some sort of religious belief and those who would abandon it altogether. For both Fromm and Cohen, as well as for Borg, theological contemplation became an obstacle to belief. It may seem incongruous that theology, the study of God, often shrivels one's belief in God, but it is true. Trying to understand God through the intellect alone is a futile endeavor that has lead many theologians down the wrong path. One such theologian was Paul Tillich, who devoted his life to a theological pursuit of preserving little more than a shadowy semblance of God.

Paul Tillich's Theology of Doubt

Paul Tillich (1886–1965), it can be argued, stretched the limits of Christian theology further than any other modern theologian. He was one of the most renowned American theologians in recent generations—the only one to be featured on the cover of *Time* magazine. Born and raised in Germany, the son of a Lutheran pastor, he was dismissed from his teaching position at the University of Frankfurt due to his opposition to Hitler. Fearing arrest, he came to New York in 1933 to teach at Union Theological Seminary and later at Harvard Divinity School and the University of Chicago. His death in 1965 merited a story on the front page of the *New York Times*.

Tillich vigorously tackled issues of belief and unbelief and the nature of God, and his theology is sometimes cited as part of the "death of God" school of thought. But Tillich's efforts were in some ways opposed to that kind of thinking. Indeed, regarding his role as a theologian, he said, "Sometimes I think my mission is to bring faith to the faithless and doubt to the faithful."[10] Yet, the result of his characterizing God as the "ground of all being" virtually denied the very existence of a personal God.

Tillich wrote extensively about issues of doubt and unbelief, and he argued that faith is a condition that requires doubt for its very potentiality. Faith and doubt are in tension, in a dialectic relationship, and this gives faith its vitality. In *The Protestant Era*, he summarizes his "theology of doubt":

> Not only he who is in sin but also he who is in doubt is justified through faith. The situation of doubt, even of doubt about God, need not separate us from God. There is faith in every serious doubt, namely, the faith in the truth as such, even if the only truth we can express is our lack of truth. But if this is experienced in its depth and as an ultimate concern, the divine is present; and he who doubts in such an attitude is "justified" in his thinking.[11]

Thus, Tillich concluded, "there is no possible atheism." According to Martin Marty, Tillich "would see the reflective and impassioned atheist gripped by an attachment to 'ultimate concern' and thus—by Tillich's definition—religious."[12]

The doubt of which Tillich spoke was not based on abstract theory. He continually encountered students and parishioners who were struggling with massive doubts about the personal God of which the Bible speaks. And his theology was fashioned largely in an effort to respond to such doubt. God became the "Ground of Being," "the name for that which concerns man ultimately." God is not "an Object which we may know or fail to know, but Being-itself, in which we participate by the very fact of existing." Indeed, "God does not exist. He is Being-itself, beyond essence and existence."[13] If this kind of double talk was aimed at helping people who were struggling with doubts, it fell short of its purpose.

Grace Cali, who served as Tillich's secretary during his seven years at Harvard, has testified to this. Raised by parents who had served in Baptist pastoral and missionary ministries, she was reexamining her beliefs when she first met Tillich, but she confessed that with him, "I got more than I could handle. His concept of God as Being-itself was threatening to obliterate any meaningful concept of a God I could relate to personally." One day she challenged him, confessing her "awful feeling of emptiness" in trying to relate to his infinite God, Being-itself. "My finite self needs a personal God."[14]

Responding to her, Tillich insisted that "God as Being-self and God as person are really not contradictory." God, he argued, is known through his attributes, and those attributes are "most powerfully expressed in Jesus."[15] But like so many before and after him, Tillich failed to do the impossible: fashion God (the Christian God of Scripture) into a truly meaningful deity for the philosophical mind. He was rightly accused of turning God into an "abstract and uninvolved deity" and of offering his readers a definition (Ground of Being) but not a relationship.

Tillich's Remote God

For Cali, Tillich's God was too remote, too impersonal. Perhaps this was the case also for Tillich himself. Indeed, some of his critics believed that his personal life was a reflection of his impersonal God. His marriage vows did not include sexual fidelity, according to his wife Hannah, a professing atheist, whose published accounts of their life together appeared several years after his death.

During his life he had made every effort to keep his personal life away from public scrutiny, so much so that he was humiliated when he learned the American press had discovered that his first marriage had ended in divorce. But for all his secrecy, he could not hide his sins from himself or from his impersonal God, who may have been far more personal than he imagined. Cali writes of this side of Tillich:

> His propensity for making intimate friendships with innumerable women was a constant source of guilt and anxiety. . . . To face them openly was torture and a key to his personal anguish and depressions. Only by an elaborate system of self-delusion could he find it bearable to live with himself. . . . The black depressions were so severe at this period that I feared a breakdown.[16]

Tillich sought to offer an alternative to atheism, but what he and his followers found was a definition of God, not *God*. This alternative was no better—perhaps worse—than atheism.

Marcus Borg, the fictional Peter Fromm and Paul Tillich each illustrate the effort to retain a semblance of Christian faith in the midst of doubt and unbelief. If I were being judgmental at this point, I would say to each of them (whether dead, alive or make-believe), *"Make up your mind; fish or cut bait! Be a Christian or be an atheist; don't muddy the water."* But I know my own heart all too well. I'm an evangelical who struggles with doubt and unbelief. Should it surprise me that some would reinterpret the faith rather than bail out of the faith altogether? And who am I to push them?

For many whose faith is flagging, however, the only alternative is to abandon faith altogether. They question the honesty of professing faith while harboring serious doubts. They take the words of Thomas Paine seriously:

> It is impossible to calculate the moral mischief, if I may so express it, that mental lying has produced in society. When a man has so far corrupted and prostituted the chastity of his mind, as to subscribe his professional belief to things he does not believe, he has prepared himself for the commission of every other crime.[17]

I respect those who are convinced that their only honest option is to cut their Christian ties altogether. One of those who I have come to know through his writing and through correspondence is Elmer Miller. His journey away from the evangelical faith of his youth was spurred not so much by theology as by biblical studies and textual criticism.

Doubt in a World of Certainty

The setting was Eastern Pennsylvania on the edge of Lancaster County, the heart of Mennonite country, during the post-war era of the late 1940s and early 1950s. It was in this atmosphere, amid tradition and stability and certainty—and change—that Elmer Miller began his youthful search for truth. His questions, however, were dismissed by church leaders, and he was often regarded a troublemaker. But young Elmer was deadly serious about his faith—so much so that his escape from the narrow and demanding Mennonite subculture was made possible by another narrow and demanding subculture, as he would describe it: "Youth for Christ and its strictly fundamentalist view of the Bible." Indeed, he insists that it was the fundamentalist, literal approach to Scripture more than the Mennonite allegorical approach that eventually led to his doubt and unbelief.[18]

But in the meantime, he enrolled at Eastern Mennonite College to pursue his calling to missions. His commitment was whole-hearted: "The drive to evangelize the world 'out there' led me to street corner preaching, which I practiced into my third year of college." This enthusiasm for ministry and biblical truth corresponded with an insatiable thirst for knowledge during his college and seminary years. One particular incident is riveted in his memory. He was alone in the college library during Christmas break. His interest in biblical languages drew him to the reference section, where he found lexicons and commentaries and concordances, and soon he was lost in the issue of language equivalency—how, for example, an Old Testament Hebrew word might be translated in the New Testament. It suddenly occurred to him that translating a text was a very human effort.

The overwhelming sense of solitude I experienced that bleak December afternoon was not about the absence of people around me, but rather about the implications of what I later came to recognize as linguistic relativity. I knew I could no longer conceptualize biblical texts in the same way I had been, and was still being taught. . . . The sense of excited confidence that my conclusion was necessarily the only logical one, mixed with the lonely awareness that the implications could undermine ties with family and closest friends, was an emotion that is difficult to explain to anyone who has not experienced a sense of alienation from his or her roots. Knowledge can be bittersweet.[19]

During his final seminary term in 1956, Elmer began to question his plans to enter the ministry. How could he become a Mennonite minister when he was struggling with major doubts? But an irresistible opportunity presented itself: mission work in Argentina that would allow him to pursue further training in linguistics. He accepted the call, and he and his wife, Lois, served for several years as Mennonite missionaries, but during that time his doubts only increased. He left his mission work behind but continued to study the Toba people of Argentina and further his graduate studies. His resignation from mission work also signaled his departure from the faith. Faith in God was not a prerequisite for the teaching and administrative posts he would hold in the years that followed in the anthropology department at Temple University.[20]

In recent years he and his wife have returned to the church, to a liberal Mennonite church that offers them a sense of community. It is a community that allows them to connect with their heritage without demanding adherence to particular beliefs, not even the belief in a personal God. In some respects his philosophy is summed up in the final paragraph of his book *Nurturing Doubt:*

Doubting is the "philosophical attitude par excellence." It *must* become a way of life that tempers response to conflicting as well as contradictory discourses in a multicultural world. This attitude should govern all knowledge held with regard to people and ideas constituted as Other. In its absence dogmatism gets entrenched, crimes are committed, and wars are fought all in the name of unquestioned truth.[21]

If the only options are doubting, on the one hand, and accepting the dogmatism of unquestioned truth, on the other, few people would argue for the latter. But I would argue that the doubting Elmer describes can easily develop into a "philosophical attitude par *insolence*"—one that arrogantly assumes that there is an objective means of doubting that leads to objective truth. Such doubting can easily become a way of life that allows little space for mystery and faith.

Elmer felt his only alternative was to walk away from faith, to leave the ministry and to pursue his doubts. Yet others continue on in ministry while holding faith and doubt in tension. Is this dishonest? Is this "mental lying," as Paine would suggest? We need to take Paine's challenge seriously, for there certainly are those who would pretend to believe—for the sake of their profession—things they do not believe. They are properly censured by Paine.

But to honestly and openly acknowledge doubt and unbelief while at the same time affirming faith and continuing in ministry is a path that many choose to follow. It is a path that often leads to inner conflict and soul-searching, as is seen in the testimony of Father Michael Paul Gallagher. But more importantly, as his story demonstrates, it is a path that sheds light on coming to terms with the life of faith lived amidst the tensions of belief and unbelief.

Disbelieving the Words of Jesus—While Saying Mass

Unlike Elmer Miller, who entered ministry with faith-threatening doubts, Father Michael Paul Gallagher's struggle with atheism came long after his seminary education was completed and when he was already settled in ministry. His crisis of doubt and unbelief erupted suddenly—after a long, frustrating day that had followed a short night of sleep; as in Miller's situation, the immediate context of Fr. Gallagher's crisis related to biblical more than theological issues.

> The actual trigger for atheism came paradoxically with the reading of the Gospel at Mass. It was about the Sadducees disputing with Christ over resurrection from the dead, and, with a little form-criticism in my

head, I found myself disbelieving that these words were ever spoken by Jesus: they were surely put into his mouth by some controversy in the early Church. How much was added? The question soon became magnified into 'how much was fabricated?' From that inner standpoint I stayed unusually alert to the words of the Mass, but in a deeply doubting vein. I found myself, as it were, watching from the outside, and hearing words with a certain nostalgia for their meaning, almost as if I had been an atheist for years and was now revisiting a familiar scene of worship. In one sense I struggled with the thoughts and movements of spirit, but it remained an alarming and lonely experience to be there with my community, and yet to feel cut off from the core of why we were gathered there. . . .

After receiving communion I found myself praying or trying to pray, using the famous words from the father of the possessed boy in the gospels: 'Lord, I believe, but help my unbelief" (Mark 9:24). . . .

What did I understand or begin to understand after communion and at the close of my Mass in atheistic mood? I understood that faith was a more extraordinary gift than I had ever realized. I glimpsed the potential doubt that can never be separated from faith in this life. Most of all I came to see, yet again, that faith is something quite different from mere accuracy of objective truth. . . . As I sat there after communion I came up against the fact that if faith were possible at all, it would be more a matter of life and of love than of truth on its own.[22]

Reasonable Faith

When Fr. Callagher speaks of "objective truth," he raises an important issue. Christianity is a historical religion based on truth claims, but does this make it a "reasonable faith" that will satisfy those who demand objective truth? The twentieth-century Christian philosopher Alvin Plantinga, harking back to John Calvin, argues "that belief in God may be properly basic and thus not based on reasons at all."[23]

Calvin did not base his case for the existence of God on reason and natural theology, as many of his theological predecessors had. Rather, he argued that the belief that God exists is a basic belief—*sensus divinitatis*—and that the almost universal disposition to believe in God is grounds in itself to believe in the existence of God. "There is within the

human mind, and indeed by natural instinct, an awareness of divinity,"
he wrote in his *Institutes of the Christian Religion*. "To prevent anyone
from taking refuge in the pretense of ignorance, God himself has
implanted in all men a certain understanding of his divine majesty."[24]

But belief in a supreme God that comes through general revelation
and is affirmed by one's inner awareness of divinity should not be
equated with the special revelation of Scripture—a belief in the Triune
God of the Bible. It is at this point that some sort of "leap of faith" is
essential to bridge the gap between general and special revelation.
Many apologists have convincingly shown that this special revelation
of Scripture is reasonable, but to insist that it is so reasonable and
rational as to be accepted on its merits alone is claiming too much.
Acceptance of special revelation is a mystery, best explained as the
illumination of the Holy Spirit, a necessary illumination for those of us
who are easily overwhelmed by rational thoughts.

A Challenge from F. W. Robertson

Calvin is helpful to those who are seeking an understanding of faith in
an environment that both demands proofs for God and offers proofs
for God—proofs that simply do not exist. But on a practical level, how
does the Christian who has continual nagging doubts or sudden
onslaughts of atheism continue on in the faith, especially when one's
vocation is Christian ministry? On this point I have found the words of
F. W. Robertson particularly helpful. He was known as one of
England's greatest preachers of Victorian times. He was a man who
held his audience captive. But he was also a man who struggled with
doubts about the very God of whom he preached. His questions concerning *truth* reflect the questions of Fr. Gallagher and all those of faltering faith. Robertson openly confessed his own doubts; but more
than that, he offered advice that is as helpful today as it must have
been to those in his parish church who heard his words during a Sunday morning sermon:

> But there are hours, and they come to us all at some period of life or
> other, when the hand of Mystery seems to be heavy on the soul. . . . Well

in such moments you doubt all—whether Christianity be true: whether Christ was a man or God or a beautiful fable. You ask bitterly, like Pontius Pilate, What is Truth? In such an hour what remains? I reply, Obedience. Leave those thoughts for the present. Act—be merciful and gentle—honest; force yourself to abound in little services; try to do good to others; be true to the duty that you know. *That* must be right, whatever else is uncertain, and by all the laws of the human heart, by the word of God, you shall not be left in doubt. Do that much of the will of God which is plain to you, and "You shall know the doctrine, whether it be of God."[25]

The quote by Sergei Bulgakov that opens this chapter speaks of loss of faith during seminary education. As a seminary professor, I do not take those lines lightly. Like Robertson, there are moments when I doubt all. It is then that I sometimes ask myself as I'm looking out my office window, *What on earth am I doing here? They'd fire me if they only knew.* But then I'm challenged further as a teacher to be more than a *professor* of right words. I know that at such a time, I, like Robertson, must leave those thoughts for the present. I must be merciful and gentle and abound in little services—knowing that such is right, no matter what else is uncertain. This is a powerful challenge to all those who are in Christian service, whether lay ministry or professional. This is a powerful challenge to my fellow seminary professors. We should not be threatened by the ultimate "what if" question. *What if* our biblical beliefs are false? If they are, could we still look back on our lives with sense of satisfaction and security, knowing that we had faithfully cared for creation and served our fellow human beings—ever abounding in good deeds?

9

The Challenge
of Psychology
& Social Issues

The most powerful argument against Judeo-Christian
faith that I know is that of Sigmund Freud. . . .
Reading *The Future of an Illusion* is a sobering experience.
It is the strongest argument against
religious faith in existence, as far as I know.
One comes away feeling like rather a fool
for continuing to be a believer.

— FLEMING RUTLEDGE

The most fascinating psychological study of belief and unbelief I have encountered is found in the novel *The Brothers Karamazov* by Fyodor Dostoyevsky. It is the story of three brothers who have very different views of life and of God. This is not a book for a timid reader. My paperback version is more than nine hundred pages long, even in small print. (I kept thinking, as I was reading, that this great Russian novelist might have an even larger following if he had pared back some pages, but the book is definitely worth plowing through.) Dostoyevsky himself is a fascinating person, and the book reflects his own psychological makeup; three aspects of his personality are incarnated in the beliefs and personalities of the three brothers. The book is, as Konstantin Mochulsky suggests, a "spiritual biography."[1]

Dostoyevsky grew up in Moscow. His mother died in 1837, when he was sixteen; his father, a physician, was killed by his serfs a few years later in a peasants' revolt. This was an era of great scientific and philosophical changes in the world, which led to the "shattering of humanism." Indeed, as Mochulsky writes, "Before his eyes humanism tore itself away from its Christian roots and was transformed into a struggle with God. Having begun with the emancipation of man from 'theology' and 'metaphysics,' it ended by enslaving him to the 'laws of nature' and 'necessity.' "[2]

Young Dostoyevsky went through an initial period of enchantment with utopian socialism, a form of Christian humanism, but he quickly moved on to atheistic communism. It was during this time that he was arrested for illegal political activities and sentenced to death. He was only twenty-eight the day he waited on the scaffold, but at the last moment the death sentence was commuted and he was instead exiled to Siberia.

As he was boarding the train to leave, a devout Christian woman slipped him a copy of the New Testament. Thus began the third phase of his life. Amid the awful living conditions—the hours of arduous toil, the lack of food, the stench of the squalid cell packed body to body, the frigid temperatures of the winter and the heat of the summer—he found God.

After his term of exile, Dostoyevsky sought to unravel his own issues of belief and unbelief through his novels. "The main question which has tormented me consciously or unconsciously through my entire life," he wrote, is "the existence of God." But God is never nonexistent in the novels. Indeed, "God torments" all his characters. Yet there is a sense in which the characters are also left in a world that has been abandoned by God. With this juxtaposition of certainty and uncertainty, Dostoyevsky digs deep into the psychology of belief and unbelief.

> Dostoyevsky's psychological art is famous throughout the world. Long before Freud and before the school of psychoanalysts he plunged into the depths of the subconscious and investigated the inner life of chil-

dren and adolescents; he studied the psychics of the insane, maniacs, fanatics, criminals, suicides. . . . But his analysis was not limited to individual psychology; he penetrated the collective psychology of the family, of society, of the people. His greatest insights concern the soul of the people, the metapsychic "unity" of mankind.[3]

Does God exist? This tormented question is asked and answered—in different ways—throughout *The Brothers Karamazov*. One particular scene features Mr. Karamazov and his two sons Ivan and Alyosha after they have had an audience with an old monk whom Alyosha reveres. Ivan is a cynical atheist; Alyosha is a devoted Christian. The father, knowing his two sons very well, asks whether there is a God. Ivan responds in the negative.

"What about you, Alyosha—is there a God?"
"Yes, there is."
"And what about immortality, Ivan? I mean, isn't there any immortality at all? Not even a tiny little bit?"
"No, there's no immortality either." . . .
"Now you, Alyosha. Is there immortality?"
"Yes."
"There is God and there is immortality then?"
"Yes, both God and immortality. And immortality is in God."
"Hm. Most likely it's Ivan who's right. Think how much faith and energy men have devoted to that dream, how much strength has been wasted on it, and for thousands of years! Once more, for the last time: Is there or isn't there a God? I want a final, definite answer."
"For the last time—there is no God."
"Well, who can be playing that joke on men, then, Ivan?"[4]

Psychological and Social Ramifications of Religious Faith

Why did Ivan deny the existence of God, and why did Alyosha believe so fervently in God? What influenced their very different perspectives on religious faith? They are both products of the same gene pool and the same environment. Yet undoubtedly psychological and social factors predisposed them toward belief or unbelief. Does one believe in order to fulfill an underlying psychological need for love or in order to develop business contacts and professional associates? Does another deny God because a father is distant and aloof or because personal habits do not accord with religious tenets? And what, we might rightly ask, is the reality of one's belief and unbelief in the deepest recesses of the heart and mind? Can we even know that of ourselves?

A psychological or sociological reflection on religion must take into account the nature of the religion—whether it is civil religion, upheld for political reasons and the welfare of the state, or whether it is personal faith that is affirmed or denied despite the negative reaction it may illicit. Christian thinkers through the centuries (some might say beginning with Jesus) have made a sharp distinction between civil religion and personal faith. Søren Kierkegaard compared Christendom to Christianity, and Karl Barth defined religion as unbelief in comparison to the revelation of the Word of God.[5]

Any effort to make a strict line of demarcation between public and private religion, however, is dubious at best. Rarely are personal beliefs (or unbelief) entirely private matters, nor ought they be. Faith is formed in community, and that community often extends far beyond a local congregation of believers. As such personal faith easily infringes on what might be termed civil religion. Religious beliefs, whether private or collective, are complex, and they are endorsed and rejected in the public arena for many reasons, even as they are embraced and abandoned in the private realm for many reasons.

The mixing of private and public religious faith has been a controversial issue in North America in recent decades. Many people who fear the influence of religion in the public arena insist that one's faith should be confined to the personal realm. They emphasize the negative effects of a religion that influences government decisions and public opinion. Indeed, some North Americans have made a conscious effort to single out religious opinion as a form of speech that must be eliminated from the public square.

Such exclusionary tendencies are not new. Karl Marx was the ultimate master of this strategy. He regarded religion, be it civil religion or personal faith, as a weapon of social control and, as such, a toxin to be eliminated from society. Even Christian socialism was a masked attempt of the rich to enslave the poor, as he powerfully penned in *The Communist Manifesto:* it is "but the holy water with which the priest consecrates the heart-burnings of the aristocrat." Marx abhorred all religion, but he took particular aim at Christianity; and in *Das Kapital,* he supported his thesis on religion with a quote from W. Howitt: "The barbarities and desperate outrages of the so-called Christian race, throughout every region of the world, and upon every people they have been able to subdue, are not to be paralleled by those of any other race, however fierce, however untaught, and however reckless of mercy and of shame, in any age of the earth." But religion was more than an oppressor; it was an intoxicant. In his paradigm of class struggle, Marx saw religion as the worst enemy of progress: "Religion is the sigh of the oppressed creature, the sentiment of a heartless world, and the soul of soulless condition. It is the opium of the people."[6] It was Sigmund Freud, however, more than anyone else, who seized the task of defining religion in psychological and sociological terms; and he possessed at least a façade of professional objectivity that Marx did not.

Freud's Biased Unbelief

Sigmund Freud (1865–1939), who is known as the "father of psychoanalysis," was born and raised in a Jewish home in Vienna, but there is no evidence that religious faith ever took hold in his own life. His father Jakob had been at one time a practicing Orthodox Jew, but by the time Freud was born, his father was known in the community as a progressive, free-thinking, liberal-minded man, a factor that might have significantly influenced his young son. The most notable aspect of his childhood and youth was utter poverty—an affliction that followed him into young adulthood. Despite the poverty, however, Freud was able to enroll at the University of Vienna in 1873 as a medical student, amid the optimism that science held the keys to the future. Of Charles Darwin's theories, Freud was convinced "they held out hope of an extraordinary advance in our understanding of the world."[7]

Freud specialized in psychiatry, which was in its primitive stages at that time. Then there were only two prescribed cures for mental patients: hypnotism and electrotherapy. The field was wide open, and he quickly made his mark in it. "Psychoanalysis was conceived by Freud and it came to vigorous manhood during his lifetime."[8] From the beginning, his understanding of religion had a profound effect on his psychoanalysis, and much of his reaction to religious belief came from his own background, as H. L. Philip suggests:

> Freud became an atheist at a very early age, so early indeed that it is dif-
> ficult to believe that he was mature enough, or that he possessed suffi-
> cient knowledge, to justify such conclusions against the general
> consensus of belief. When we remember that he had always been made
> to feel, by his situation as a Jew in a predominantly Catholic commu-
> nity, that he was permanently in a minority his reaction is easy to
> understand, and if his father had become a complete free-thinker (as
> his grandchildren claim) the change would not be so great after all.
> Nevertheless, his atheism does not seem to be so completely rational as
> he himself appeared to think. It was adopted too early in life, and the
> nature of his writings about religion lacks those qualities of objectivity
> and calm which we find elsewhere in his books.[9]

"A Universal Obsessional Neurosis"

Religion is "a universal obsessional neurosis"—this was the underlying thesis of a paper Freud published in 1907. "Religion is not just
explained but explained away," writes Philip. "It is a pathological
condition to be dispersed by analysis as soon as possible so that
man, no longer hampered by its unhealthy influence, can move on
to greater progress." Religion, Freud argued, was merely an illusion.
He did not even consider the possibility that religious beliefs might
be true.[10]

Freud's harshest attack on religion came two decades later, when he
published *The Future of an Illusion*. He was past seventy when he
wrote it, and according to Philip, "it reads like the statement of the

beliefs of a disillusioned old man." Here he developed his concept of the father-god created to fill the human need of security. He placed religion alongside other cultural creations: "I have tried to show that religious ideas have sprung from the same need as all other achievements of culture: from the necessity for defending itself against the crushing supremacy of nature" and "the eager desire to correct the so painfully felt imperfections of culture." Religious beliefs, said Freud, are wish fulfillments: "they are illusions, fulfillments of the oldest, strongest and most insistent wishes of mankind."[11]

When I contemplate Freud and his "father-god" theory of insecurity, I am reminded of Helen Barrett Montgomery, a noted missions leader, denomination president, Bible translator and prolific author in the late nineteenth and early twentieth centuries. She testified to fatherly images of God, but she did not remotely fit Freud's profile of an insecure individual controlled by an unhealthy influence. She was the most celebrated, outspoken, well-traveled leader of the women's missionary movement and inspired millions of women and men to become involved in humanitarian endeavors.

Her father most inflamed her strong self-image, her intellect and her lifelong devotion to God. Indeed, her love for her father allowed her to comprehend her love for God.

> I loved both parents with all the affection within me. But I am not quite sure that my mother's authority was completely successful. She was obeyed because she belonged. My father, on the other hand was adored. To this child God always looked like her father, and obedience to her father became the basis of submission to the will of God. There was reverence, there was fear, the right kind of fear, a dread of doing what was wrong in my father's sight.[12]

Montgomery's testimony is very different from my own. My father was very distant, and I might have wanted God to fulfill in me something that my father did not, but God often seemed to be far more distant than my aloof and unapproachable father. Whatever sort of Freudian wish fulfillment was present in me did not come to fruition.

Religion and the Sense of Absolute Dependence

When we think of the psychology of belief and unbelief in modern times, Freud naturally comes to mind. But long before he came on the scene, the German theologian Friedrich Schleiermacher (1768–1834) delved into the matter. Like many other German philosophers, Schleiermacher was born and bred in the incubator of evangelical pietism: his father an army chaplain and both grandfathers Lutheran ministers. He initially reacted against his pietist training but later sought to combine the pietistic religious experience with theological liberalism. Unlike great theologians of earlier centuries who focused primarily on God, Schleiermacher emphasized religious experience. He, along with his circle of Romantic writers, "rebelled against the rationalistic views of the Enlightenment, and stressed the role of mystery, imagination and feeling." As an apologist for the faith in a post-Enlightenment world, he sought to steer a course between biblical orthodoxy and moralistic religion. Of his contribution to the philosophy and psychology of religion, Barth wrote, "He did not found a school, but an era."[13]

To Schleiermacher, religious experience was the very essence of religion, and the starting point of religious experience was a sense of dependence on God. This was the principal approach for understanding religion both at the present time and historically. Everything was viewed through the spectacles of the perceived feeling of dependence, though this was not regarded in a negative light as it later was with Freud. Schleiermacher would have seen Montgomery's perception of God as a positive example of this feeling of absolute dependence.

The Shallowness of Unbelief

Another thinker who weighed in heavily on the psychology of belief was William James (1842–1910). He graduated from Harvard Medical School in 1869, and three years later returned to teach, a tenure that last thirty-five years. He is a founder of the field of psychology of religion, and in that role (and through his books), he placed a great emphasis on feeling and emotion as factors in religion. Like Schleiermacher, James was not concerned with theological or biblical matters in and of themselves. Rather, religion was a subjective domain, and thus he took very seriously people's accounts of spiritual experiences. He personally had a preference for the mystical tradition, though his research was an earnest attempt to approach the topic scientifically. His best-known work on this topic is his classic *Varieties of Religious Experiences*. In the last chapter of that book he addresses the topic of disbelief in God, arguing that such unbelief is a product of a limited view of the universe and its complexities. Indeed, unbelief is a shallow and unimaginative perspective that is overly dependent on science.

What James is saying has very significant psychological and social implications. From both a personal level and from a societal level, it would be possible to argue from his studies that the individual or the society that does not stifle the natural inclination to believe might have a deeper and more imaginative perspective on life. The individual or society that stifles belief is often infected by a hollow humanism. Some of the greatest thinkers of past centuries have been ones who believed in God. Atheists have their lists of great thinkers, but the fact that they need to put them on a list indicates the paucity of their numbers. Is it fair to suggest that some of the greatest civilizations are ones that bowed before a concept of God, while certain lesser civilizations, such as the former Soviet Union, denied tribute to God? Perhaps the generalization is stretched to far. But the premise ought to be a challenge to Christians as they reflect on faith, both private and public.

James clearly enunciated the benefits of belief, as is shown in Paul Pruyser's summary of his perspective:

> Belief may be untidy, ad hoc, and concrete, but the bit of experience it deals with is "a solid bit as long as it lasts." Unbelief on positivistic grounds may be orderly, general, and abstract, but what it deals with are "but ideal pictures of something whose existence we do not inwardly possess." But James's great stress on motor activity would make him also say that in the end a man's beliefs appear in what he does (with all possible contradictions among his doings) rather than in the ephemeral accounts of his verbalized world view.[14]

In *The Will to Believe,* James defined belief as exercising the will, which involved choices, ventures, commitments and risks in one's quest to know the truth and avoid falsehood. But by this definition, he did not identify unbelief as the opposite. Indeed, here he suggested that unbelief—a deliberate conscious agnosticism—can be as adventurous and risky and passionate as belief. "We can thus complement Bacon's phrase," writes Pruyser, "that there is a *superstition in avoiding superstition* by the proposition that there can be a *faith by avoiding faith.*"[15]

Carl Jung's Search for a Soul

Perhaps the most noted name in the field of psychology of religion in recent decades is that of Carl Jung (1875–1961). His concept of "modern man in search of a soul" was a development welcomed by many evangelicals who were seeking to integrate faith with a study of social sciences; but Jung himself was no evangelical. The son of a Swiss Reformed minister, he recognized a positive purpose for religion in society; but, like Schleiermacher and James, Jung had long abandoned a faith that was rooted in historic Christian orthodoxy. Yet when asked late in life whether he believed in God, he responded: "I don't need to believe, I know." He was not interested in theological constructs of God. He had no interest in a God—a transcendent being who was "wholly other." But he was interested in a God who was experienced: "I must concern myself with him, for then he can become important, even unpleasantly so, and can affect me in practical ways."[16]

What stands out most about Jung—especially in comparison to Freud—is his positive view of religion as it relates to an individual's well-being. Wallace Clift captures his contribution in this arena:

> Jung was perhaps the first psychotherapist to focus on what has become widely recognized as *the* problem for individuals today—the problem of meaninglessness. . . . Outer circumstances did not give life meaning, Jung found. It did not matter whether his patient was rich or poor, had family and social position or not. Rather, it was much more, Jung said, a "question of his quite irrational need for what we call a spiritual life, and this he cannot obtain from universities, libraries, or even from churches."[17]

The guidance churches offered, according to Jung, may relate to experience, but it's someone else's experience. What his patients needed was not teaching or doctrine but rather guidance in interpreting their own experiences. They needed "images of wholeness offered by the unconscious, which, independently of the conscious mind, rise up from the depths of our psychic nature." In working with his patients, he became what he referred to as a "pastor of souls." His specialty was helping people find a religious outlook on life that was unique to their own experience.[18]

Jung found that among his adult patients—those thirty-five and older—"there is not one whose ultimate problem is not one of religious attitude." Thus in regard to unbelief and loss of faith, he could confidently say, "Indeed, in the end every one suffered from having lost that which religions . . . have given to the believers, and none is really cured who has not regained his religious attitude," which, he added, "has nothing to do with creeds or belonging to a church." Christianity and all religions, he insisted, "are psychotherapies, which treat and heal the sufferings of the soul, and those of the body that come from the soul."[19]

Faith and Well-Being

Was Jung correct? Does faith truly have a positive effect on a person's social and psychological well-being? A believer might readily answer this question by pointing to the benefits of living a Christian life. Unbelievers may scoff at such certainty, but studies would seem to support such benefits of religious faith—and it may be a factor in the retention of faith. Many people who struggle with doubts nevertheless hold on to their beliefs because they find support and security and a certain kind of serenity within the community of belief. For their book *Amazing Conversions: Why Some Turn to Faith and Others Abandon Religion,* Robert Altemeyer and Bruce Hunsberger conducted a study on two groups of people: those without a religious background who became strong Christians ("Amazing Believers") and those with strong religious backgrounds who abandoned the faith ("Amazing Apostates").

We found that these rare groups differed in important ways, other than the religious beliefs themselves. For example, Amazing Believers apparently turned to religion for emotional and psychological reasons. Many of them reported very difficult pasts, including substance abuse, psychological problems, death of loved ones, dysfunctional families, criminal behavior, and so on. Religion offered them comfort, security, friends, sympathy, a helping hand—things that they sorely needed in their lives.

On the other hand, the Amazing Apostates left their religious backgrounds for very different—primarily intellectual—reasons. They had apparently taken apart the religious infrastructure in their lives "brick by brick," thinking their way through religious teaching after religious teaching. In the end, they simply could not believe the religion they had been taught, and many turned instead to science and logic as their guides to life.[20]

Lifestyle Issues and the Loss of Faith

The "Amazing Apostates" that Altemeyer and Hunsberger studied fit the same profile that I have discovered in my research. Intellectual reasons are a major factor in walking away from faith, and these intellectual factors are often closely related to psychological and sociological issues. It would be impossible to imagine how many once-professing Christians have abandoned their beliefs after having studied Freud and his negative views on religion. In both the fields of psychology and sociology, religion has been severely assailed. But beyond these *intellectual* factors, there are very practical, everyday psychological and sociological factors related to lifestyle issues that enter the mix.

The most obvious lifestyle behavior related to unbelief is that of living as if there is no God—the most common way of life today, at least in the very materialistic Western world. This is an unconscious form of unbelief, not a determined act of walking away. Christians, myself included, too easily go through life as practical atheists, living as though they are the captain of their fate. Any sense of utter dependence on God, as Schleiermacher spoke of, is almost nonexistent in an age when well-being seems to be far more dependent on medical specialists or air-traffic controllers or the whims of the stock market.

Schleiermacher defined sin as a craving for independence from God, a condition that is closely related to unbelief. "Why is it so hard to believe?" asked Blaise Pascal. "Because it is so hard to obey." People walk away from faith because their lifestyle does not conform to the standards of their beliefs. This was true for J. Budziszewski, a writer and university professor, who testifies that he had for a time abandoned his faith in order to sin without guilt—and he generalizes his situation to fit others:

> As I got further and further from God, I also got further and further from common sense about a lot of other things, including moral law and personal responsibility. . . . By now I had committed certain sins that I didn't want to repent. Because the presence of God made me more and more uncomfortable, I began looking for reasons to believe that He didn't exist. It's a funny thing about us human beings: not many of us doubt God's existence and then start sinning. Most of us sin and then start doubting His existence.[21]

It is appropriate for the professor to testify of his own unbelief, but we should be cautious about his generalizations. The implication that people walk away from faith in order to sin is a common accusation, but it is not found in my own research. Many people with no obvious moral or ethical deficiencies walk away from the faith.

There are other individuals, however, whose loss of faith appears to parallel a turn toward a promiscuous lifestyle. The individual who stands out most in my mind is John Humphrey Noyes, a figure I studied in graduate school and have since written about, as it relates to his founding a nineteenth-century "cultic" movement, the Oneida Community. His loss of faith and his "free love" lifestyle coincided—though he later came back to a "faith" that included free love.

Noyes might have abandoned the faith altogether, but he did not. Rather, after a lapse, he redefined the faith to fit his own lifestyle. There are those today whose spiritual pilgrimage follows a similar pattern—though rarely with such a complex effort to justify a new moral code. Instead, they would point to Christianity as harmful to their psychological well-being. They would insist Christianity offers anything but solace and positive benefits for those whose lifestyle does not conform to biblical morality.

"My Sin of Homosexuality Became Intolerable"

David Dean's testimony is typical of a spiritual pilgrimage that centers around lifestyle and abandoning faith. When he enrolled at Moody Bible Institute, he was, by his own account, a "full-fledged Bible-thumping fundamentalist." At Moody, he writes, "my beliefs were being validated, I was surrounded by like-minded people, and there were no outside views to challenge what I was being taught. It was the perfect microcosm for the maturing fundamentalist." In this atmosphere, Dean initially seemed to thrive:

> Everything was going wonderfully until I discovered a reality about myself that all the prayers in the world could not change, and that was my sexual orientation. . . . The immeasurable pain I was carrying because of my sin of homosexuality became intolerable. . . . All I knew was that I wanted relief from the guilt of my sin and suicide seemed to offer the best answer.
>
> The height of my depression developed the fall semester of my second year at Moody Bible Institute. I would find myself in my dorm room crying because I felt that I was unworthy of God. I began to entertain thoughts of suicide on a daily basis. . . . So on one gray and cold Saturday in autumn, I found myself walking along Oak Street Beach crying out to God demanding, "Why me?" I continued to walk to Fullerton Pier where I sat and watched the waves splashing onto the pier. An incredible sadness enveloped me as I walked to the edge of the pier and considered jumping in the crashing waves. All I can say is that God must have been with me in that moment because somehow I found myself sobbing and wanting to live.[22]

After graduating from Moody, Dean continued on in his biblical studies, "continued to pray, and pray, and pray, for the removal of my sin of homosexuality." But in spite of his prayers, he writes, God "remained silent in his heavenly expanse, not caring about me." Then, Dean "abandoned Christianity" altogether: "To me it became a religion of false hopes and lies. To know and experience an intimate God was a fabrication of fanatics." A liberal philosophical version of Christianity did not appeal to him either. "Why bother with the holy, impersonal other?"

Since walking away from faith, Dean testifies that he has come back to religious faith—a faith that affirms his homosexual lifestyle: "I walked away from the religious right and fundamentalism about seven years ago. Since then I've been rediscovering a loving God who accepts me."[23]

Feminism and Goddess Worship

Feminism (or more precisely, radical feminism), like homosexuality, has been a lifestyle-related issue that has prompted individuals to walk away from the faith. For some, lesbianism is a factor; and like David Dean, they redefine traditional moral standards. In other cases, the issue is Christianity itself, and no amount of reinterpreting can fix the problem. This was the case with a woman who told her story to a reporter from the *Chicago Tribune*. Like Dean, she had close ties, through her education and later employment, with Moody Bible Institute, but she lost her job and her marriage due to her loss of faith:

> I was a faithful churchgoer. I participated in the youth club, went to church camp and Bible school. I went to a church-related college and worked in religious publishing for 12 years. There was obviously something there for me. But I became more and more disenchanted. It's hard to say how it got started, except to say that I found myself in this inner desert. It's like I was drying up inside, all the while following the tenets of evangelicalism.
>
> I left the church because I felt it was overly restrictive. I went to Episcopalianism and was horrified to discover that my real problem was with Christianity. I got to where I could no longer say the Nicene Creed, which begins "I believe in God, the father almighty."
>
> This was like looking over the edge of a cliff for me. I was raised

Christian and felt like there was no other way. None of the other world religions would work, because they all had Father God, too.[24]

This woman goes on to testify that the only religion she found satisfying was goddess worship. She had found herself in an "inner desert," "drying up inside," and Christianity did not meet her needs. Here, as in many other instances, we find psychological issues tightly intertwined with lifestyle issues. Both are factors in explaining why some people walk away from faith.

As I have researched the phenomenon of walking away from faith, I have found that the reasons and results people describe vary significantly depending on the worldview out of which the individual is functioning. Those who are troubled by scientific and philosophical complexities (fueled by modernism) often deny religious belief altogether. On the other hand, those whose issues relate to psychological and lifestyle factors (fueled by postmodernism) redefine the terms of their religious faith to better fit their lifestyle and psychological needs. In some respects the two sides are represented by Freud and Jung respectively, the latter being more threatening to historic biblical Christianity. Freud offered one option—that of rejecting religious faith altogether. Jung paved the way for reinventing religious faith as being designed to meet the needs of the individual whatever those needs might be, and as such historic Christianity, with its strict moral standards, is easily rejected in favor of a "designer" spirituality.

Blooming in Frosty Weather

As I contemplate matters of psychological makeup and lifestyle and how they, along with modernism and postmodernism, influence people in their struggle with doubt and unbelief, I am brought back to the writings of my favorite poet, Emily Dickinson. She was engulfed in the modern worldview of Darwinian evolution, and she faced it head-on, never attempting to make Christianity conform to her own personality and needs. She recognized who she was and was unwilling to pretend she was something else. She was honest in her struggle to believe, and she expressed her faith—such as it was—not through a rational argu-

mentation nor through shallow emotionalism, but rather through the
mystery of poetic lines that reflected on her psychological makeup. I
am convinced that she bloomed, as does my favorite autumn flower,
the purple gentian. I resonate with her as she reflects on her own wintery spirituality—a spirituality conditioned by both nature and nurture,
by both her psychological make-up and her surroundings. Like her, I
can never be the rose of summer, but through God's grace I will bloom
in frosty weather.

> God made a little Gentian—
> It tried—to be a Rose—
> And failed—and all the Summer laughed—
> But just before the Snows—
>
> There rose a Purple Creature—
> That ravished all the Hill—
> And Summer hid her Forehead—
> And Mockery—was still—
>
> The Frosts were her condition—
> The Tyrian would not come
> Until the North—invoke it—
> Creator—Shall I—bloom?[25]

10

Disappointment with God & with Fellow Christians

[If God] lets us remain long in grief and be almost consumed by it,
we cannot but feel, humanly speaking, as if he had forgotten us.
When the anxiety this provokes seizes the mind of a man,
it plunges him in profound unbelief,
so that he no longer hopes for any remedy.

— JOHN CALVIN

The most provocative book I've ever read on loss of faith due to disappointment with God is Shusaku Endo's *Silence*. The title of the book says it all: silence—the silence of God. The book is a novel about Roman Catholic priests who secretly slip into Japan during the seventeenth century, in the days when the Christian message was silenced and Christians faced fierce persecution and execution. This was in the period following the heyday of Christianity in Japan, sparked by the missionary work of Francis Xavier.

In *Silence*, one of those who enters Japan is Sebastian Rodrigues, a Portuguese priest. One of his early letters to his superiors that is smuggled out of Japan touches on the problem of suffering and evil—specifically persecution and *silence*—as it was raised by a Japanese Christian:

I do not believe that God has given us this trial to no purpose. I know
that the day will come when we will clearly understand why this persecution with all its sufferings has been bestowed upon us—for everything
that Our Lord does is for our good. And yet, even as I write these words,
I feel the oppressive weight in my heart of those last stammering words
of Kichijiro on the morning of his departure. . . . Why has Our Lord
imposed this torture and this persecution on poor Japanese peasants? . . .
Already twenty years have passed since the persecution broke out; the
black soil of Japan has been filled with the lament of so many Christians; the red blood of priests has flowed profusely; the walls of the
churches have fallen down; and in the face of this terrible and merciless
sacrifice offered up to Him, God has remained silent.[1]

Later Fr. Rodrigues writes of Christians who were drowned slowly
in the black waters of the sea. He was spared, but he was forced to
watch their terrible watery execution:

They were martyred. But what a martyrdom! I had long read about martyrdom in the lives of the saints—how the souls of the martyrs had gone
home to Heaven, how they had been filled with the glory in Paradise. . . .
But the martyrdom of the Japanese Christians. . . . What a miserable
and painful business it was! The rain falls unceasingly on the sea. And
the sea which killed them surges on uncannily—in silence. . . . Behind
the depressing silence of this sea, the silence of God. . . . the feeling that
while men raise their voices in anguish God remains with folded arms,
silent.[2]

As the book progresses, Fr. Rodrigues becomes more and more disillusioned. His first contemplation on the silence of God are spoken
with the words of a believer—a believer, who like the psalmist, wonders
where God is in the vast universe. But with each execution, his questions become more despairing. The silent God becomes a God who
perhaps does not even exist:

No, no! I shook my head. If God does not exist, how can man endure
the monotony of the sea and its cruel lack of emotion? . . . From the
deepest core of my being yet another voice made itself heard in a whis-
per. Supposing God does not exist. . . .

This was a frightening fancy. If he does not exist, how absurd the whole thing becomes. What an absurd drama become the lives of Mokichi and Ichizo, bound to the stake and washed by the waves. And the missionaries who spent three years crossing the sea to arrive at this country—what an illusion was theirs.[3]

In the end Fr. Rodrigues apostatizes in the face of persecution, as has another priest, Fr. Ferreira—but the persecution they seek to avoid is not their own. That would have been far easier to endure. Fr. Rodrigues apostatizes to save Japanese Christians from torture. Fr. Ferreira's words to Fr. Rodrigues—before Fr. Rodrigues has apostatized—say it all: "The reason I apostatized . . . are you ready? Listen! I was put in here and heard the voices of those people for whom God did nothing. God did not do a single thing. I prayed with all my strength; but God did nothing."[4]

The problem of pain and evil as it relates to the perceived silence of God is surely the most troubling conundrum that Christians confront. It should not surprise us then that people walk away from their faith during times when they feel this silence most profoundly—or are subtly pushed away by a community of faith that lacks understanding.

Silence in the Book of Job

Losing faith is one way of responding to God's silence in the face of pain and suffering. Others seek to theologically and philosophically come to terms with that which is beyond human understanding. Still others shake their fist in the face of God, consumed with anger more than unbelief. And, amazing as it may seem, some sense the presence of God in an even greater measure during times of great loss and sorrow—when it would seem that God was silent in regard to their pain. For still others, God's seeming silence brings a numbing uncertainty accompanied by a determination to persevere in the faith.

Glimpses of all of these responses can be seen in the Book of Job, which more than any other biblical document carries a theme of the

problem of evil, with the related issues of disappointment with God
and the enigma of bad things happening to good people. In reflecting
on Job, Thomas Dow points out that the very arguments we sometimes
use to prove God's existence fall apart when we are most vulnerable in
times of misfortune:

> There seemed to be no Grand Scheme left to believe in. And if no
> Grand Scheme, perhaps there was no Grand Architect, no Master
> Builder with a plan for each life and a plan for the whole.
>
>   All of us can identify with Job at this point. We have all, at one time
> or another, wondered if there is any ultimate meaning to life. Sometimes
> it all seems so piecemeal, so ragged at the edges, so unlike the ordered
> design we describe in our theological arguments for God's existence.[5]

Lament for a Son

Biblical scholars, theologians and philosophers have all grappled with
theodicy—attempting to make some sense out the problem of pain and
of evil. For a person of faith, it truly is the ultimate enigma. There simply is no satisfactory resolution to the problem. But we can find words
and stories that offer insights on how to come to terms with what is
utterly incomprehensible.

In referring to his son's death, rabbi Harold Kushner reminds his
reader that we are not promised a life that is free from pain. "The most
anyone promised us," he writes, "was that we would not be alone in
our pain, and that we would be able to draw upon a source outside
ourselves for the strength and courage we would need to survive life's
tragedies and life's unfairness." His purpose in writing *When Bad
Things Happen to Good People* was to share "with others the story of
how we managed to go on believing in God." Their son Aaron died two
days after his fourteenth birthday of *progeria*, a congenital condition
that did not allow his body to grow normally. "In a sense," writes
Kushner, "I have been writing this book for fifteen years."[6]

Nicholas Wolterstorff had no such preparation for his lament for a
son. Wolterstorff, one of the leading Christian philosophers in America
today, taught at Calvin College for many years before accepting a posi-

tion at Yale Divinity School. His books, which are often heavy and academic, deal with philosophical issues related to belief and unbelief. He was back in Grand Rapids this past summer and I spotted him—at a distance—in church. I immediately thought of his writing. Two of his books, which I had checked out from the library, were on my desk at home. But the book I associate with him most often is not a heavy philosophical work—though it deals with belief and unbelief. It bears the stark title *Lament for a Son.*

Nick's son Eric, who was twenty-five, died on June 11, 1983, while mountain climbing in Austria. *Lament for a Son* is truly a lament—as powerful a lament as I have ever encountered. "I believe in God the Father Almighty, maker of heaven and earth and resurrecter of Jesus Christ," he writes. "I also believe that my son's life was cut off in its prime. I cannot fit these pieces together. I am at a loss. . . . To the most agonized question I have ever asked I do not know the answer. I do not know why God would watch him fall. . . . My wound is an unanswered question."[7]

The tragedy changed Nick's faith. When a friend asked him why he did not simply abandon his faith in God in the midst of such suffering, he reflected seriously on the question. Perhaps the friend thought it would be easier not to have to deal with a personal God at all. But such was not an option—especially for a philosopher whose faith in God had been tested, at least intellectually, many times before.

> I'm pinned down. When I survey this gigantic intricate world, I cannot believe that it just came about. I do not mean that I have some good arguments for its being made and that I believe in the arguments. I mean that this conviction wells up irresistibly within me when I contemplate the world. The experiment of trying to abolish it does not work. When looking at the heavens, I cannot manage to believe that they do not declare the glory of God. When looking at the earth, I cannot bring off the attempt to believe that it does not display his handwork.
>
> And when I read the New Testament and look into the material surrounding it, I am convinced that the man Jesus of Nazareth was raised

from the dead. In that, I see the sign that he was more than a prophet. He was the Son of God.

Faith is a footbridge that you don't know will hold you up over the chasm until you're forced to walk out onto it. I'm standing there now, over the chasm. . . .

For a long time I knew that God is not the impassive, unresponsive, unchanging being portrayed by the classical theologians. I knew the pathos of God. . . . But I never saw it. Though I confessed that the man of sorrows was God himself, I never saw the God of sorrows. Though I confessed that the man bleeding on the cross was the redeeming God, I never saw God himself on the cross, blood from sword and thorn and nail dripping healing into the world's wounds. What does this mean for life, that God suffers? I myself am only beginning to learn.[8]

Everyday Silence

The silence we encounter when we contemplate the death of a child is deafening. But there is also a silence that is often felt in the less horrific tragedies of life, like when we pray and wonder whether our prayers have gone any further than the ceiling. Is there a personal God who cares about my everyday needs, who hears my prayers regarding my job interview, my mammogram results, my canceled insurance, my wayward son, my crime-ridden neighborhood? It is tempting to think that our personal concerns are too small for God's attention. And when we hear only silence, though our problem be large or small, we frequently feel forgotten.

Sometimes the silence and absence is implied by one's failure to pray—one's failure to recognize the reality of God's presence. This was true of my friend Judy Kupersmith, who has abandoned the faith of her childhood—a faith that continued through her early adult years. From the age of six she was nurtured in a legalist Wesleyan Methodist environment where belief in God and prayer was as natural as breathing—though not for her personally:

> To be perfectly honest, I think I prayed as much and probably more than anyone else my age. And I listened with my ears and with my heart. Truthfully I never heard anything. I always marveled at those folks who

said, "I KNOW what God wants me to do; he told me while I was praying. He leads me every step of the way." Well, I never heard anything
and never knew for sure what to do. So . . . what is the next best thing?
Find someone you KNOW is holy and who has an inside track with God
and have them pray for YOUR guidance.[9]

Judy turned to Janet, her pastor's wife, for guidance, and she followed her as a model in life. At Houghton College, Judy dated a young
man who was studying for pastoral ministry. Janet, writes Judy, "was so
delighted that we might both be preacher's wives. And it made us even
closer. I just knew that making Janet happy was the same as making
god happy. So, the romance continued." They were married, and like
Janet, Judy became a Wesleyan pastor's wife—but not for long.

> Now this story really gets long and complicated. Let me cut to the punch
> line. Two and one half years later, our marriage was annulled because it
> had never been physically consummated. . . . I was in big trouble with
> the denomination. I was a scandal. But I was one of the few young girls
> in our church who got in such big trouble for NOT doing "it." Those
> years were by far the most miserable of my whole life—to this day. This
> experience did not make me lose my faith or any of my beliefs. But now
> I knew that I was going to hell for sure.
>
> Later, I got saved . . . again![10]

After the marriage was annulled, Judy remarried and "the fruit of
that union was two practically perfect children. Then divorce. Then
the '70s. A little marijuana. A little valium . . ." and a slow movement
away from her faith.

> BUT THE DEFINING MOMENT came in 1976. I returned home from
> a convention. Let myself into my apartment only to interrupt an intruder
> who robbed me, raped me and beat me. While lying face down on the
> floor with pictures of my babies in full view, I talked and cried and
> cajoled and tried to save my life. I did. It was later, weeks later, when I
> was able to reflect on that night that a sudden realization hit me. I had
> been in mortal danger—AND IT HAD NOT EVEN ENTERED MY
> MIND TO PRAY. Well, it was like a burden rolled off my back. I no
> longer believed. I was free. I had saved myself, in my own mind. Imme-

diately after the event, my friends continued the saving process. AND STILL IT DID NOT OCCUR TO ME TO PRAY.[11]

Here was a woman raised in a religious environment of *knowing* God through prayer—a God who hears and answers prayer. Yet in the moment of her greatest desperation, she did not even think to reach out to God. Where was God during this terrible rape and assault?

For Judy, the sense of disappointment with God was not isolated from a sense of disappointment with God's people. In the years following her marriage annulment, some of the very church leaders who were supposed to be involved in her healing process took advantage of her vulnerabilities. As a naive young pastor's wife, such hypocrisy (which she is uncomfortable talking about to this day) set the stage for her subsequent loss of faith. She blamed herself, but God, as represented by the "men of God" in her life, was diminishing in stature and on his way to becoming nonexistent for her.

Portofino

Sometimes the abuse perpetrated by a "man of God" does not lead to the abandonment of faith, but the effects are nonetheless devastating. I thought about this as I recently reread Franky Schaeffer's novel *Portofino*. This has been characterized as an autobiographical novel—reflecting not only on himself but on his mother, Edith, and his late father, the well-known Christian apologist and writer Francis Schaeffer. This book *is* fiction, I kept reminding myself. But it is difficult to keep that in mind, especially when I read of the family's denominational affiliation and ministry: they are fundamentalist Presbyterians who are missionaries in Switzerland, as were the Schaeffers. The following description of the father in the novel resembles the author's own father:

> He had come to live in Switzerland after the war to be a missionary to Swiss Roman Catholic youth . . . a Reformed Presbyterian minister who traveled around Europe preaching the gospel to youth wherever local Christians need encouragement in their outreach to lost Roman Catho-

lics. . . . Dad taught the Bible, the Calvinist principles of the doctrine of
Total Depravity, and Calvin's Institutes to lost Roman Catholics.[12]

The narrator, a boy named Calvin, recalls his mother on vacation in
Portofino, the Italian village on the Mediterranean where the family
spent two weeks each summer: "After Mom had eaten a little, she
would sit back in her deck chair, a queen among grateful subjects, and
we, ranged on towels about her, would keep eating while she read
aloud." I remember years ago a colleague referring to Edith Schaeffer
as "the queen bee." But I remind myself that the mother in the book is
Elsa, not Edith. Elsa is particularly known for her long prayers—especially before meals in the resort dining room.

But Calvin's father is the towering figure. Indeed, his black moods
and madness dominate the book. The reader turns the page always
wondering whether he will be in his "Mood" again:

> Our family life revolved around Dad's Moods. . . . Anything could sum-
> mon the storm clouds of a Bad Mood. . . . At home in Switzerland we
> often would go to each other's rooms and huddle together against the
> rise and fall of Dad's angry voice punctuated by the low murmur of
> Mom's rejoinders. . . . Then we would hear unspeakable things that left
> us no place to look for the shame of it all. It was agony to even glance at
> your sisters when Dad was being really bad because we were all so
> embarrassed that we had such a wicked father. . . . Last year he
> slammed the glass door between [their] room and the balcony so hard it
> shattered and once he had thrown a potted ivy plant at Mom.[13]

One time in Portofino, the father's Mood becomes so black after
they arrive that he makes the family pack their bags in the middle of
the night and go outside to wait for the early morning bus to take them
back to Switzerland. In the end, after waiting for hours, he backs down
just as the bus arrives. On another occasion, while dining at the resort,
when Elsa offers him her plateful of chicken (because he had ordered
his meal late), he takes the plate and breaks it on the floor, chicken
and broken glass flying everywhere. And if that were not enough, he
then "swept all the dishes crashing onto the tiled floor." But there were

other times when he was not in the Mood: "Mom seemed kind of anxious . . . nervous that Dad would smash stuff again. But Dad was in a much better mood; he even leaned over and kissed Mom and said she looked beautiful."[14]

I am not a literary critic, and what I see in poetry and prose is not necessarily what other people see. But here we have a very domineering father figure, who could almost be equated with God in the mind of Calvin, the narrator, who is utterly insecure about his own standing before God. Sometimes this father figure is kind, but more often he is cruel—and this disposition most definitely affects the faith of his son. Calvin is not attracted to the stern religion of his father or to the syrupy piety of his mother. Rather, he is captivated by the religion of the Catholics he befriends in Portofino. He goes into the Catholic church and crosses himself before the statue of Mary, even though he knows his parents consider Catholics outside the fold—not part of God's elect. They are the objects of the family's missionary endeavors.

At one point Calvin is daydreaming about himself and his Catholic friends—how they will go to hell because they have not studied John Calvin's *Institutes* to learn about Reformed theology. But in his imaginings, he hears the Lord say of John Calvin, "He's not one of the Elect, his mind was unregenerated, he is the *original* vessel of Wrath." The narrator loves the world of the Catholics in Portofino. In the last chapter, he is saying his goodbyes and preparing to leave with his family, but his heart remains in the unregenerate world of Portofino.[15]

The book is about much more than hypocrisy. It is a boy's story, a journey of faith and folly—and it is a very funny one, despite the dark episodes. Franky Schaeffer has been criticized severely by some for writing the book. Some angrily ask, If it truly is an autobiographical novel, why does he need to air the dirty linen? And if it is not, why is he spreading such false "rumors"? Whatever the case, the book offers an all-too-real depiction of a "man of God" and his representation of God to a vulnerable child.

The significance of *Portofino* for this study is that it illustrates how the sin and hypocrisy of Christian leaders affects the faith of followers.

Other published accounts, real and fictional, too numerous to mention, show similar patterns; in some instances the followers leave the faith altogether. In *Don't Call Me Brother*, for example, Austin Miles lays out a lengthy catalogue of all the sins of well-known and not so well-known preachers and evangelists. "[I] had been driven to outrage and revulsion by what I had witnessed and experienced in the name of Christianity," he writes. He cites Billy James Hargis, a Baptist televangelist and Christian college president in the mid-south who traveled around the country singing patriotic music with his college's choir—until the news broke that he was having sordid sexual encounters with both young men and young women in the traveling choir. Jim and Tammy Bakker are also on his list of close acquaintances who drove him away from the faith he once professed.[16]

Where Is God in the Midst of Pain and Evil?

Why doesn't God intervene and put these people out of business once and for all? Why doesn't God pour his wrath out on the wicked and make the righteous to prosper? These questions are as old as the Bible itself. Sometimes it seems as though God has gotten things backwards: evil flourishes and goodness is not rewarded.

The disillusioned doubter may find it difficult to make sense out of a seemingly inattentive, silent God whose foremost followers are so utterly flawed. And this assessment of God and his followers is made not merely by accusing, disgruntled "walk-aways"—it is the picture often portrayed in Scripture. For Adam and Eve in the Garden, sin was only a temptation away; and from there everything went downhill, with the first murder recorded in Genesis 4. The Old Testament prominently features sins of deceit and discrimination and sexual exploitation—sins often associated with God's people. Even in Scripture there is little sense of justice for those who seem to be most exploited. We do not even hear their voices. Where is God in the midst of this pain and evil? We read of God's people turning their backs on God. Did the sins of the leaders influence this unfaithfulness?

Despite the unfaithfulness of his people, God did not turn his back on them. Throughout the Scriptures we see God's concern for the oppressed and exploited, the poor and the widows, but their cries of pain are, for the most part, left out of the stories. Like most historical records, the Bible features the stories of prominent and powerful men (occasionally their wives are included). What about the "little" men and women? Did they often feel betrayed by their leaders and abandoned by God? We can only imagine they did.

We know that some of the most prominent biblical characters harbored such feelings: Job and the psalmist powerfully articulated their sense of abandonment. The psalmist's laments are often quoted by other biblical characters who are encountering a profound sense of silence and disappointment with God. In themselves, these laments do not offer any real resolution, but they remind us that we are not alone in our feeling of abandonment.

A Cry of Absence

A provocative book that deals with the psalmist's laments and with issues of death, doubt and disappointment with God is *A Cry of Absence: Reflections for the Winter of the Heart* by Martin Marty. Although Marty is known primarily as the nation's premier historian of American religious history, he reflects in this book on many of the darker psalms and begins by describing the anguish surrounding the terminal illness and death of his wife, Elsa:

> SHE: What happened to Psalm 88? Why did you skip it?
> HE: I didn't think you could take it tonight. I am not sure I could. No: I am sure I could not.
> SHE: Please read it, for me.
> HE: All right
> *. . . I cry out in the night before thee . . .*
> *For my soul is full of troubles . . .*
> *Thou has put me in the depths of the Pit,*
> *In the regions dark and deep . . .*
> SHE: I need that kind the most.

Marty goes on to say that each night they read a psalm in turn—she read the odd numbered ones, he the even numbered. "But after a particularly wretched day's bout that wracked her body and my soul, I did not feel up to reading Psalm 88. . . . We continued to speak, slowly and quietly, in the bleakness of midnight. . . . We agreed that often the starkest scriptures were the most credible signals of the Presence and came in the worst times."[17]

Although the book relates primarily to the terminal illness and death of Marty's wife, it reflects more broadly on how people relate to God and asks the reader "to undertake a journey of the soul."[18] Marty wrote the book during the winter months following Elsa's death, rising at four o'clock in the chilly Chicago mornings, the wind and snow blowing against his study window. The lines of John Crowe Ransom were appropriate to the setting and to his spirit:

> Two evils, monstrous either one apart,
> Possessed me, and were long and loath at going;
> A cry of Absence, Absence, in the heart,
> And in the wood the furious winter blowing.[19]

For Marty the "cry of absence" in the most personal sense related to Elsa, but it had wider implications in his relationship with God. And it is this latter perspective that makes so powerful the book's challenge to believers who struggle perennially with a sense of absence and the silence of God. For those people, "the divine is distant, the sacred is remote . . . God is silent." They are ones "who live with dullness of soul, feel left out when others speak only of such bright spirituality." Here he writes of two very distinct types of spirituality—the summery and the wintery.

> The wintery sort of spirituality, let it be remembered, stakes out its place on the landscape next to persons who have seen God excluded from their horizons. That exclusion is the signal of their winteriness. They have not given up on the search for God. They remain committed to the Christian meanings, and they find many occasions to worship and affirm. That is the sign of their spirituality. . . . They cannot satisfy their hunger by reading the descriptions of summery piety. They have to find their Yes on the colder, more barren landscape.[20]

The best answer Marty can offer is for people to come to terms with God and with themselves. Those who are troubled by a sense of abandonment and silence need not strive for a summery spirituality—nor need they contemplate the option of walking away from the faith. There is a place for them on the barren wintery landscape, where the January thaw may provide a welcome respite. But "the spiritual January thaw will not last," writes Marty. "Enjoy the warmth and sound it brings, the heart tells itself, but know that this is not a dispelling of winter, only an interruption."[21]

The Unanswered Question

From an intellectual standpoint, one can discuss the issues relating to disappointment with God and the sense of silence, but ultimately one will find no answers. I am convinced of that. I have searched the most insightful authors seeking clues, but all they can say individually and collectively is that such things are beyond our comprehension. I believe Annie Dillard sums up this problem better than anyone else. In *Holy the Firm,* Dillard introduces an utterly unsolvable "story problem": a little girl named Julie has been admitted to the burn unit of the hospital—her face is badly burned, so badly that no drugs are able to relieve the pain. Then Dillard takes us back to Jesus and the blind beggar:

> "Who did sin, this man or his parents?" they ask him. Jesus spit on the ground, and with a finger full of mud, rubbed the eyes of the man and healed him. "Neither has this man sinned, nor his parents: but that the works of God should be made manifest in him."[22]

Then comes Dillard's commentary, ending with the question posed in her unique way:

> Really? If we take this answer to refer to the affliction itself—and not the subsequent cure—as "God's works made manifest," then we have, along with "Not as the world gives do I give unto you," two meager, baffling, and infuriating answers to one of the few questions worth asking, to wit, What in the Sam Hill is going on here?[23]

Dillard goes on to conclude, and rightly so, that none of this—none of life's pain and sorrow and evil—makes any sense. "We do need reminding, not of what God can do," she writes, "but of what he cannot do, or will not, which is to catch time in its free fall and stick a nickel's worth of sense into our days."[24]

The problem of pain and of evil is the ground of all battles for belief. Whether the wrong is perceived to be a random occurrence or to be perpetrated by Hitler or a television evangelist, it is only natural for one to wonder why God did not prevent it. The only question really worth asking is "What in the Sam Hill is going on here?" No thoughtful philosopher or theologian has the answer. The best response is to offer no answer at all. One can only say—along with Dillard and with a sigh of resignation—"God does not catch time in its free fall and stick a nickel's worth of sense into our days."

So why bother with faith? This is the question my friend Judy Kupersmith asks me. She knows that faith does not come easily for me. If it did, she would not be so perplexed by it. But she simply cannot comprehend why anyone would persist in faith amid struggles with doubt and unbelief. What is the point of a faith that finds its home on the barren wintery landscape? "What in the Sam Hill is going on here?" she might well ask me. I have no answer but the wordless sigh of resignation, *God does not . . . stick a nickel's worth of sense into our days.* I do not know why some people more than others are afflicted with a sense of God's absence, but as for me, I will seek to be faithful to God even if my only habitation is "on the landscape next to persons who have seen God excluded from their horizons."

Part Three

The chapters in this section seek to explain the new life of unbelief as well as the new life of returning to faith—a faith that often looks different from and feels more vital than the earlier faith. It is important that Christians understand people who walk away from faith before plunging into personal interaction with a preprogrammed response. We need to ask, How do we best come to terms with matters relating to loss of faith? How can we effectively respond to an individual who has walked away? What preventative measures can be taken with those who are struggling with doubts?

The chapters that follow present both sides—the side of unbelief and the side of belief. Chapter eleven looks at the new life of unbelief from the perspective of the unbeliever. Here the testimonies of pain and anguish as well as peace and joy and happiness are presented as valid reflections by individuals who are best equipped to know their own hearts. The next chapter focuses on the "evangelistic" outreach of some of these individuals who once professed faith. These missionaries of unbelief are persuasive in their discussions with Christians who are struggling with doubts. Chapters thirteen and fourteen seek to respond to some difficult questions and to tell the stories of individuals who have returned to faith. We cannot manufacture easy answers (as chapter thirteen demonstrates), but we can find ways to come to terms with the difficult questions—indeed, we can even find opportunities to live a vibrant life of faith amid the tensions of doubt and unbelief. The final chapter focuses on the stories—the testimonials—of three women who have lived through doubt and unbelief and have *returned*, so to speak, to a life of faith. Their stories offer a powerful image of sovereign grace in the lives of flawed individuals who commit their lives to God in faith.

11

The New Life of Unbelief

Seeking Happiness Outside the Family of Faith

After many years spent living in "the World,"
I have learned that there is such a thing as happiness, peace,
and even unconditional love, and that Calvary Chapel—religion
in general, for that matter—holds no monopoly on it.
Though it's taken almost half my lifetime—and endless hours of therapy—
to shed the anger, guilt, and self-hatred . . . my new life is
demonstrably richer, fuller, and more meaningful
than my narrow, fear-driven experience, intoxicating though it was,
within the inner circle of Calvary. I am not alone.

— D A V I D   T E M P L E T O N

What is the new life of unbelief like? Many Christians have sought to answer or make allusions to this questions without ever taking seriously the stories of those who have made the transition from belief to unbelief. Most Christians imagine a post-faith life as full of unhappiness and insecurity and hopelessness. But many who have walked away from faith give testimonies that are not negative at all—except for the initial pain of making the decision and telling friends and family. Once the initial shock is over, however, and the individual has settled into the new life of unbelief, there is frequently a profession of greater happiness and security. Many Christians would argue that such a claim is all a façade, that there is a self-delusion of serenity that does not measure up to reality. Such may be the case, but the same might also be alleged of Christians who profess happiness and security.

I am skeptical of public professions of a higher life of tranquillity, whether given by believers or nonbelievers. I know all too well that behind the scenes these public testimonials are often a sham. Those who have walked away from the faith often claim to have found true peace before their post-faith peace has been tested by a real crisis. Now that they have lost their faith, how do they come to terms with the loss of a child or loved one? How do they face their own mortality? Does it make no difference that they have lost the hope of ever meeting loved ones again? Is there no downside to living a life that that has turned away not only from God but also from the faith and traditions of one's heritage? One cannot fully answer these questions on behalf of those who have walked away without doing research and conducting studies and surveys that go beyond the scope of this book. But a first step in seeking understanding those who have abandoned the faith is to take seriously some of their testimonies.

Loss of Faith and Contentment
Many people who have lost faith would not necessarily describe their "new life" in terms of happiness or contentment. They would insist— and rightfully so—that one cannot pretend to continue believing something or continue living a lie for the sake of contentment; in the end, there is no real contentment in false pretense. Yet there are those, I am sure, who for the sake of comfort remain within the community of believers despite their serious doubt and unbelief. What, it is fair to ask, is their state of contentment?

Does "losing faith" entail real loss? Many who have walked away from the faith insist that they do not like the term *loss*—because they do not feel they have *lost* anything. In a recent e-mail message from Dan Barker (whose story is told in chapter twelve), he writes, "As you know, I feel no sense of loss in giving up my faith. There is no virtue in faith—it always leads to more problems than answers. I feel relieved. 'Saved,' if you will. Reason and kindness are good enough for me."

My friend Judy Kupersmith, from Tampa, offers a similar testimony—though in comparison to Dan Barker, she feels much more warmth for Christians. And in her case, we are in frequent contact and I am aware of her daily frustrations and joys. She has lived with her elderly mother and has faced the usual frustrations regarding health issues that might be expected, though more often I hear of their good times together. And she has recently become a grandmother three times over; and here, her biggest frustration is that one of the little ones lives much too far away from the doting grandmother. To even imply that she somehow derives less joy from her little ones than I do from my little Kayla would be entirely without warrant. Indeed, I sometimes envy the sense of contentment she has in life that too easily alludes me.

In response to a questionnaire that I sent her, she wrote this about the quality of her life of unbelief:

> I found peace when I began to look within myself and outward to other people for all the things I need. My inner contentment is found completely in the natural, not the supernatural. The last 16+ years have been so restful and so productive since my energies could go into things other than seeking a spiritual "something." It has been a most interesting journey from that little corner church with the shouting Wesleyan Methodists to where I am now. The journey has been without resentment or anger or bitterness—which seems so prevalent in "recovering" Christians. I am still connected to the people from that part of my life. And though I intellectually completely disagree with them, I can still love them and tolerate their beliefs for them. . . . They have a much harder time accepting me than I do them. Guess it is because I have been where they are; they have not been where I am now.[1]

But are Judy and Dan representative of those who have abandoned the faith? The hard, cold evidence is not easily available, but some studies would show that there is true *loss* involved in losing faith. Robert Altemeyer, a Canadian researcher, developed a "Happiness, Joy and Comfort" questionnaire in the late 1990s, which he administered to several hundred parents of university students. He asked them how "happiness, joy and comfort" were influenced by *traditional religious beliefs* versus *logic and science*. There were sixteen categories that included such things as these:

1. They tell me the purpose of life.
2. They help me deal with personal pain and suffering.
3. They take away the fear of dying.

The results showed that "religion brought them substantially and significantly more happiness, joy, and comfort than did logic and science." In only one of the sixteen categories did logic and science reach the halfway mark on the scale—that category being "They bring me the joy of discovery"—while in all the categories religion was above the halfway mark. But an even more disturbing result for the nonreligious side is that logic and science did worse than religion in "satisfying answers to all the questions in life" and explaining "the mysteries of life"—and this from a well-educated group of people."[2]

This questionnaire considered only factors relating to one's satisfaction with life. Among all the characteristics and attributes of life, how high should we rate satisfaction? To be fair, it should be pointed out that other studies have shown that the more religious a person is, the more prejudiced the person is likely to be—especially when that person is categorized as a religious fundamentalist; and for this group of people, studies indicated that authoritarianism was also a characteristic. So some might argue it is a mixed bag—many nonreligious people testify to contentment, and many religious people abhor prejudice and authoritarianism. Another problem with the survey was that it pitted traditional religious beliefs against logic and science, the latter reflecting a modernist worldview. Today many people would identify themselves more in postmodernist categories and might likely attribute their happiness, joy and comfort to an ill-defined "spirituality."

Losing Faith by Erosion

Perhaps more studies need to be done and more numbers need to be

charted. But in many ways, the new life of unbelief is best told in stories, not statistics. It is helpful to hear of the pain and struggle, and,
yes, of the peace and satisfaction that some testify comes from walking
away from the faith. In many instances, the transition from belief to
unbelief is a long and difficult road. Every story has its own plot and
cast of characters, but the stories share similar themes. The metaphors
used to describe these themes vary, but one of the most fitting comes
from Rudolf Nelson, who speaks of "erosion":

> I had difficulties with Christian belief almost as far back as I can
> remember, although for long periods of time I buried them. . . . [By]
> 1967 . . . I was forced to acknowledge that for some twenty years my own
> faith had been suffering a steady process of erosion. The word *erosion*
> almost always carries pejorative connotations, and I certainly did not
> use it in those years to describe what was happening to me. I would
> have been much more pleased with the self-congratulatory notion that I
> was a sculptor chipping off superfluous matter in the effort to uncover a
> beautiful work of art. In the sculpture metaphor, what I was losing was
> not worth keeping anyway, and I would be left with a small core of
> Christian affirmations in which I *really* believed. But then parts of the
> core started to chip away too. I wondered if there was enough stone left
> to make a work of art. The erosion metaphor was the right one after all.
> It is one thing, though, to lose a few inches a year off the Atlantic shore-
> line. It is quite another thing to feel ominous subterranean rumblings
> and discover that the river of doubt has been eating away under the
> ground and that one's whole house of faith inevitably will soon be
> poised on the edge of the abyss.[3]

Another metaphor for the loss of faith is death. Indeed, for family
members the loss of a loved one to unbelief can be worse than death.

Loss of Faith Worse Than Death

Families and church communities are often profoundly affected when
a person walks away from the faith and begins a new life of unbelief.
On a website titled "The Anguish of Leaving the Faith," a man by the
name of James posted correspondence relating to his and his wife's

"deconversion." Here we see many of the emotions that erupt and complications that arise in the process of abandoning the faith. In fact, he and his wife initially concealed their unbelief in order to soften the blow to their families:

> It is because we wanted to maintain good family relations that we did not reveal our loss of faith when it first occurred. We wanted to slowly move away from the faith to give you all a chance to get used to the idea and spare you the shock. But we were found out by accident, and so now we all must deal with it.[4]

In this correspondence, James reminds his in-laws that he "was a Christian" for twenty-three years and that he was "very serious about living the Christian life." It was not his neglect of his faith that created doubts but his study of Scripture—while "giving Christianity every benefit of the doubt." He tried to overlook the difficulties he encountered, assuming he had not yet discovered their resolutions. "However," he writes, "the more I studied, the more numerous and prominent the difficulties became." Then almost a year before the correspondence began, his life changed dramatically: "One day last Christmas season I sat down and opened my Bible for personal devotions and suddenly recognized that I did not believe it anymore."[5]

Pain and anger were evident in the first letter he and his wife received from her parents after they learned of the dramatic changes that had occurred.

> This letter is in response to your apparent new belief/practice that the Bible is not true and that there is no God. We will preface our remarks by saying that everything we write is because of our deep love for you. First I will state our feelings. These include the following: very upset (wake up at night worrying), grieving, angry, sad, and worst thing that has ever happened to our family. . . .
>
> James, we hold you responsible because we firmly believe that Alison would never have come up with this on her own. . . . We have a major disagreement within our family for the first time. We have been in harmony up to now. Now we do not agree with your beliefs and are very concerned with the way our grandchildren are being raised. If this

belief/way of life continues then we are worried and afraid that your great family will suffer. In fact, I predict that it will, as much as I hate to make such a prediction. . . . I am sending three books which I hope and pray that you will read.[6]

That James's in-laws were blaming him, rather than their daughter, for walking away from the faith was not without foundation. He made no secret of the fact that Alison had followed him "into unbelief" soon after he had "lost faith." Her reason (which was described in a later letter) was that she trusted his knowledge of the Bible and thought his "new position had to be well grounded in fact." And she knew this was not a matter he decided on a whim. "She had seen me struggle to resist coming to this conclusion, but the contrary evidence overwhelmed my intellect, and, if I may paraphrase Josh McDowell, my heart cannot worship what my mind cannot accept."[7] One week after he received the letter excerpted above, James responded by seeking to explain his rationale for walking away from his church community and also to confess how painful this ordeal was for him and Alison.

I know that my very existence, as a Christian who rejects the faith based on knowledge of the faith, is threatening, and I understand why you all have reacted so strongly. Alison and I have experienced many of the same emotions about this that you have. Our loss of faith is something that happened to us while we were doing the things that Christians are supposed to do—not something that we willfully or maliciously decided. (Why would we? It would have been much easier to continue on as believers.) The whole process has been wrenching for us, and, like you, I have lost many hours of sleep because of it. However . . . to affirm something that is impossible for me to believe would be lying, and I cannot do it with a clear conscience.[8]

After receiving the above-mentioned books from his father-in-law, James wrote to thank him, adding that he would not read anything that was sent unless the arrangement was mutual: "I will read a book or chapter or essay of your choosing for every book or chapter or essay of my choosing that you read."[9]

In a letter to his pastor, James insisted that he felt no animosity toward him and apologized for not having broken the news to him personally. (The pastor heard about it from James's father-in-law.) James's reason for not disclosing the matter to the small group that he was leading (telling them instead that he was stepping down because it had become "too stressful") was straightforward: "I did not want to shake the faith of my small group members, especially while we ourselves were in the throes of coping with the collapse of our entire worldview."[10]

James was also concerned that the matter would get back to his children: "We decided that it would be too traumatic to tell the children, since we had raised them to love Jesus. Instead we are teaching them to think critically and helping them come to their own conclusions as they are ready." One very poignant admission that James made in his correspondence related to his reason for not having come immediately to talk with his pastor: "Your duty and theirs would have been to shepherd us back into the fold, and so we had to struggle through the loss of faith on our own. In this limited sense, loss of faith is harder than the loss of a loved one, since there is no support of (believing) friends or family to carry one through a loss of faith."[11]

James found his support group outside the church—on the Internet. In late March 1998, more than a year after his Christmas-season loss of faith and some four months after his family had discovered his secret, James wrote a letter to Internet "walk away" supporters.

Hi, folks! I'm declaring myself healed of the Christian delusion and I am leaving the ex-tian list. I want you to know that I think you folks are the greatest. Losing faith is a lonesome thing, and the existence of this list and the people who post to it gave me countless emotional boosts when I needed them most over the past year.

For some time now I have felt strong and happy and confident and free, and I believe that I am no longer in need of support. The ghost of my old Christian faith has faded away, and I have really already moved on to living and enjoying life in the here and now without superstition. Hence my own personal emotional state is healthy and vigorous, if I may be allowed to diagnose myself.

As for relationships . . . my spouse and kids are happy and healthy without superstition. . . . I am confident . . . of maintaining mutually respectful relations with my believing relatives. . . . I feel now as if I have been born again into a new life. Losing faith is like losing weight—both improve one's health and make one feel wonderful.[12]

My heart breaks when I read this last letter. I am too skeptical to believe that life is as rosy for James's family as he implies it is. It seems to me that they walked away for all the wrong reasons and that those around them were ill-equipped to deal with what is too often perceived to be a "worse than death" situation. Why, I ask, did he have to go outside the community of faith for support? How differently things might have ended if their support group had been not unbelievers on the Internet but believers *in the flesh*—believers who know that a community of faith which wholly trusts in God's sovereign grace need not be threatened by unbelief.

"Pleasantly Surprised" by New Life of Unbelief

"January 1982 was a momentous month for me." This is the opening sentence of another testimony posted on a website by a man named Edie. "It was during that time I became a born again Christian. I remember the day well. It was about two weeks before my birthday, and I was horribly depressed. I was only 14 at the time, and the country was in a recession that kept my parents scraping for every dime—life looked pretty hopeless."[13]

Edie's biological father had "made a clean exit" from his life when he was a toddler; Edie felt insecure, "so the thought of a heavenly Father that would reach out, hold me, approve of me and take care of me was too good to be true." He quickly became very active in a Baptist church and "deeply entrenched in Fundamentalism." After high school he was involved with Youth with a Mission, and through that organization he took courses in biblical studies. He later enrolled in a Christian college, where he continued his study of the Bible and theology. "I had been warned," he writes, "how education often resulted in the loss of faith. But rather than take that as a sign that something was amiss with the Christian faith, I took it as an indication that the devil was indeed still dabbling with the minds of humanity in a last ditch effort to 'take some with him.' "[14]

Edie's doubt began after he received an e-mail message from an individual associated with a website that had a link to "Walk Away" (an online support group for ex-fundamentalists).

> Christians made up the majority of deconverts. Now, I could understand why someone would leave legalistic Fundamentalism—I had done so myself, but I hadn't sacrificed my faith by "throwing the baby out with the bath water" like many of the ex-Christians did. I found myself saying, "if they knew what *I* know, or if they were like *me*, they wouldn't have left." Basically, I thought it couldn't happen to me, and that I was "different" and "special." These people *obviously* didn't have the wealth of knowledge, experience and "relationship with Jesus" that I had, or they would never have left. . . . I decided to take the ultimate challenge where my faith was concerned: I was going to face the objections of the deconverts openly and get to the bottom of this. . . . I had such faith in my beliefs that I determined I was going to come up with an answer, and follow that trail no matter where it led.[15]

That trail led to what Edie and many others refer to as "deconversion," a process that was aided significantly by his new acquaintances on the Internet. Like many others, he paints a very positive picture of the new life of unbelief:

> When I finally realized I could no more believe in Christianity . . . than I could . . . fly like Superman, it was a little scary. . . . It was like I closed my eyes and held my breath as I took the final plunge, wondering what terrible feelings lurked below the murky surface. I was pleasantly surprised. . . . There was no magical "change" or urge to rush out and "sin" because I didn't have some frowning Daddy in the Sky telling me not to. In fact, my morals and convictions regarding being kind, loving and respectful to others shifted very little, and only then to become greater and more inclusive. . . . Can you imagine how freeing it is to know that there is no judgment at the end, that I don't have to wonder if my homosexual friends are going to hell. . . . Another wonderful result is that I no longer have to "hide" from scrutiny or truth for fear that I'll be

led astray. If someone presents persuasive evidence to me on *anything*, I'm free to consider and weigh it accordingly. . . . I've heard believers ask, "aren't you afraid you might someday be proven wrong about Christianity? My response: "No. Are you?"

Hey, I've been wrong before—I spent 15+ years devoted to Christianity. There could be some evidence out there that overturns not only the "lacking evidence" but the *negative* evidence against Christianity. I intend to have my eyes open for it. After all, to put a new twist on Pascal's Wager, what have I got to lose?[16]

A basic tenet of Christianity is that faith offers freedom. From the King James memory bank I started in as a child, I can easily quote John 8:36: "If the Son therefore shall make you free, ye shall be free indeed." Yet these people, who walked away from the faith, are testifying to a newfound freedom. There is clearly a difference in the meanings of "freedom." Christians are often tempted to dismiss rather than seek to understand this very different concept of freedom. Steve Locks offers a similar perspective.

"All the Problems and Clutter . . . Disappeared"

Steve's first exposure to Christianity was in a "moderately high Anglican church," where he found the music very appealing. He joined the choir and was confirmed. But during his university years, he had his "first decent exposure to arguments from atheists. . . . I got to know some more informed freethinkers. (Now I loath the term 'non-Christian' with its negative connotations. It is like calling a woman a 'nonman' as if it is a defect!)."[17]

The more he talked with freethinkers, the more frustrated he became:

> I was perturbed that I could not give an adequate coherent account of even the basics of Christianity. . . . I almost deconverted whilst at university due to what seemed a more coherent explanation of Christianity as a human phenomenon. I was kept back though by the feeling that, as Thomas Merton said, "by denying God we are denying ourselves." If I wasn't a Christian I would be missing something important

in life, therefore there had to be something in it. I finished my degree
and got a job. . . . I read veraciously. [*sic*] I got through Bonhoeffer, all
of C. S. Lewis, G. K. Chesterton, "the cloud of unknowing," Thomas à
Kempis and other classics. . . . I also joined an evangelical church!
Although not really my scene, I actually found it quite exciting when I
tried it out. I was struck by how strongly the people there really
believed in their religion. I had not encountered that strength of belief
before. . . . I felt I had a special relationship with God through accepting Christ.[18]

Steve continued his discussions with freethinkers, defending his faith,
but knowing little about theirs:

Eventually I bit the bullet. I felt that I had to be allowed (by God) to
examine the other side of the argument. I trusted him to help me come
to a deeper faith. . . . I put myself in his hands to stop me being misled.
I also kept a journal all through this period, which makes a fascinating
(for me) insight into my deconversion. I read books on the psychology
of religion and the history of Christianity from as neutral as possible
sources. Meanwhile I had an (almost) "deconversion experience." . . . I
read Russell's "Why I am not a Christian." When I came to the passage
where Russell says that Christ had a serious moral defect, he believed in
hell—my stomach churned. . . . The fact that Jesus, as depicted in the
gospels, believed in hell is to me such a serious religious problem that it
was one of the things that finally broke up my Christianity. . . . This was
the last straw.[19]

At first, Steve sought to become a missionary of unbelief: "I felt that
I must let everybody know, especially as I was in a position to talk
about it since I had known what it was like from the inside." Even as
he had read books by Dietrich Bonhoeffer and C. S. Lewis to
strengthen his Christian beliefs, Steve now read more works by Bertrand Russell, William James, David Hume, Friedrich Nietzsche, Thomas Paine and Robert Ingersoll. At the same time, he sensed his whole
perspective on life was changing—for the better.

Due to my total change of world view I also had some very weird experiences that were not like anything I had expected. I was struck enor-

mously by what I called "existential shock." I was completely amazed at
the mere fact of existence. . . . It was being struck by the amazing "sac-
rament" of life—or the utter shock and opportunity of existence over its
alternative. . . . I felt transformed, awed, excited—the whole world
seemed more special than can ever be said. Life was far more poignant
without Christianity than it had ever been with it. I was not expecting
this to happen to me. I thought these experiences were what converted
people to religion, not what you got when you left! . . . All the problems
and clutter associated with religion disappeared of course, though I
won't pretend it was easy explaining my new position to my Christian
friends. (Some still don't know.) . . . The greatest benefit I discovered
was the disappearance of a spiritual barrier for me between people.
When I had strong religion . . . I was in a "spiritually superior state."
Now I see Christians just as people but with a mistaken belief. . . . I now
see us all as vulnerable human beings full of hopes and fears and psychological tangle.[20]

The people whose testimonies I have quoted above should not be
taken as official representatives for all who have abandoned the faith.
Indeed, many tell an entirely different story—especially those who later
returned to the faith. For some the new life of unbelief allows for freedom from "the problems and clutter associated with religion"; but for
others the situation is precisely reversed. This was true for Wetherell
Johnson, who could not endure a life without belief in God.

"Life Was Utterly Without Meaning"

The late Wetherell Johnson was the founder and director of the world's
largest Bible study organization, Bible Study Fellowship. As a young
British woman, she struggled with deep doubts in her Christian life.
She had been educated in France, where "the heavy study left no lei-
sure for thought or emotional introspection." When she returned to
England, she realized how much she had changed. "I had time to recognize that when I gave up belief in the Lord Jesus Christ and the
Bible, I had no philosophy to fill the vacuum that remained. Life was
utterly without meaning."[21]

This doubt soon prompted her to cry out in the night, "God, if there be a God, if You will give me some philosophy that makes reasonable sense to me, I will commit myself to follow it." After that, she testifies, "God met me in a mysterious way which I cannot fully explain." One result of this experience was an intense desire to learn and understand Scripture. She enrolled in five correspondence courses and continued on in a study of the Bible which then spread to thousands of women and men all over the world.[22]

Johnson's is one that we should keep in mind as we interact with people who profess to have walked away from the faith. But we should not overlook, or deny the validity of, the stories of individuals who tell of peace and happiness after abandoning their beliefs. Not all people experience the same sense of meaninglessness that Johnson did. When David testifies (in the epigraph to this chapter) that his new life is "richer and fuller" and James claims he feels "strong and happy and confident and free"—both since walking away from their Christian faith—we should take them at their word, listen to their stories and learn from them. Sometimes the very things that distressed them most about their faith communities were not authentic Christian beliefs and practices in the first place. We need to challenge these individuals in our words and actions—even as we invite them to challenge us.

12

Missionaries
of Unbelief

The Appeal of the
Message & the Messenger

Virtually everyone knows that religious believers have
often sought to convert others to their convictions.
It is less commonly recognized that atheists, too,
have for centuries had their own proselytizing agenda,
aimed at tumbling the gods from their altars
and setting up reason in their place.
The motives animating the atheist project are—
like those inspiring religious propagandists—many and varied.

— RODGER BEEHLER

Missions is one of my areas of specialty. I have taught courses on missions. I have lectured and preached on missions. And I have written numerous works on missions, including a textbook on the history of missions and other books and articles on women in missions, the missionary family, urban missions, Mormon missions and missions to Muslims and Jews. But until I began working on this volume, I had never even thought of the concept of "missionaries of unbelief." Even as *conversion* is a goal of Christian missionaries, so *deconversion* is a goal of missionaries of unbelief. It is not enough for many people to simply abandon the faith; missionaries of unbelief seek to lead others to their way of thinking. In the case of Dan Barker, the role came naturally. Once he had broken his ties with Christianity, he moved easily from his previous ministry as a Christian evangelist to his work as an atheist evangelist.

The "Friendly Neighborhood Atheist"

The words of the much beloved Christmas carol "O, Little Town of Bethlehem" were written by Philips Brooks, one of America's most celebrated nineteenth-century preachers. He was recognized as a "brilliant, soul-winning, character-building minister" who served as the Episcopal bishop to Boston, delivered lectures on preaching at Yale Divinity School, and preached at Westminster Abbey and the Royal Chapel at Windsor before Queen Victoria. A century after these lyrics were written, Dan Barker copyrighted new lyrics to the tune, beginning with the words "O, shining star of solstice time." Other titles of his copyrighted songs are "Nothing Fails Like Prayer" and "Friendly, Neighborhood Atheist."

I met Dan Barker for the first time this evening. We greeted each other briefly before and after he lectured at the Calkins Science Center on the campus of Grand Rapids Community College. As I reflect back on the evening, I smile and affirm a comment that I recently made in a class—that *I've never met or known an atheist I didn't like.* I am sure there are plenty atheists out there whom I would not care for, but I have simply not met them. As for Barker, he was funny and casual and secure and gave no evidence of being bitter or resentful of his past life as a professing Christian. To the contrary, he spoke with fond memories of his experiences as the child in a fundamentalist family, and he emphasized that he has remained close to some of his Christian friends. During the question-and-answer time, I prefaced a question to him by saying that as I was listening to his story, I was saying "Me, too." But Barker and I have gone in two very different directions. He has walked away; I have not (nor will I).

Barker is America's premier evangelist of unbelief. There are other such evangelists. Some might argue that John Shelby Spong, an Episcopal bishop, deserves that title instead. Through his books and speaking he has carved out a career in debunking such beliefs as the infallibility of the Bible, the virgin birth and the resurrection of Christ. But Spong has not yet overtly denied belief in God, and he was not previously recognized as an evangelist of belief, as were both Brooks and Barker—"brilliant, soul-winning, character-building" ministers. Besides their both being brilliant, Barker (a member of several "High-IQ societies") and Brooks have much in common: both were widely traveled preachers and evangelists, both were authors of books, and both were songwriters.

And indeed, both brought their messages before the cultural icons of their day: Brooks to Queen Victoria, and Barker to the queen of daytime television, Oprah Winfrey. But the message that Barker brought into the presence of "royalty" was very different than Brooks' message. Barker's fame was derived from his change of belief and vocation, as is indicated in the subtitle of his autobiography, *Losing Faith in Faith: From Preacher to Atheist.*

Barker was born in 1949 and was raised in southern California. He began his evangelistic work at age fifteen and was, for a short time, associated with the ministry of faith-healer Kathryn Kuhlman. In 1975, after graduating from Azusa Pacific University, he was ordained to the ministry; and in the years that followed he served on the staff of three different churches. For eight years he toured as a full-time Christian evangelist and was recognized as an accomplished pianist, arranger and songwriter—the composer of more than two hundred published and recorded songs. His music has been performed by the choir of the Crystal Cathedral on Robert Schuller's television broadcast, and he has worked with Pat Boone and other Christian celebrities. He continues to receive royalties from Manna Music for his children's musicals "Mary Had a Little Lamb" (1977) and "His Fleece Was White as Snow" (1978), which are still performed in churches throughout the world.

Today Barker uses his evangelistic skills, in speaking and writing, to lead people away from the faith. The testimony of Rhonda Jockisch, posted on a website, is typical. She was a college graduate with a good job, and she was in the habit of reading her Bible daily.

I should have been on top of the world, and yet I was miserable, full of guilt at all my supposed sins. . . . Then I got a computer and started talking with some humanists/atheists. . . . One of them recommended . . . *Losing Faith in Faith* by Dan Barker. And after reading that book, I knew that if Dan Barker was telling the truth, that there was no way Christianity could be true.[1]

Barker serves on the staff of *Freethought Today* in Madison, Wisconsin, and writes and speaks for the atheist cause. He also volunteers his time at retirement homes, where he gives free concerts to the residents. His debate topics include "Does God Exist?" "Is the Bible an Acceptable Guide for Morality?" "Did Jesus Rise from the Dead?" and "Jesus of Nazareth: Messiah or Myth?" And Barker does not address his missionary message only to adults: he continues to write books and music for children. One of his books is titled *Just Pretend: A Freethought Book for Children.*

How does an evangelist make a 180-degree turn from preaching Jesus as Messiah to preaching Jesus as myth? From telling children that the gospel is good news to telling them it is bad news? Barker is eager to give his testimony to all who will listen:

It was some time in 1979, turning thirty, when I started to have some early questions about Christianity. . . . I just got to the point where my mind was restless to move beyond the simplicities of fundamentalism. I had been so involved with fundamentalist and evangelical matters that I had been ignoring a part of myself that was beginning to ask for attention. It was as if there was this little knock on my skull, and something was saying, "Hello! Anybody home?" I was starving and didn't know it, like when you are working hard on a project and you forget to eat and you don't know you are hungry until you are really hungry. I had been reading the Christian writers (Francis Schaeffer, Josh McDowell, C. S. Lewis, etc.), and really had not read much of anything else besides the Bible for years. So, not with any real purpose in mind, I began to satisfy this irksome intellectual hunger. I began to read some science magazines, some philosophy, psychology, daily newspapers (!), and began to catch up on the liberal arts education I should have had years before. This triggered a ravenous appetite to learn and produced a slow but steady migration across the theological spectrum that took about four or five years.

I had no sudden, eye-opening experience. When you are raised like I was, you don't just snap your fingers and say, "Oh, silly me! There's no God."[2]

As time passed, Barker moved further away from his conservative Christian heritage. "As I traveled across the spectrum," he recalls, "I kept drawing my line higher and higher. I studied some liberal theologians, such as Tillich and Bultmann." Finally he came to the point where he could say, "I was not uncomfortable with Tillich's idea that God is the 'ground of all being,' or some other vague notion." Although Barker was no longer preaching "soul-winning" sermons, he continued to accept invitations to perform music and speak at "fundamentalist and conservative evangelical churches." But his conscience bothered him: "Even then, I felt hypocritical, often hearing myself mouth words about which I was no longer sure, but words that the audience wanted to hear."[3]

In the summer of 1983 Barker finally admitted to himself that he was an atheist—though he kept it to himself for several months. "Between the summer and Christmas of 1983," he writes, "I went through an awful period of hypocrisy. I was still preaching, and I hated myself. . . . I knew I should have just cut it off cleanly, but I didn't have the courage."[4]

It was on a November night of that year, while on a preaching tour in Mexico, that he had an experience which made him suddenly realize that he had to immediately sever his association with the Christian faith. His bed was a cot in a church. He could not sleep. As he stared at the ceiling, he suddenly came to a "startling reality" that he was alone—"completely and utterly alone . . . no supernatural realm, no God." He had another preaching engagement in December, but after that, he never preached again. In January, he sent a letter to everyone he knew—"ministers, friends, relatives, publishing companies, Christian recording artists, fellow missionaries—and told them I was no longer a Christian, that I was an atheist or agnostic."[5]

A "Home" Missionary of Unbelief

On meeting Barker, it is quickly apparent that his long ministry as a warm, good-natured, charismatic evangelist prepared him well for his new ministry as a missionary of unbelief. And even as he came across as trustworthy and believable then, so he has since his "deconversion." Indeed, his story is very unique as it relates to his influence on others, particularly his close family members. In most instances, Christian family members dig in their heals and do not even politely listen to the one who has walked away from the faith. But in Barker's case, many listened, and some were deconverted.

Barker's parents had been lay evangelists with the Assemblies of God, and when they received his letter, he writes, "they were shocked." They had been proud of his celebrity as a traveling evangelist and musician, and now they felt the disappointment and shame of what seemed to be his ultimate failure—a failure of faith. "My mother," writes Barker, "immediately hopped on a bus, traveling from Phoenix to my home in California, and we had a long, emotional discussion into the early morning hours. She would never be the same." After that late-night discussion, she never again went back to church, and she told an interviewer the reason: "The answers he gave me impressed my heart and mind. . . . I had so much love for my son that I knew in some way he was right."[6]

For Barker's father, the process of "deconversion" was slower. He told the same interviewer, "I tried to straighten him out. It worked the other way around." Barker, however, insists he did not seek to "deconvert" them: "I never suggested to my parents that they should become atheists. They did their own thinking." As Barker's father was rethinking issues, he remembered playing in dance bands before he entered the legalism of the Christian community.

> One night, just before he dumped the whole system of belief, Dad drove to church, took his trombone case out of the car and walked toward the building where he could hear the praying, singing, and preaching. When he got to the door it struck him that he did not belong there any more. Hoping that no one would notice, he quickly turned around and went home.[7]

His younger brother Darrell also walked away from the faith and later became a chapter director of Atheists United. Of this turn of events, Barker writes:

> The gradual change in my parents and my brother Darrell was tremendously heartening. I never would have predicted such an outcome. My parents had been fervent evangelists for Jesus for years, and Darrell had been a street preacher with a missionary organization. . . . The fact that these born-again, door-to-door preachers were open to change gives me hope.[8]

In 1985, Barker's marriage ended, due, not surprisingly, "mostly to the tension between viewpoints." In 1987, he married Annie Laurie Gaylor, the editor of *Freethought Today*. At the time he wrote his autobiography in 1992, Barker's older brother was continuing on in his faith, as were Barker's four children, who were living in California with his ex-wife: "They go to church with their mother, who works at a Christian school, and their stepfather, a youth director at a Baptist church."[9] The children have since moved away from active church involvement.

Barker's story is one that we as Christians would rather not hear. We like "testimonies,"—stories told by teary-eyed, quivering-voiced young people who have been saved from their waywardness or by former skeptics who have been gloriously transformed by Jesus. We want to hear about *conversion*—being saved, becoming born-again, inviting Jesus into your heart and then reaching out to family and friends and leading them to the foot of the cross. We are not equipped to deal with the reverse. We have no framework for *deconversion*. It simply is not supposed to happen. How, we ask, could a person who has experienced the power of the gospel in his own life and in the lives of others turn his back and renounce the very faith he once publicly proclaimed?

We need to also ask, How does a Christian deconstruct Barker's account of deconversion? One of the first questions I ask myself is why stories like this are not more widespread. It is easy to find stories of people who have walked away from cultic groups. Do fewer people walk away from the Christian faith? Probably not. But it is more socially acceptable to debunk a cult than to debunk Christianity. So it is reasonable to assume, I believe, that there are many people who have walked away from faith, thinking thoughts like Barker's, but not expressing them openly. Barker, like most Christians, did not feel free to talk candidly about his doubts when they first surfaced.

For Barker, deconversion was a slow process. For others, it happens much more quickly—sometimes in the very act of defending the faith to atheists, as was the case with Chris's deconversion. Whether losing one's faith happens slowly or in an instant, the community of believers needs to be aware of the possibility that some may walk away from faith and, accordingly, it needs to create an atmosphere that allows doubt to be discussed, not dismissed.

An Internet Evangelist Loses Faith

Chris grew up in a Christian family with Pentecostal and fundamentalist connections. During his teen years he made a personal profession of faith. "Doing so," he writes, "meant repenting, asking Jesus into my heart as Lord and Savior, reading the Scriptures, praying, living right, and sharing the gospel. But it was this last step that led to his undoing. While discussing faith via the Internet, the tables were turned: Chris, the Christian evangelist, was "deconverted" by Rich, the atheist evangelist.

> I became an atheist after a result of an online discussion with another atheist in the summer of 1996. I guess in a way I was "defending the faith" and doing what I should be doing—taking the gospel to the lost. However, in the course of the discussion, this atheist . . . pointed out that if I even expected him to take me seriously, then I'd have to take his points seriously too. I knew that the Bible was the basis of my faith, from the time I was young I always believed there was something "special" about the Bible, and I had some idea of the sorts of Josh McDowell–type arguments were meant to defend that. However, this was the first time I really looked critically on that belief in my life.[10]

Chris was not prepared for the issues that Rich raised. Indeed, his story is not unusual. Evangelists of unbelief are seeking for the kind of interaction that Chris offered. They reason that they have nothing to lose. For Chris, the loss was nothing less than his faith.

> Instead of finding the evidence pointing in overwhelming fashion to Jesus, as I had expected, I found myself facing more and more tough questions. . . . These weren't by any means "new" questions that no theologian has ever heard of; in fact, many people I read had pat answers to these questions. They all had one thing in common: they were very unconvincing. After several months of consideration, prayer, study, reflection, and deep soul-searching, I decided that I couldn't remain intellectually honest and still believe there was something special about the Bible which made it authoritative concerning spiritual matters. Along with this rejection of the Bible came a rejection of God.[11]

In some respects Dan Barker and Chris each fit the profile of a "walk-away," especially in relation to their church community and education. Where intellectual pursuits are confined largely to the Bible and religious reading, where a dichotomy of sacred and secular is strictly maintained, where tough questions are silenced—here faith-threatening doubts often emerge. Out of this background arises one who finds an exciting new world of learning and thus eagerly spreads the word to others trapped in what is scorned as anti-intellectual religious fundamentalism. But where a well-rounded liberal-arts education is viewed as a necessary component of a Christian worldview and where hard questions are encouraged—here the Christian faith is more secure. But even in such settings some still struggle to maintain their faith. Indeed, some would argue that such an open environment encourages a bright young student like Peter De Vries to seek success in "worldly ventures" where dangers lie in wait for him on every side.

Missionary for "Christian Atheism"

Peter De Vries was not a missionary in the sense that Dan Barker is. His message was set forth in fiction—humorous fiction more often than not. Like Barker, though, he was nurtured in American evangelicalism, but at the opposite end of the spectrum. His heritage—family, community, church and schooling from elementary through college— was firmly grounded in the Christian Reformed Church. He was born in 1910, and during his youth the church still strongly retained its Dutch heritage, marked by a strain of pietism and mixed with legalism and separation from the world. "We went to church five times a week," he writes, "three times on Sunday."[12]

Like many of his friends, De Vries enrolled at Calvin College after his graduation from a Christian high school. (I know this college well. I live one block from the old campus where De Vries roamed the halls, and for a dozen years I taught part time at the present campus, three miles from my home.) Then, as now, the school was known for its high academic achievement, and De Vries had many opportunities to inter- act with bright young students and faculty members. It was during this time that he began to question his Christian heritage.

Before his college years, however, he had faced a serious crisis of faith—the death of his older sister at age eighteen. He later recalled how his parents responded to the tragedy:

> My father became very, very religious, so that even prayers at the table and the school were not enough. We had to end the day by kneeling on the kitchen floor with our elbows on the chairs. My mother never sang in church again after my sister died.[13]

De Vries struggled as a writer after college until, in his early thirties, he began working for the *New Yorker*. Here "he continued as a main- stay, composing captions for the famous humorous drawings until his death in 1993." His primary creative energy, however, was devoted to his works of fiction: he wrote more than twenty novels during a period of four decades. "His mode was the comic narrative, a tale told tongue- in-cheek with characters adroitly named—or misnamed—in true Dick- ensian fashion. . . . His themes were never far removed from a satirical representation of his religious upbringing."[14]

The Blood of the Lamb is De Vries most autobiographical novel. "This book," wrote a reviewer at the *New Yorker*, "is written at white heat, in grief-stricken anger against God." Like the narrator, Don Wanderhope, De Vries grieved the death of his eleven-year-old daughter to leukemia. In the book, Wanderhope sustains no consolation from this offering of a sacrificial lamb, from which comes the title of the book. Some months after his daughter's death, Wanderhope takes out a tape recording of her piano playing, followed by her own reflections, which he has not heard before. She speaks directly to him, saying that she had browsed through a copy of his old college magazine and seen an editorial on his philosophy of life. She asks if he remembers it, and tells him that it brought her courage to face what she knows is coming. Then she reads the piece to him:

> I believe that man must learn to live without those consolations called religious, which his own intelligence must by now have told him belong to the childhood of the race. Philosophy can really give us nothing permanent to believe either; it is too rich in answers, each canceling out the rest. The quest for Meaning is foredoomed. Human life "means" nothing. But that is not to say that it is not worth living. What does a Debussy *Arabesque* "mean," or a rainbow or a rose? A man delights in all these, knowing himself to be no more—a wisp of music and a haze of dreams dissolving against the sun. Man has only his own two feet to stand on, his own human trinity to see him through: Reason, Courage, and Grace. And the first plus the second equals the third.[15]

It is in his novel *Slouching Towards Kalamazoo* that De Vries most clearly set forth his "gospel" message, the message of truth he seeks to offer his readers. The narrator of this book is the son of a minister. (At age fifteen, the narrator impregnates his much older teacher.) Amid these circumstances, his father agrees to participate in a public debate with the town atheist, who is having a "platonic" affair with his wife. The debate judges call it a draw, but in the process of the debate, the minister has been won over to the other point of view. He confesses his loss of faith to his wife:

> "He's right. There is no God. Or none justifying the religion I've been preaching. I've always had my doubts, as you know, every thinking and educated man does, but I don't anymore. Only certainty. Christianity *is* a hodgepodge of odds and ends of pagan religions amalgamated into a

myth for which Western civilization was ripe. It's an opium for poor
mankind unable to take reality neat. I've been feeding hungry bellies
with promises of heavenly feasts. . . .

"The Bible is a goulash of hokum, contradictions, and tribal supersti-
tions." He kicked at a footstool. "My ministry is a joke. The only thing I
can honorably do is resign."[16]

De Vries did not demonstrate the same atheistic zeal that Barker,
the seasoned evangelist, does. Rather his was the subtle satire that
seeks doubt over certainty. "He looked for converts to what he calls
'Christian atheism.' "[17]

> Or turn it around and call them atheistic Christians, adherents of a faith
> and a religious discipline all the more necessary to a species sprung
> mysteriously into being in a universe devoid of any provable gover-
> nance, or any evidence of meaning or purpose properly so called. Let,
> then, the Church serve in a Void: it was all the more essential for that.
> Voltaire was right. If there were no God, it would be necessary to invent
> one. And invent Him mankind jolly well had, to see him through this
> vale of tears.[18]

In Christian atheism, De Vries sought to bring faith and reason
together in a new gospel. Here the morals and ethics and disciplines of
faith are combined with the rationality and intellectual freedom of reason—a "combination of faith and skepticism." The individual brought
into the novel as the model of this new religion is Bertrand Russell,
"the great all-time infidel humanitarian of the twentieth century,
claimable as a Christian atheist despite his pains to explain why he
wasn't a Christian." De Vries's "creedless creed" was straightforward
and perhaps much more appealing than the atheism preached by
Barker:

> We live as *though* life had meaning, and lo—it does! We live as though we
> are Christian soldiers following in our Captain's command, and lo—we
> are! Our best writers have told us this life is a flimflam, even some of the
> Old Testament prophets, but to the extent that we're wise to the scam, it
> isn't. Hemingway called life a dirty trick, Mark Twain a swindle, Fitzger-
> ald a fraud, Shakespeare a tale told by an idiot, and on and on. . . .

The point I'm trying to make is that it takes more faith to live life without belief in the cozy self-delusions of what has traditionally been called faith. That is our doctrineless doctrine, our creedless creed.[19]

That Russell was De Vries' model for "the great all-time infidel humanitarian of the twentieth century" is not surprising. Russell is also the model for a missionary of unbelief. His name is probably mentioned more than any other as the individual who was most persuasive in influencing a loss of faith. He was an atheist with passion, who sought to make unbelief attractive. "Russell has probably exerted more influence in the twentieth century," writes J. C. A. Gaskin, "than any other contemporary academic philosopher. . . . His cool pursuit of the reasonable and the justifiable make Russell . . . the wise man of the century."[20]

Russell was an atheist with a heart; he was the friendly neighborhood atheist that Barker seeks to be today—an effective missionary of unbelief. Christians ought to be aware of these missionaries' activities and should be prepared not just to counter them, but to listen to them. But this can be dangerous. Many of these very missionaries themselves have abandoned the faith as a result of the missionary activities of other unbelievers. We must guard our own faith. But we should not let these individuals intimidate us. They struggle with their own doubts and uncertainties, as did Russell: "The center of me," he confessed, "is always and eternally a terrible pain—a wild pain—a searching for something beyond what the world contains."[21]

"Really, a young atheist cannot guard his faith too carefully," writes C. S. Lewis. "Dangers lie in wait for him on every side."[22]

13

Answering Doubt & Unbelief

Confronting the Serious Issues

An honest religious thinker is like a tightrope walker.
He looks almost as though he were walking on nothing but air.
His support is the slenderest imaginable.
And yet it really is possible to walk on it.

—LUDWIG WITTGENSTEIN

I am often troubled when I read books and articles on doubt—even as I was as I read an article by Mark Buchanan in *Christianity Today* entitled "The Benefit of the Doubt." Buchanan emphasizes the positive side of doubt, insisting, as many others have, that it can strengthen one's faith. That may be the case, but most people who have had serious doubts do not speak of it as having actually strengthened their faith. They may end up with a different faith, but whether that new faith is actually stronger depends to some degree on how one defines faith. Perhaps the most uncontested benefit of doubt is that it allows one to more effectively reach out to others who are struggling with doubt.

But more troubling to me than Buchanan's emphasis on the benefits of doubt is his seeming dismissal of the doubter—or perhaps, if I characterize it more charitably, his lack of understanding of the doubter. Of doubt, he writes, "It can become a way of holding God for ransom. . . . Indulged too long, doubt becomes just a parlor game." In my studies, I have seen that with most doubters, the only way in which they are "holding God" is in their *holding on for dear life*, fearing that their belief in God is slipping away. And while some may be playing a "parlor game," the majority are encountering a life-and-death battle for their beliefs. Buchanan goes on to say:

> Here lies the basic flaw of all doubt; it really can never be satisfied. No evidence is ever fully, finally enough. Doubt wants always to consume, never to consummate. It clamors endlessly for an answer, and so drowns out any answer that might be given. It demands proof, but will doubt the proof proffered. Doubt, then, can become an appetite gone wrong; its craving increases the more we try to fill it.[1]

I myself have not often encountered anyone with a doubt like this, unless the doubter is a youth or a young adult who is rebelling against a childhood faith that was never really a faith at all. For the one who truly believed and lived a life of faith, doubt is rarely something that "wants always to consume," that "clamors endlessly for an answer"; it is seldom "an appetite gone wrong." No, that is not it at all. The majority of serious doubters I have encountered are people who are deeply distressed, for they desperately want to hold on to their faith. They don't "demand proof"; rather they cling to anything that will help them hold on a little longer. They frequently experience a profound sense of God's absence: they want to believe in a personal God, but they encounter only silence and hiddenness and infinite distance.

As I read the conclusion to Buchanan's article I felt a sense of sadness for those readers who are agonizing over their doubts and who have searched the article for help. For many such people with fragile faith, Buchanan's argument may have set them back even further in their struggle with ever-present doubt. Here he tells, secondhand, the story of a man who cannot be convinced that Jesus' resurrection is true, believing rather that "those who encountered the risen Christ were in altered states of consciousness." Buchanan offers no evidence that this man was not truly sincere in his unbelief, but of his unbelief, he writes:

> That's not honest doubt. That's something very different—intellectual dogma, doctrinaire agnosticism, hidebound ideology, scholarly Trivial Pursuit. That's the refusal to be convinced even if someone rises from the dead.
>
> Over that, I'll take Thomas and his doubt any day.[2]

Thomas saw the risen Christ in the flesh. This man of whom Buchanan speaks did not. And we do not know whether Thomas continued to struggle with doubts—he may have his whole life long. I admire Thomas, but my heart goes out to the man Buchanan describes, and I will gladly walk along with him, though he may never find the "proof" to believe. God alone is the judge of "honest doubt." It is not for me to judge what is in someone else's heart.

Buchanan's response is a more *hard-line* approach than the one I would take, though surely there is biblical and historical precedent for such a response. In fact, some religious groups, from the Amish to Jehovah's Witnesses and Muslims, would *shun* those who walk away from the faith. A good case can be made that such a response is effective not only as a preventative measure but also in influencing individuals to return to the faith. For many, the isolation from family and friends serves as a very efficient deterrent.

But such a response does not demonstrate understanding for the person who is sincerely struggling with doubt and unbelief. It minimizes real concerns, and it ignores the very difficulties faced by many of the disciples, who found Jesus' teachings hard to grasp: "This teaching is difficult; who can accept it?" (Jn 6:60). Yet when these matters are seen in terms of life and death and eternal destiny, it is very difficult for some people to remain calm.

How *Not* to Respond to Those Who Walk Away

The difficulty in remaining calm and composed is demonstrated in the case of James and Allison (see chapter eleven). After they walked away, James received a letter from his pastor, with whom he had worked closely as a small-group leader. How should a pastor respond to such disclosures? I try to put myself in the position of that pastor. At minimum I would want to begin a letter with an affirmation of my love and friendship as well as some words of appreciation for the years of service that James and his wife had given to the church. I would, above all, try to listen—to listen to their story and try to comprehend what they were saying. I would interact with them, asking them whether they might possibly be demanding too much from their faith, for example, expecting *proofs* that the Christian faith never promises. I would express my deep disappointment, and at the same time, I would promise to be available to help them during these troubled times. But these are not the sentiments James found in the opening paragraphs of his pastor's response.

> You have not had a "Loss of faith." You have believed a lie (Romans). You are a smart man James, but you are not smarter than Jesus! Even if you reject Jesus as deity he was by all historical accounts the most profound and wise teacher who has lived. He taught that you should fear God. You are a smart man, but not likely any smarter than King David, King Solomon, Moses, the Apostle Paul, and other historical figures who were smart enough to believe in God. You are not a novelty James. Even Nebuchadnezzar had a battle with pride and the false belief that there is no God. He returned to his senses. You are a smart man, but you are not omnipresent. Therefore, you cannot KNOW there is no God somewhere in the universe, can you? (Be logical!) Therefore you cannot be an Atheist. No honest, rational, logical person would ever claim omnipresence except God himself. You are not really ready to make such an irrational claim as Atheism are you James? At best James, you might qualify as Agnostic. . . . You are a smart man. Seek wisdom. Don't be the fool who has said in his heart that there is no God! You are a smart man James, but you are not smarter than God. Humble yourself under his mighty hand! . . . I will count it a privilege and an act of friendship to help you back when you are ready.[3]

In his response to his pastor, James answered each charge one by one, and concluded by reemphasizing what a painful struggle this had been: "The loss of a church family was the hardest part for Alison. It's too bad that Christianity is too narrow to extend fellowship to former believers who have rejected the faith based on knowledge of the faith." He then asks whether the church is really a "church for the unchurched."

To answer James's question: *Yes, the church is for the "unchurched."* It is especially for those in the community of believers who are struggling with doubt and unbelief. In the case of James and Allison, things might have turned out differently if those around them had shown more understanding and less anger. But how do we respond specifically to those with faltering faith or those who think they have lost their faith? It is critical that we begin by assuming their struggle is genuine—not by presuming they are insincere or dishonest—and that we then respond with understanding, keeping the following factors in mind:

- The truth or falsehood of Christianity is not *proven* by rational arguments.
- The element of mystery in faith should be celebrated, not avoided.
- Doubt and unbelief are natural components of faith.
- Those mature in faith must be open about their own struggles with doubt.
- Faith is a collective endeavor that involves community and service.

I have culled this little "grocery list" from numerous sources, but of the writings I've studied, the source that supports these ideas most effectively is the correspondence of Flannery O'Connor.

Flannery O'Connor on Doubt and Unbelief

Flannery O'Connor (1925–1964), a celebrated fiction writer, offers profound insights on belief and unbelief in her extensive personal correspondence. She is not an apologist who seeks to argue someone back to faith. Faith is faith, and there is never enough evidence or proof to bring someone who needs proof back to faith. That is not to say that apologetical works—both classical and contemporary—do not help many people. But to the one demanding proof, O'Connor would offer a very different approach.

Her "gravest concern," she once wrote to an acquaintance, was "the conflict between an attraction for the Holy and the disbelief in it we breathe in with the air of the times." Although she was sometimes criticized for the violence in her novels and short stories (especially in the story "A Good Man Is Hard to Find"), she was a devoted Roman Catholic who made no apologies for her Christian faith:

> I see from the standpoint of Christian orthodoxy. This means that for me the meaning of life is centered in our Redemption by Christ and what I see in the world I see in its relation to that. I don't think that this is a position that can be taken halfway or one that is particularly easy in these times to make transparent in fiction.[4]

O'Connor corresponded with people who struggled with doubt and unbelief, and it was in her letters that she made her best "arguments" for faith. To Louise Abbot she confessed the "torment" doubts caused her—and all those who truly want to believe. She spoke of doubt as the greatest suffering one could endure, but this suffering was part of the cost of religion. Most people, she insisted, "think faith is a big electric blanket, when of course it is the cross." O'Connor realized that the cross makes little sense to the one struggling with doubt, but she remarks that "these things are mysteries and that if . . . we could understand them, they wouldn't be worth understanding." But in the end her counsel was quite simply to exercise her will: "If you feel you can't believe, you must at least do this: keep an open mind. Keep it open toward faith, keep wanting it, keep asking for it, and leave the rest to God."[5]

Faith "Like the Tides of an Invisible Ocean"

In July 1955, O'Connor began a nine-year correspondence with a woman previously unknown to her, with whom she would develop a deep and intimate friendship. In this woman, who was also a writer, O'Connor found someone "who recognizes my work for what I try to make it," and the woman found in O'Connor a "God-conscious writer near at hand." When O'Connor's letters were collected and edited after her death, this woman asked to remain anonymous. She is identified simply as "A." In January 1956, six months after their relationship began, O'Connor wrote to A. that she was sending her *The Church and Modern Man*, dealing with such things as "dogma and free will." She went on to say, "I have a good many books that you might be interested in but I haven't put them forth because I thought they were 'too Catholic' and I did not want you to think I was trying to stuff the Church down your throat." By May 1956, less than a year after their acquaintance began, A. had decided to join the Catholic Church, and O'Connor wrote, "I'll be real pleased to be your sponsor for Confirmation."[6]

O'Connor did sponsor her friend, but this commitment to the church was short-lived. By 1958, A. was becoming disillusioned with the church, as is evident in O'Connor's responses to her questions:

> All your dissatisfaction with the church seems to me to come from an incomplete understanding of sin. . . . You are asking that man return at once to the state God created him in, you are leaving out the terrible radical human pride that causes death. . . . The Church is founded on Peter who denied Christ three times and couldn't walk on water by himself. You are expecting his successors to walk on the water.[7]

By the autumn of 1961, A. had decided to leave the church. O'Connor assured her that she thought no less of her because of this decision. But she also expressed her great sorrow. A. was clearly the loser, and as her friend, O'Connor was deeply pained by the loss that she described as "a narrowing of life for you and a lessening of the desire for life." She reminded her friend that while faith is a gift, it is also a volitional act of the will, and its loss is "basically a failure of appetite, assisted by sterile intellect." These were harsh words, and O'Connor did not end there: "Some people when they lose their faith in Christ, substitute a swollen faith in themselves." She insisted, however, that she was not accusing A. of this. She went on to remind her that faith has its ups and downs—"like the tides of an invisible ocean"—and that leaving the church during a down time is not the solution: "All I can suggest to you, as your one-time sponsor, is that if you find in yourself the least return of a desire for faith, to go back to the church with a light heart and without the conscience-raking to which you are probably subject."[8]

Unbelief Is Part of Faith

One of O'Connor's most profound letters on faith was written to a college student. It is a letter that should be copied by Christian parents and friends and given to young adults who are struggling with doubts and unbelief. It is a letter that Christian teachers in secondary schools and colleges should have at their fingertips—for themselves and for their students.

> To Alfred Corn, 30 May '62
>
> I think that this experience you are having of losing your faith, or as you think, of having lost it, is an experience that in the long run belongs to faith. . . . I don't know how the kind of faith required of a Christian living in the 20th century can be at all if it is not grounded on this experience that you are having right now of unbelief. . . .
>
> As a freshman in college you are bombarded with new ideas. . . . After a year of this, you think you cannot believe. You are just beginning to realize how difficult it is to have faith and the measure of a commitment to it, but you are too young to decide you don't have faith just because you feel you can't believe. About the only way we know whether we believe or not is by what we do, and I think from your letter that you will not take the path of least resistance in this matter and simply decide that you have lost your faith and that there is nothing you can do about it.
>
> One result of the stimulation of your intellectual life that takes place in college is usually a shrinking of the imaginative life. . . . The intellectual difficulties have to be met, however, and you will be meeting them for the rest of your life. . . . If you want your faith, you have to work for it. It is a gift, but for very few is it a gift given without any demand for equal time devoted to its cultivation. For every book you read that is anti-Christian, make it your business to read one that presents the other side of the picture.[9]

Being Vulnerable to the Vulnerable

What is the best way to respond to those who have walked away from the faith? This question has challenged me as I have worked through this book. After all, this study would not be complete if it did not seriously address the matter of *coming back* to faith and tell stories of how that sometimes happens.

As a Reformed Christian who takes very seriously the doctrine of the sovereignty of God, I perhaps have more room to relax in the role of evangelist or mentor or friend than do those who would emphasize free will and human responsibility for saving souls—or bringing "walkaways" back to the community of faith. If the matter were up to me I would be inclined take charge and try to get things done. I'm impatient. When a committee meeting is scheduled to start at 2:00, I am likely to speak up by 2:05 and ask whether someone intends to call the meeting to order. And as a mother, I have had to restrain myself from interfering in the life of my son too much. So my natural inclination is to dig in and accomplish the matter at hand.

But as I interact with those who have walked away from the faith, my theological foundations and my personal experience counsel me to back off—to focus more on caring than commanding and more on listening than talking. So I must restrain my tendency to interfere or to prove that my way is right. However, there are occasions when someone is argued into the faith. In *Letters from a Skeptic*, for example, Gregory Boyd, a minister and seminary professor, systematically presents his reasons for believing to his father. The books comprises their letters—the father's questions and the son's answers—but the reader knows from the book's preface what will happen:

> Exceptionally intelligent, intensely skeptical, very strong-willed and 70 years old—could a more *unlikely* candidate for conversion be found than my father? He had given me little grounds for hope. My father never showed any openness to the Gospel. He harbored only resentment toward the church and was outspoken in his animosity toward what he called "born-again types." The few talks about the faith he and I had had during the 14 years I had been a Christian up to the time of our correspondence began had all been somewhat awkward, very short, and totally futile. I had, quite frankly, all but given up hope for his salvation.

Nevertheless, beginning on March of 1989 I felt strongly led of the Lord to attempt one more time to share the Christian faith with my father, this time not in a face-to-face manner but through the mail. . . . To my surprise, my father accepted my invitation. Almost three years and 30 letters after our correspondence began, Edward K. Boyd made Jesus the Lord and Savior of his life on January 15, 1992.[10]

As I read through the letters, I often found myself siding with the father, who posed some very thoughtful questions, and I wondered how his son's answers were actually going to bring him to faith as the preface promised they would. If I were to identify one turning point in the correspondence, it came past the halfway point in the book. Here the father is getting personal:

Why does God put us in a position where we have to *try* to believe in Him? . . . What's so great about "faith" that He desires it above an *obvious* revelation of Himself? And when He does reveal Himself—supposedly in the Bible—He does so many damn bizarre things that no one who wasn't there to see it can be expected to believe it. Yet "salvation" supposedly hangs on this![11]

In his return letter, the son diverts from his usual apologetics and includes in his response a very honest confession that may have helped his father break through his unbelief at least subconsciously, though his father's response back to him would not necessarily indicate such: "I'm afraid I just can't 'suspend' my judgment on all the stories in the Bible. For me, Christianity stands or falls as a whole." In his response letter, he admitted his own struggle to believe; and whether or not his father consciously realized it, these words may have been the first that really joined them together in their religious pilgrimage:

Throughout my graduate schooling there were several occasions when my faith was on the line. I'd confront new evidence or new perspectives which seemed to contradict what I believed. And for a while, my evangelical faith would go into a sort of "state of suspension." . . . In fact, to be perfectly honest with you, I still experience this "suspension." . . . So don't let my apparent certainly in our dialogue fool you. I'm a convinced

Christian for sure. . . . But faith has never come easily for me either. I saw and heard myself all over the pages of your last letter.[12]

It is this kind of confession that often speaks the loudest when we interact with those who never believed or those who have left the faith community. Many people who walk away from the faith do so at great risk and after considerable investigation, contemplation and inner turmoil. Our effort to argue them back into the faith often prompts them to work harder to challenge Christianity and to support their unbelief. Sometimes we need to suspend our arguments and disclose our vulnerabilities.

Is the Gospel Inviting?

As we contemplate the phenomenon of people abandoning their faith, we need to look at ourselves and ask what it is about the gospel, about our own testimony, about our faith community, that is not appealing. I need to ask what is unattractive about me as a Christian in my faith community. "I like their Christ," mused Mahatma Gandhi, but "I don't like their Christians." Friedrich Nietzsche phrased the objection somewhat differently: "I will believe in the Redeemer when the Christian looks a little more redeemed."[13]

Why do people walk away? Why are unbelievers not attracted to my church? What is it about Christianity—as it is represented in my culture—that makes it so unappealing to so many people? We do well to take the humor of Walker Percy very seriously:

> Take Christians. I am surrounded by Christians. They are generally speaking a pleasant and agreeable lot. . . . But if they have the truth, why is it the case that they are repellent precisely to the degree that they embrace and advertise the truth? One might even become a Christian if there were few if any Christians around. Have you ever lived in the midst of fifteen million Southern Baptists? . . . A mystery: If the good news is true, why is not one pleased to hear it?[14]

Percy's point is well taken, though many Christians would be quick to respond that the "good news" was never necessarily supposed to be pleasant to hear—that it naturally appears to be, according to Scripture itself, "foolishness" and a "stumbling block." But is it possible to have it both ways, to have a gospel of the cross so compelling that people are drawn to it, to have the kind of message and messenger that Percy is seeking? When I think of my own religious pilgrimage, I see myself years ago as one of the Christians of whom Percy is speaking—"repellent precisely to the degree" that I was embracing and advertising the truth. If I had been able to be more relaxed and less concerned about my own importance, I might have been less repellent.

When the focus is on God rather than on oneself—not only in one's outward witness but also in one's inward identity—one is less likely, I believe, to be repellent. Too often the gospel message becomes intertwined with a personal agenda. While it is true that Christians should have a certain sense of ownership of the gospel message, there is another sense in which the gospel cannot be owned. The gospel is not like a political opinion that I hold and try to foist on others. Rather it is divine truth that I seek to reflect in word and deed. Roy Berkenbosch touches on this ideal in his idealistic portrayal of Reformed Christians:

> Reformed Christians are captivated by the biblical vision of a God of grace. God has good intentions toward humankind . . . that are never derailed by our inability to deserve them. . . . The big blessing here is that we can rest. I need not take myself too seriously as long as I can remember how seriously God takes me. The kingdom of God will come in all its wonder whether I am on board or not, for it is not made by human hands. It has little to do with how spiritually high I feel, how well I am contemplating the divine mysteries, or even how faithfully I observe the spiritual disciplines. The gospel is about what God has done and continues to do, not about our own actions.[15]

Humility and Honesty in Matters of Faith

How, then, shall Christians respond to those who have walked away from faith? Sometimes the attitude in which a response is given is more important than the response itself. My own demeanor is, I hope, first and foremost one of humility and honesty. I simply do not have all the answers, and I understand why many people would regard the answers I do have to be no more than mindless gibberish. Sometimes I almost think that myself. This does not mean that I do not express strong beliefs and enjoy lively debates, but that when I do so, I interact with others in a spirit of mutuality as opposed to the attitude of Christian superiority that I once had—an attitude one cannot easily disguise.

Along with humility is a deep sense of my own limitations, especially when it comes to converting someone to Christianity. Thus I can engage in meaningful dialogue about matters of faith with my agnostic friend Judy Kupersmith and not feel that I am responsible in bringing her back to faith. That is in God's hands. I am open and honest with her about my own doubts and unbelief, knowing that such confessions do not hurt God's reputation. And I can wish her "Happy Easter," with my favorite words, "Christ is risen. He is risen, indeed," and know that she will accept those words from me without feeling that I am trying to cram my faith down her throat. My love for her and my friendship with her is not contingent on her making a profession of faith.

When I am with Judy, I am not thinking about what I should say to convince her of the truth of Christianity or what I should do to show her that truth. Rather I'm just enjoying our being together—and I can say with certainty that the feeling is mutual. Our friendship, a friendship between a Christian and an agnostic, is in some ways unusual, especially because we frequently discuss belief and unbelief. To Judy, I am the one person who understands her fundamentalist heritage—the one who listens without being threatened by her criticism and even ridicule of her legalistic Christian heritage.

I take Percy's challenge seriously: that the stumbling block to the gospel is not the message so much as it is the messenger. It may seem like a modest goal, but I trust that somehow through God's grace I can faithfully reflect the gospel message without repelling others—especially as I interact with those who have walked away from the faith.

14

Real Stories of Returning to Faith

*My own recovery, I realize, was greatly furthered by the love,
understanding, and support of those around me.
But I was also indebted to many unknown friends who had gone before
me and left their testimony to illumine the shadowy path.*

—ANNE MORROW LINDBERGH

Looking back over the previous chapters, I notice that stories of men are featured more often than stories of women. The themes I chose just happened to involve more men than women. Thus it is with no apologies that this chapter, which explores the struggles and difficulties—and yes, the victory—in finding faith, features three women. Though I have never met these women in person, I have come to know them through their writings. They are my "friends," and I call them by their first names: Kathleen, Madeleine and Annie. Kathleen and Annie are my generational peers. We survived adolescence in the late 1950s and were college "co-eds" of the 1960s. Madeleine is of the generation of our mothers. But for me, friendship has always easily spanned generations, especially as I have found friends—dead and alive—through my reading.

This is not a chapter on apologetics and proofs for God that may bring someone to belief from a rational course. Those books have already been written. These are women's stories (though thoroughly ungendered in their appeal) that embody more emotion than rational argument, more mystery than certitude, and sometimes more humor than solemnity. They are stories of finding faith as well as stories of returning to faith—stories for the believer and unbeliever alike. None of the characters in the dramas below has *arrived*. They are all on journeys, with detours and traffic jams and accidents and breakdowns, studying the road maps and heading for the same destination. I too am on that same journey, helped along by their noted landmarks and scribbled directions.

A Confession of "Amazing Grace"

One of the most effective means of evangelizing is through confession. Indeed much more effective than debate is confession—a confession in story form, immersed in humility. One such confession that has challenged me in my journey of faith is a spiritual autobiography by Kathleen Norris titled *Amazing Grace*. Here she tells about her slow return to the church after many years away. "Whenever I filled out a form that requested my religious affiliation, I would write 'nothing.'" Her return came in fits and starts, and even as her book concludes, she does not exude an air of confidence. Her pilgrimage is tenuous, as she feels it must be. In the preface she writes:

> If this book is in a way, my "coming out" as a Christian, I need to remind the reader (and myself) that this was not a forgone conclusion as I began to write it. If anything it seemed unlikely to me that I would ever find a place for myself within the religious tradition of my inheritance. In my previous books, *Dakota* and *The Cloister Walk*, I told the story of the move I made with my husband, David, from New York City, where I had worked for six years following graduation from college in Vermont, back to my ancestral home in South Dakota. My four grandparents had come to the state during homestead days to work as teachers, doctors, and Methodist ministers. Since 1974, I have lived in the

house where my mother was raised, and have found to my surprise that my move back to my roots proved to be in part a coming to terms with my religious inheritance. In 1985, I joined the Presbyterian church in my small town, which I had been attending sporadically since my move to South Dakota.[1]

As I read *Amazing Grace*, I began to resonate with Kathleen. Indeed, we have some of the same "friends"—particularly one nineteenth-century poet. "I latched on to Emily Dickinson," Kathleen writes. I also appreciate her straightforward talk and her refreshing perspectives on life. She is a feminist, yet she has an appreciation for the King James Version of the Bible despite its noninclusive language and the Lord's Prayer, beginning with "Our Father." The theme of *Amazing Grace* is reclaiming religious heritage. "Human inheritance is both blessing and curse," she writes. "My inheritance, my story, is of a Protestant Christianity—Methodist, Congregational, and Presbyterian. . . . I am now glad to identify myself as an ordinary Christian. . . . It's been a lively journey. And I am the person who departed, so long ago, and not the same at all."[2]

Kathleen's story of walking away from the Christian community in which she was raised is one that has been echoed countless times: "Despite having loved church as a child, I found it remarkably easy to walk away from it all when I went to college." But even before her college years, she had a "heady first encounter with Enlightenment and modern humanistic philosophies." At age sixteen, her faith began to waver. "A dose of the Enlightenment, a bit of Bertrand Russell, a dollop of Marx, a dash of Camus, and away with God!"[3]

What makes her story different from the stories of so many, however, is that she does not testify to losing her faith. After spending time with the Benedictines when she was in her mid-thirties, she began to "recognize that religious conversion had been alive in me during the years when I would have claimed to have no religion at all." Again she testifies, "I came to understand that God hadn't lost me even if I seemed for years to have misplaced God." In speaking of God, she quotes Catherine M. La Cugna: "One finds God because one is already found by God. Anything we would find on our own would not be GOD."[4]

Belief, Doubt and Sacred Ambiguity

One of the most helpful aspects of Kathleen's book is her honest struggle to believe. In a chapter entitled "Belief, Doubt and Sacred Ambiguity," she offers counsel and words of wisdom to those who find belief out of their grasp. She points out that the word *belief* is often misunderstood:

> I have come to see that my education, even my religious education, left me with a faulty and inadequate sense of religious belief as a kind of suspension of the intellect. . . . Yet I knew religious people who were psychologists, mathematicians, and scientists. So I had to assume that religious belief was simply beyond my grasp. Other people had it, I did not. And for a long time, even though I as attracted to church, I was convinced that I did not belong there, because my beliefs were not thoroughly solid, set in stone.[5]

It was through her relationship with Benedictine monks that Kathleen began to come to terms with her doubt and unbelief. They were far less concerned about her doubts than she was. "They seemed to believe that if I just kept coming back to worship, kept coming home, things would eventually fall into place." But that she would be "coming back to worship" was not a foregone conclusion. She offers a gross understatement when she concedes that for someone "anguishing over issues of belief and doubt, worship can become impossible." Not only was it impossible in her case, but the very effort sometimes triggered depression that continued for days.[6]

What seemed to help most was *remembering*, remembering her childhood—the Bible stories, the believing in God and the Sunday morning singing in church. This is where I resonate so completely with Kathleen. Her story is my story too. These had been "the great joys" of her childhood. "But if I had to find one word to describe how belief came to take hold in me," she writes, "it would be 'repetition.' " The repetition of the words of the hymn "Amazing Grace" and the repetition of the words of the creeds and the psalms and the Bible stories all served to develop her Christian faith.[7]

But even as she absorbed the religious heritage of her childhood, she was not free from doubt and unbelief. She was sometimes tempted to give up her struggle completely. Her resolution came from what might seem like an unlikely situation—one I readily identify with as a writer *and* believer.

> I would recall the wise words of William Stafford, who once said that he never had writer's block, because when a poem failed to come, he simply lowered his standards and accepted whatever came along. So, I lowered my standards. . . . Fortunately, believing, like writing, is more process than product, and is not, strictly speaking, a goal-oriented activity. There is no time limit.[8]

But if she lowered her standards for belief, it seemed reasonable that she should lower her standards for unbelief as well: "Perhaps my most important breakthrough with regard to belief came when I learned to be as consciously skeptical and questioning of my disbelief and my doubts as I was of my burgeoning faith."[9] Kathleen, who was away from the church for almost twenty years, is able to speak about unbelief in a way that challenges other "walk aways" to contemplate their own situations. In reflecting on apostasy, "the abandonment of one's religious faith," she writes:

> There is a certain pride inherent in apostasy, which often manifests itself as a remarkable faith in oneself, as in "I alone know what is right for me." Teachers, traditions, the family stories, and the beliefs of the common herd are all suspect; suspicion rather than trust is what defines the apostate. And it defines our age. The individual stands alone, a church of one, convinced that he or she is free of the tyranny of any creed or dogma. . . . If I had to come up with a synonym for apostasy . . . it is simple vanity.[10]

Roots

Perhaps the most important reason that Kathleen Norris's story speaks to the "walk-away" is because she emphasizes tradition—ancestry and roots. In apostasy, "the individual" stands alone. But in returning to faith, one is acknowledging the need for community, and frequently that community includes one's family, living and dead. So it was for Kathleen:

> Fear is not a bad place to start a spiritual journey. . . . It has meant coming to terms with my fundamentalist Methodist ancestors, no longer ignoring them but respecting their power.
>
> Conversion means starting with who we are, not who we wish we were. It means knowing where we come from. . . . And this is what I hope I have done, beginning with my move back to Dakota. My path of conversion may have a few elements of Indianness, because of the spirits of the land where I live, and because I understand that my faith comes from my grandmothers. . . .
>
> It came as an unwelcome surprise that my old ones led me back to church. It continues to surprise me that the church is for me both a new and an old frontier. And it astonishes me as much as it delights me that moving to the Dakota grasslands led me to a religious frontier where the new growth is fed by something very old, the 1,500-year tradition of Benedictine monasticism.[11]

In this area of coming to terms with one's tradition, Kathleen speaks with particular understanding and familiarity to the one who has walked away from faith. Some people have warm memories of childhood faith and all the rituals that attended it, while others may have many more negative than positive memories. Kathleen serves as a model in both her affirmation and recognition of her tradition and her pursuit of a fresh understanding of the faith.

Step by Step . . . I Made My Way Back to Church

For Kathleen, faith and community go together. She has absorbed the concept of community from the Benedictine monastery and recast it in her own ancestral religious community in her small-town South Dakota Presbyterian church. The church is a community of *corporate* belief. Individual belief and spirituality are part of a woven fabric of faith, and the weaker strands are secured by overlapping and by ties and knots that hold tightly. Yet there is always a careful balance: when too many strands are frayed by faithlessness and fractiousness, the fabric falls apart. But the tightly woven community of faith is the ideal; here we seek true communal worship:

> Communal worship is something I need; that it is an experience, not a philosophy or even theology. Whatever the pitch of my religious doubts, it is available to me for the asking. It seems a wonder to me that in our dull little town we can gather together to sing some great hymns, reflect on our lives, hear some astonishing scriptures (and maybe a boring sermon; you take your chances), offer some prayers and receive a blessing. . . .
>
> Step by step, as I made my way back to church, I began to find that many of the things modern people assume are irrelevant—the liturgical years, the liturgy of the hours, the Incarnation as an everyday reality—are in fact essential to my identity and my survival. I am not denying the past, or trying to bring it back, but am seeking in my inheritance what theologian Letty Russell terms "a usable past."[12]

The Crosswicks Confessions

When I first read the *Crosswicks Journals* many years ago, I knew I had found in the author a kindred spirit. I marked up the books and made good use of quotes in my teaching and speaking. But now as I have occasion to reread the books, I'm seeing things that I passed right by years ago. Madeleine L'Engle is firstly a mother and secondarily a writer and teacher and speaker (who often gives lectures at Wheaton College and other Christian schools). It was in those capacities and in her perspective on life that I identified with her. But now I discover that she, like me, was also a shopkeeper: she ran a general store with her husband. My store is a gift and garden shop that I have developed with my son. She writes that she, in her "reading Schopenhauer behind the counter, or writing in a journal between customers, must have seemed a very peculiar bird to the people who came in to our store."[13] I too have written in my journal between customers; and she and I are no doubt among a dying breed of shopkeepers who have read Schopenhauer behind the counter.

Like Kathleen, Madeleine writes very forthrightly about her struggle to believe. Long into her pilgrimage of faith, she confessed to her friend Luci Shaw that she had been living "in a sense of the absence of God."[14] Such feelings for her had been part of a way of life, from her earliest efforts to believe and continuing throughout the journey.

In the beginning of her journey, her reasoning was more pragmatic than "spiritual." She had attended church as a child, but "since the crisis in faith . . . that so often comes during college, I had seldom darkened the doors of a church when a service was going on." That was before she became a mother.

> But when our children were born, two things happened simultaneously. We cleaned up our language. . . . And we discovered that we did not want our children to grow up in a world which was centered on man to the exclusion of God. . . . I found myself explaining to the young minister that I did not believe in God, "but I've discovered that I can't live as though I didn't believe in him. As long as I don't need to say any more than that I try to live as though I believe in God, I would very much like to come to church—if you'll let me."
>
> So I became the choir director. Grandma was the organist. . . . She had been distressed because the church had been for so long without a choir. . . . I might not believe in God. . . . I might be terribly unsure about God, but I was happy working in his house.[15]

Because Madeleine is honest about issues of doubt and unbelief, she makes room for others to be honest and to express their own struggles. She, through her writing, has often supported me in times of weakness. "With my naked intellect I cannot believe in God," she confesses. Those nine stark words often resonate with my own faltering confession. "My intellect," she writes, "is convinced that any idea of the person's continuing and growing after death is absurd; logic goes no further than dust to dust." But all is not lost. There is another means for her—and for me—to find hope: "Images, in the literary sense of the word, take me much further."[16]

Finding God in Mystery

In seeking to come to terms with who God is, Madeleine challenges the notion that many of us subconsciously (if not consciously) believe that God is *located* somewhere in outer space, beyond the edges of the universe. This very notion contributes to unbelief, and her words are helpful to the one for whom God is remote and unapproachable.

> It doesn't work if I think of God as Out There. . . . Back when it was still possible to believe that this planet was the center of everything, that the sun and the moon and the stars were hung in the sky entirely for our benefit, it was quite possible to think of God as our Maker, Out There. . . . We have too often thought of God as being *outside* the universe, creating us, and looking at what happened to us, concerned, but Out There. But as I contemplate the vastness of the night sky on a clear, cold night, God Out There does not work. Out There is *too* far out. God becomes too remote. . . .
>
> Scripturally, God is always in and part of Creation; walking and talking with Adam and Eve, taking Abraham out to see the stars, wrestling with Jacob.
>
> And the most glorious possible demonstration of God *in* and *part of* Creation, God came to us in Jesus of Nazareth, fully participating in our human birth and life and death and offering us the glory of Easter.[17]

A God of Mystery

It is through art and literature—through the aesthetic senses—that we often come closest to God. And a touch of humor often helps. In her book *Circle of Quiet*, Madeleine repeats Dorothy Sayers's story of a Japanese man who is politely listening to a Christian who is trying to explain of the concept of the Trinity. The Japanese man is puzzled: "Honorable Father, very good. Honorable Son, very good. Honorable Bird I do not understand at all." Madeleine goes on with her own commentary:

> Very few of us understand Honorable Bird, except to acknowledge that without his power and grace nothing would be written, painted, or composed at all. To say anything beyond this about the creative process is

like pulling all the petals off a flower in order to analyze it, and ending up having destroyed the flower.[18]

In her writing, Madeleine seeks to unravel the mystery of God. "Her stories," writes Donald Hettinga, "are her responses to this God of Mystery. Her questions are not pat ones; they are questions that probe reality, questions that essay her faith—questions of the nature of God and the nature of evil, questions of love and questions of pain." But for Madeleine these questions remain unanswered: "The questions worth asking are not answerable." For her the God who is known is always juxtaposed with the God who is unknown:

> The mystery is tremendous, and the fascination that keeps me returning to the questions affirms that they are worth asking, and that any God worth believing in is the God not only of the immensities of the galaxies . . . but also the God of love who cares about the sufferings of us human beings and is here, with us, for us, in our pain and in our joy.[19]

Pilgrim at Tinker Creek

While recovering at home from outpatient surgery some time ago, I listened to the taped reading of Annie Dillard's Pulitzer Prize-winning book, *Pilgrim at Tinker Creek*. The book had been sitting unread on my bookshelf. I had started it years earlier, but I tend to do things in a hurry, and if there is one book that cannot be read in a hurry, it is this one. So, lying in bed, unable to sit up and read, I listened unhurriedly to Annie's words.

In many ways I identify with her. We were born a few months apart. She has her Tinker Creek; I had my Yellow River. Hers is a stream running through a valley in Virginia's Blue Ridge Mountains; mine is a river running through the forests and meadows of the two-hundred acre farm on which I grew up in northern Wisconsin. I loved that river in every season, and I spent countless hours getting to know its movements and melodies and rhythms, its forms and hues and temperament. I was a child then. I live far away from the river now. But Annie brings me back into a world I then perceived only dimly, one that has now passed me by. And as I go back to that world, I see more clearly through her eyes not only nature but human nature—and more than that, hints of God, hints that reach our senses all along the banks of Tinker Creek. Here are some of the words I listened to as I was recuperating:

> The sky is deep and distant, laced with sycamore limbs like a hatching of crossed swords. . . . My back rests on a steep bank under the sycamore; before me shines the creek . . . and above it rises the other bank, also steep, and planted in trees.
>
> I have never understood why so many mystics of all creeds experience the presence of God on mountaintops. Aren't they afraid of being blown away? . . . It often feels best to lay low, inconspicuous, instead of waving your spirit around from high places like a lightening rod. . . . Invisibility is the all-time great "cover." . . . And we the people are so vulnerable. Our bodies are shot with mortality. . . . That is why physical courage is so important—it fills, as it were, the holes—and why it is so invigorating. . . . The courage of children and beasts is a function of innocence. . . .
>
> When we lose our innocence—when we start feeling the weight of the atmosphere and learn that there's death in the pot—we take leave of our senses. Only children can hear the song of the male house mouse. Only children keep their eyes open.[20]

An American Childhood

Annie grew up in Pittsburgh—an environment very different from the rural setting in which I grew up. But our spiritual formation was similar. She tells of going to Bible camp every summer with her sister: "If our parents had known how pious and low church this camp was, they would have yanked us," she writes. The children all sang "rollicking hymns," prayed, and learned Scripture verses to the point that she had lodged in her brain "miles of Bible in memory."

"I had got religion at summer camp," she recalls, but time took its toll. "As the years wore on, the intervals between Julys at camp stretched," and in between were all the attractions of the world. "When I was fifteen, I felt it coming; now I was sixteen, and it hit. . . . I was what they called a live wire. I was shooting out sparks that were digging a pit around me, and I was sinking into that pit."[21]

From that point, her life began to unravel: "I quit the church. I wrote the minister a fierce letter." This was at the very time she was struggling with the question that would continue to haunt her: "If the all-powerful creator directs the world, then why all this suffering?" But most of her struggles were less philosophical.

> Funny how badly I'd turned out. . . . I woke up and found myself in juvenile court. I was hanging from crutches; for a few weeks after the drag race, neither knee worked. . . .
>
> I'd been suspended from school for smoking cigarettes. . . . Both my parents wept. . . . Why didn't I settle down, straighten out, shape up? I wondered, too. . . .
>
> Late one night, my parents and I sat at the kitchen table; there was a truce. We were all helpless, and tired of fighting. . . .
>
> "What are we going to do with you?"
>
> Mother raised the question. Her voice trembled and rose with emotion. . . .
>
> She sighed and said again, looking up and out of the night-black window, "Dear God, what are we going to do with you?" My heart went out to them. We all seemed to have exhausted our options. They asked me for fresh ideas, but I had none. I racked my brain, but couldn't come up with anything. The U.S. Marines didn't take sixteen-year-old girls.[22]

Philosopher at Tinker Creek

Annie has since grown up, and she has some of the clearest insights on belief and unbelief that I have ever encountered. And some of her insights are no insights at all—they are simply statements of fact. I concluded chapter ten with her reflections on pain and suffering—an issue that has troubled her since youth. Her verdict: "We do need reminding, not of what God can do, but of what he cannot do, or will not, which is to catch time in its free fall and stick a nickel's worth of sense into our days."[23]

It is Annie's humor that I enjoy the most. It is all too easy for Christians—and the church that is made up of Christians—to take themselves and their acts of piety too seriously. How silly we must often

look in the eyes of God—and I mean all of us, not just those who are
exercising the gift of "holy laughter" or the pastor who is sitting on the
church roof to raise money for a new "ministry" van. We all look silly.
We need to examine ourselves and our feeble attempts to connect with
God. And that which is truly feeble, Annie points out, may actually
connect with the heart of God more effectively than that which is so
smooth and professional. One of her stories illustrates this well:

> We had a wretched singer once, a guest from a Canadian congregation, a
> hulking blond girl with chopped hair and big shoulders, who wore
> tinted spectacles and a long lacy dress, and sang, grinning, to faltering
> accompaniment, an entirely secular song about mountains. Nothing
> could have been more apparent than that God loved this girl; nothing
> could more surely convince me of God's unending mercy than the con-
> tinued existence on earth of the church.
>
> The higher Christian churches—where, if anywhere, I belong—come
> at God with an unwarranted air of professionalism, with authority and
> pomp, as though they knew what they were doing, as though people in
> themselves were an appropriate set of creatures to have dealings with
> God. I often think of the set pieces of liturgy as certain words which
> people have successfully addressed to God without their getting killed.
> In the high churches they saunter through the liturgy like Mohawks
> along a strand of scaffolding who have long since forgotten their danger.
> If God were to blast such a service to bits, the congregation would be, I
> believe, genuinely shocked. But in the low churches you expect it any
> minute. This is the beginning of wisdom.[24]

Annie captures the continuity of history and our place in history
before God as well as any writer I know. I am a historian more than by
profession: I cannot think apart from history. Without history there
would be no future, no faith, no God. Annie's writing and thinking is
permeated by a sense of history—sacred history that comes in very
shabby clothes:

> A blur of romance clings to our notions of "publicans," "sinners," "the
> poor," "the people in the marketplace," "our neighbors," as though of
> course God should reveal himself, if at all, to these simple people, these

Sunday school watercolor figures, who are so purely themselves in their
tattered robes, who are single in themselves, while we now are various,
complex, and full at heart. We are busy. So, I see now, were they. Who
shall ascend into the hill of the Lord? Or who shall stand in his holy
place? There is no one but us. . . . There never has been. There have
been generations which remembered, and generations which forgot;
there has never been a generation of whole men and women who lived
well for even one day. Yet, some have imagined well, with honesty and
art, the detail of such a life, and have described it with such grace, that
we mistake vision for history, dream for description, and fancy that life
has devolved.[25]

"Yet, some have imagined well," she writes, "with honesty and art"
especially "artists and visionaries." These three women—Kathleen,
Madeleine and Annie—are artists and visionaries who have imagined
well. They speak of their own experiences through stories that have a
universal quality, stories that stir spiritual curiosity in those whose
senses have been numbed by rational arguments and complex explanations. They have walked away from the faith of their childhood and
returned with fresh insights, ever aware of their own vulnerabilities.
They are struggling to make sense out of life, sense out of faith, sense
out of God's reign in this world. Their struggles and challenges are
mine, and they nudge me along in my pilgrimage of faith.

Postscript

As I close this volume, I conclude with the opening lines: "Lord, I believe." I can say these words with confidence, but I will never exclude the self-effacing words that follow: "Help my unbelief." This six-word confession does not suggest that my belief is tentative—indeed, precisely the opposite. I confidently declare my faith while humbly recognizing my dependence on God. The second half of the confession is not equal to the first half; rather it is a qualifier. It does not take away from the force of the statement, "Lord, I believe." In fact, I believe it adds to it. It recognizes that without *help* from the Lord, my belief is utterly insufficient. It acknowledges that my belief does not rest on my ability to believe.

It is unfortunate that this confession is cited most often in discussions of wavering or faltering or weak faith. It is quoted in every book on doubt but rarely quoted in books celebrating the power of faith. Yet it ought to be part of our mindset—if not in our words—with every declaration of faith we make.

As a Christian I confess, along with the church through the ages, the Apostles' Creed. But even this powerful declaration of faith, it seems to me, ought to include a humble acknowledgment of our propensity for unbelief—and our need for help.

I believe in God, the Father almighty,
   creator of heaven and earth.

     Lord, help my unbelief.

I believe in Jesus Christ, his only Son, our Lord.
   who was conceived by the Holy Spirit
   and born of the virgin Mary.
   He suffered under Pontius Pilate,
   was crucified, died, and was buried;
   He descended to hell.
   The third day he rose again from the dead.
   He ascended to heaven
   and is seated at the right hand of God the Father almighty.
   From there he will come again to judge the living and the dead.

     Lord, help my unbelief.

I believe in the Holy Spirit,
   the holy catholic church,
   the communion of saints,
   the forgiveness of sins,
   the resurrection of the body,
   and the life everlasting.

     Lord, help my unbelief. Amen.

Notes

Preface
[1]W. P. Livingstone, *Mary Slessor of Calabar: Pioneer Missionary* (London: Hodder & Stoughton, 1915), pp. 142-43.
[2]Parker Palmer, *The Courage to Teach: Exploring the Inner Landscape of a Teacher's Life* (San Francisco: Jossey-Bass, 1998), pp. 85-86.

Chapter 1: "Lord, I Believe; Help My Unbelief"
[1]Meredith Gray, "Motherless," in *Mother: Tributes from the World's Great Literature*, ed. Lois M. Notkin (New York: Samuel Curl, 1943), p. 64.
[2]Emily Dickinson, "I Know That He Exists," in *The Poems of Emily Dickinson*, ed. R. W. Franklin (Cambridge: Harvard University Press, 1998), 1:389.
[3]Kelly James Clark, *When Faith Is Not Enough* (Grand Rapids, Mich.: Eerdmans, 1997), p. 9.
[4]Flannery O'Connor, *The Habit of Being*, ed. Sally Fitzgerald (New York: Farrar Straus Giroux, 1969), p. 451.
[5]"Jesus, Savior, Pilot Me," words by Edward Hopper, 1871.
[6]"Jesus I Come," words by William True Sleeper, 1887.

Chapter 2: A Tale of Two Evangelists
[1]Charles Templeton, *Farewell to God: My Reasons for Rejecting the Christian Faith* (Toronto: McClelland & Stewart, 1996), p. 17.
[2]Ibid., p. 4.
[3]Ibid., p. 5.
[4]Marshall Frady, *Billy Graham: A Parable of American Righteousness* (Boston: Little, Brown and Company, 1979), p. 28.
[5]Ibid., p. 48.
[6]Templeton, *Farewell to God*, p. 2.
[7]Paul C. Vitz, *Faith of the Fatherless: The Psychology of Atheism* (Dallas: Spence, 1999), pp. 6–9.

[8]Templeton, *Farewell to God*, p. 2.

[9]Stanley High, *Billy Graham* (London: The World's Work, 1957), pp. 72–73.

[10]Templeton, *Farewell to God*, pp. 2–3.

[11]Edward T. Babinski, *Leaving the Fold: Testimonies of Former Fundamentalists* (Amherst: Prometheus, 1995), pp. 285–86.

[12]Templeton, *Farewell to God*, p. 6.

[13]Ibid., pp. 7–8.

[14]Lee Strobel, *The Case for Faith: A Journalist Investigates the Toughest Objections to Christianity* (Grand Rapids, Mich.: Zondervan, 2000), p. 10.

[15]Babinski, *Leaving the Fold*, p. 289.

[16]Templeton, *Farewell to God*, p. 10.

[17]Ibid., pp. 12–13.

[18]Ibid.

[19]Ibid., p. 14.

[20]Strobel, *Case for Faith*, p. 14.

[21]Templeton, *Farewell to God*, p. 9.

[22]Strobel, *Case for Faith*, p. 15.

[23]Ibid., pp. 15–16. Templeton died on June 7, 2001.

[24]Templeton, *Farewell to God*, p. 9.

[25]Peter Berger, *A Far Glory: The Quest for Faith in an Age of Credulity* (New York: Macmillan, 1992), pp. 5–6.

[26]Ibid., p. 13.

[27]Berger, *A Far Glory*, p. 218.

[28]"Just As I Am," by Charlotte Elliott, 1836.

Chapter 3: The Smith Family

[1]Marie Henry, *The Secret Life of Hannah Whithall Smith* (Grand Rapids, Mich.: Zondervan, 1984), pp. 26, 47.

[2]Henry, *Secret Life*, pp. 119, 126.

[3]Ibid., p. 28.

[4]Ibid., p. 31.

[5]Ibid., p. 38.

[6]Ibid., p. 51.

[7]Ibid., p. 53.

[8]Ibid., p. 61.

[9]Ibid., p. 66.

[10]Ibid., pp. 72, 75.

[11]Ibid., pp. 74–75, 77.

[12]Ibid., p. 81.

[13]Ibid., p. 82.

[14]Ibid., pp. 83–85.

[15]Ibid., p. 118.

[16]Ibid., pp. 86–87.

[17]Ibid., p. 100.

[18]Ibid., pp. 159, 147.

[19]Ibid., p. 117.

[20]Ibid., p. 115.

[21]Walt Whitman, *Leaves of Grass*, in David L. Larsen, *The Company of the Creative: A Christian Reader's Guide to Great Literature and Its Themes* (Grand Rapids, Mich.: Kregel, 1999), pp. 275-76.

[22]Larsen, *Company of the Creative*, pp. 275–76.

[23]Augustus Hopkins Strong, *American Poets and Their Theology* (Freeport, N.Y.: Books for Libraries Press, 1968), p. 455.

[24]Henry, *Secret Life*, p. 145.

[25]Ibid., p. 153.

[26]Ibid.

[27]Ibid., pp. 43–44.

[28]Ibid., p. 69.

[29]George R. Hunsberger, *Bearing the Witness of the Spirit: Lesslie Newbigin's Theology of Cultural Plurality* (Grand Rapids, Mich.: Eerdmans, 1998), p. 89.

[30]Marjorie Holmes, *Who Am I God?* (New York: Bantam, 1971), pp. 25–26.

Chapter 4: Knowing God

[1]Parker Palmer, *The Courage to Teach: Exploring the Inner Landscape of a Teacher's Life* (San Francisco: Jossey-Bass, 1998), p. 86.

[2]"God vs. God" (editorial), *Christianity Today*, February 7, 2000, p. 34.

[3]Ibid.

[4]Ibid.

[5]Clark Pinnock et al., *The Openness of God* (Downers Grove, Ill.: InterVarsity Press, 1994).

[6]Timothy George, "A Transcendence-Starved Deity," *Christianity Today*, January 9, 1995, p. 34.

[7]Ibid.

[8]Christopher A. Hall and John Sanders, "Does God Know Your Next Move?" *Christianity Today*, May 21, 2001, p. 42.

[9]Jack Miles, *God: A Biography* (New York: Random House, 1995), pp. 21–22.

[10]Douglas F. Kelly, "Afraid of Infinitude," *Christianity Today*, January 9, 1995, p. 32.

[11]Clark Pinnock, "God as Most Moved Mover: How the Pentecostal Theology of Experience Is Changing Our Understanding of God," *Worship Leader*, November/December 2000, p. 34.

[12]Kelly James Clark, *When Faith Is Not Enough* (Grand Rapids, Mich.: Eerdmans, 1997), p. 8.

[13]Richard Muller, *Dictionary of Latin and Greek Theological Terms* (Grand Rapids, Mich.: Baker, 1985), p. 90.

[14]William J. Bouwsma, *John Calvin: A Sixteenth-Century Portrait* (New York: Oxford University Press, 1988), p. 155.

[15]J. Verkuyl, Contemporary *Missiology: An Introduction* (Grand Rapids, Mich.: Eerdmans, 1978), p. 36.

[16]Ibid.

[17]Ibid., pp. 35–36.

[18]Ibid., p. 35.

[19]J. H. Bavinck, *Faith and Its Difficulties*, trans. William B. Eerdmans Sr. (Grand Rapids, Mich.: Eerdmans, 1959), p. 9.

[20]Ibid., pp. 11–12.

[21]J. H. Bavinck, *The Church Between Temple and Mosque* (Grand Rapids, Mich.: Eerdmans, 1981), pp. 130, 134.

[22]C. S. Lewis, "Myth Became Fact," in *God in the Dock: Essays on Theology and Ethics*, ed. Walter Hooper (Grand Rapids, Mich.: Eerdmans, 1970), pp. 66-67.

[23]Louis A. Markos, "Myth Matters," *Christianity Today*, April 23, 2001, p. 35.

[24]C. S. Lewis, *Surprised by Joy* (New York: Harcourt Brace, 1955), pp. 228-29.

[25]Frederick Buechner, *Telling Secrets: A Memoir* (San Francisco: HarperCollins, 1991), p. 61.

[26]"How Great Thou Art," words by Stuart K. Hime, 1949.

Chapter 5: The Dark Night of the Soul

[1]Georgia Harkness, *The Dark Night of the Soul* (Nashville: Abingdon/Cokesbury Press, 1945), pp. 24–25.

[2]John of the Cross, *The Dark Night of the Soul*, in *An Anthology of Devotional Literature*, comp. Thomas S. Kepler (Grand Rapids, Mich.: Baker, 1977), pp. 284–85.

[3]Ibid., p. 286.

[4]William H. Shannon, *Thomas Merton's Dark Path: The Inner Experience of a Contemplative* (New York: Farrar Straus Giroux, 1981), p. 11.

[5]Raymond Bernard Blakney, *Meister Eckhart: A Modern Translation* (New York: Harper & Brothers, 1941), p. 85.

[6]D. L. Salvatera, "Thomas Merton," in *Dictionary of Christianity in America*, ed. Daniel G. Reid (Downers Grove, Ill.: InterVarsity Press, 1990), p. 731.

[7]Shannon, *Thomas Merton's Dark Path*, pp. 10–11.

[8]Ibid., pp. 26–27.

[9]Simone Weil, *A Spiritual Autobiography*, in *Pilgrim Souls: An Anthology of Spiritual Autobiographies*, ed. Amy Mandelker and Elizabeth Powers (New York: Simon & Schuster, 1999), pp. 500–501.

[10]Ibid., p. 503.

[11]Simone Weil, cited in Susan A. Taubes, "The Absent God," in *Toward a New Christianity: Readings in the Death of God Theology*, ed. Thomas J. J. Altizer (New York: Harcourt Brace & World, 1967), pp. 108–11.

[12]Taubes, "The Absent God," p. 107.

[13]Ibid., p. 114.

[14]*The Autobiography of Saint Thérèse of Lisieux: The Story of a Soul*, trans. John Beevers (New York: Doubleday, 1989), pp. 3, 116–19.

[15]Ibid., pp. 119–21.

[16]Henri Nouwen, "Adam's Peace," *World Vision*, August/September 1988, pp. 4–7.

[17]Michael Ford, *Wounded Prophet: A Portrait of Henri J. M. Nouwen* (New York: Doubleday, 1999), p. 167.

[18]Ibid., p. 172.

[19]Luci Shaw, *God in the Dark: Through Grief and Beyond* (Grand Rapids, Mich.: Zondervan, 1989), pp. 252, 265.

[20]Ibid., pp. 13–14.

[21]Ibid., p. 266.

[22]"Spirit of God, Who Dwells Within My Heart," words by George Croly, 1867.

Chapter 6: Biblical & Historical Reflections of Doubt & Unbelief

[1]Martin Marty, *Varieties of Unbelief* (New York: Holt, Rinehart & Winston, 1964), p. 36.

[2]William Klassan, *Judas: Betrayer or Friend of Jesus?* (Minneapolis: Fortress, 1996), pp. 3, 57.

[3]Ibid., p. 3.

[4]Gary R. Habermas, *The Thomas Factor: Using Your Doubts to Draw Closer to God* (Nashville: Broadman, 1999), p. 18.

[5]*Divine Principle* (New York: The Holy Spirit Association for the Unification of World Christianity, 1973), p. 348.

[6]Ruth Tucker, "Faith That Welcomes Doubt," *The Church Herald*, April 1991, p. 21.

[7]Eusebius, *Ecclesiastical History* (Grand Rapids, Mich.: Baker), p. 146.

[8]Ibid., pp. 258–59.

[9]Christopher B. Kaiser, "From Biblical Secularity to Modern Secularism," in *The Church Between Gospel and Culture*, ed. George Hunsberger and Craig Van Gelder (Grand Rapids, Mich.: Eerdmans, 1996), pp. 96–97.

[10]Roland H. Bainton, *Here I Stand: A Life of Martin Luther* (New York: New American Library, 1963), pp. 282–84.

[11]Ibid., pp. 286–87.

[12]William J. Bouwsma, *John Calvin: A Sixteenth-Century Portrait* (New York: Oxford University Press, 1988), p. 184.

[13]Elizabeth Wade White, *Anne Bradstreet: "The Tenth Muse"* (New York: Oxford University Press, 1971), pp. 177–78.

[14]Jim Herrick, *Against the Faith: Essays on Deists, Skeptics and Atheists* (Buffalo: Prometheus, 1985), pp. 150–51.

[15]Ibid., p. 151.

[16]Ibid., p. 155.

[17]Kelly James Clark, *When Faith Is Not Enough* (Grand Rapids, Mich.: Eerdmans, 1997), p. 12.

[18]Sergei Bulgakov, cited in *Pilgrim Souls: An Anthology of Spiritual Autobiographies*, ed. Amy Mandelker and Elizabeth Powers (New York: Simon & Schuster, 1999), pp. 92–93.

[19]Ibid., pp. 91, 94.

[20]Eugene Rolfe, cited in Marty, *Varieties of Unbelief,* p. 59.

[21]Christopher Fry, *A Sleep of Prisoners* (London: Oxford University Press, 1951), pp. 47–48.

Chapter 7: The Challenge of Science & Philosophy

[1]William A. Dembski, *Intelligent Design: The Bridge Between Science and Theology* (Downers Grove, Ill.: InterVarsity Press, 1999), pp. 49–50.

[2]Friedrich Nietzsche, cited in Will Durant, *The Story of Philosophy* (New York: Washington Square, 1964), p. 432.

[3]Durant, *Story of Philosophy,* p. 401.

[4]Ibid., p. 417.

[5]Ibid., pp. 403–4.

[6]David L. Larsen, *The Company of the Creative: A Christian Reader's Guide to Great Literature and Its Themes* (Grand Rapids, Mich.: Kregel, 1999), p. 138.

[7]Durant, *The Story of Philosophy,* p. 406.

[8]Friedrich Nietzsche, *The Antichrist,* cited in J. C. A. Gaskin, *Varieties of Unbelief: From Epicurus to Sartre* (New York: Macmillan, 1989), p. 185.

[9]Durant, *Story of Philosophy*, pp. 428–32.

[10]Friedrich Nietzsche, *Thus Spake Zarathustra*, cited in Durant, *Story of Philosophy*, p. 416.

[11]Friedrich Nietzsche, "The Madman," in *The Joyful Wisdom*, trans. Thomas Common (New York: Gordon Press, 1974), pp. 167-68.

[12]Colin Brown, *Philosophy and the Christian Faith* (Downers Grove, Ill.: InterVarsity Press, 1968), pp. 91–104.

[13]Gaskin, *Varieties of Unbelief*, p. 59.

[14]Voltaire, *Philosophical Dictionary*, cited in Brown, *Philosophy*, pp. 85–86.

[15]Steven Cahn, cited in Kelly James Clark, *When Faith Is Not Enough* (Grand Rapids, Mich.: Eerdmans, 1997), p. 11.

[16]Brown, *Philosophy*, p. 70.

[17]Ibid., p. 71.

[18]Durant, *The Story*, pp. 253, 263.

[19]Brown, *Philosophy*, pp. 91–104.

[20]Colin Brown, "The Ascent of Man," in *Eerdmans' Handbook to the History of Christianity*, ed. Tim Dowley (Grand Rapids, Mich.: Eerdmans, 1977), p. 541.

[21]Martin Marty, *Varieties of Unbelief* (New York: Holt, Rinehart & Winston, 1964), p. 58.

[22]Richard A. Muller, *The Study of Theology* (Grand Rapids, Mich.: Zondervan, 1991), p. 168.

[23]Alvin Plantinga, "Darwin, Mind and Meaning," *Books and Culture*, May/June 1996, p. 35.

[24]Ibid.

[25]Ibid.

[26]Ibid.

[27]Roger Lundin, *Emily Dickinson and the Art of Belief* (Grand Rapids, Mich.: Eerdmans, 1998, p. 4.

[28]Ibid., p. 34.

[29]Ibid., pp. 32, 34.

[30]Ibid., p. 34.

[31]Emily Dickinson, #365, in *The Poems of Emily Dickinson*, ed. R. W. Franklin (Cambridge, Mass.: Harvard University Press, 1996), 1:389.

[32]Ibid., #525, 1:534.

[33]Graham Greene, *The Potting Shed*, cited in Robert McAfee Brown, *Is Faith Obsolete?* (Philadelphia: Westminster Press, 1974), p. 89.

[34]5Huston Smith, *Why Religion Matters: The Fate of the Human Spirit in an Age of Disbelief* (San Francisco: HarperCollins, 2001), p. 59.

[35]Ibid., pp. 59–60, 62.

[36]Dale Kohler, cited in Smith, *Why Religion Matters*, p. 177.

[37]Dembski, *Intelligent Design*, p. 153.

[38]Smith, *Why Religion Matters*, p. 77.

[39]Dembski, *Intelligent Design*, p. 107.

[40]Smith, *Why Religion Matters*, p. 177.

[41]Dembski, *Intelligent Design*, p. 126.

[42]Ibid., p. 147.

[43]Ibid.

[44]Madeleine L'Engle, *A Circle of Quiet* (San Francisco: Harper & Row, 1972), pp. 57, 63.

[45]Ibid.

Chapter 8: The Challenge of Theological Complexities & Biblical Criticism

[1]Richard Dawkins, "Snake Oil and Holy Water," cited in Lee Strobel, *The Case for Faith: A Journalist Investigates the Toughest Objections to Christianity* (Grand Rapids, Mich.: Zondervan, 2000), p. 57.

[2]Marcus Borg, *Meeting Jesus Again for the First Time* (San Francisco: HarperCollins, 1994), p. 5.

[3]Ibid., pp. 7–8.

[4]Ibid., pp. 13, 15.

[5]Martin Gardner, *The Flight of Peter Fromm* (Amherst, N.Y.: Prometheus, 1994), pp. 274–75.

[6]Ibid., p. 275.

[7]Ibid., pp. 267, 272.

[8]Ibid., 272.

[9]Edmund Cohen, "Howard Walked Away," online posting (2000), Institute for First Amendment Studies <www.ifas.org/wa/cohen.html>.

[10]Paul Tillich, cited in Robert McAfee Brown, *Is Faith Obsolete?* (Philadelphia: Westminster Press, 1974), p. 89.

[11]Paul Tillich, *The Protestant Era* (London: Nisbet, 1951), p. xlii.

[12]Martin Marty, *Varieties of Unbelief* (New York: Holt, Rinehart & Winston, 1964), p. 121.

[13]Paul Tillich, cited in David L. Smith, *A Handbook of Contemporary Theology* (Wheaton, Ill.: Victor, 1992), p. 78.

[14]Grace Cali, *Paul Tillich First-Hand: A Memoir of the Harvard Years* (Chicago: Exploration, 1996), pp. 62–63.

[15]Ibid., p. 62.

[16]Ibid., p. 21.

[17]Thomas Paine, cited in Gardner, *Flight of Peter Fromm*, p. 173.

[18]Elmer S. Miller, *Nurturing Doubt: From Mennonite Missionary to Anthropologist in the Argentine Chaco* (Urbana: University of Illinois Press, 1995), pp. 12–13, 18.

[19]Ibid., p. 20.

[20]Ibid., pp. 22–23, 102.

[21]Ibid., p. 203.

[22]Fr. Michael Paul Gallagher, *Help My Unbelief* (Chicago: Loyola University Press, 1983), pp. 19-22.

[23]C. Stephen Evans, *Faith Beyond Reason: A Kierkegaardian Account* (Grand Rapids, Mich.: Eerdmans, 1998), p. 52.

[24]John Calvin, *Institutes of the Christian Religion*, cited in Paul Helm, *Faith and Understanding* (Grand Rapids, Mich.: Eerdmans, 1997), p. 180.

[25]F. W. Robertson, cited in Kelly James Clark, *When Faith Is Not Enough* (Grand Rapids, Mich.: Eerdmans, 1997), pp. 94–95.

Chapter 9: The Challenge of Psychology & Social Issues

[1]Konstantin Mochulsky, introduction to *The Brothers Karamazov*, by Fyodor Dostoyevsky, trans. Andrew MacAndrew (New York: Bantam, 1981), p. xii.

[2]Ibid.

[3]Ibid., pp. xiii, xvi.

[4]Fyodor Dostoyevsky, *The Brothers Karamazov*, trans. Andrew MacAndrew (New York: Bantam, 1981), pp. 159–60.

[5]Paul Pruyser, *Between Belief and Unbelief* (New York: Harper & Row, 1974), p. 8.

[6]Karl Marx and Friedrich Engels, *Manifesto of the Communist Party* and Karl Marx, *Capital*, in *Great Books* (Chicago: Encyclopaedia Britannica, 1952), 50:430, 372; Robert McAfee Brown, *Is Faith Obsolete?* (Philadelphia: Westminster Press, 1974), pp. 134–37.

[7]H. L. Philip, *Freud and Religious Belief* (Westport, Conn.: Greenwood, 1956), pp. 2–10.

[8]Ibid.

[9]Ibid. p. 15.

[10]Ibid., pp. 23, 34.

[11]Ibid., pp. 68, 71, 72.

[12]Helen Barrett Montgomery, *Helen Barrett Montgomery: From Campus to World Citizenship* (New York: Revell, 1940), p. 22.

[13]Colin Brown, *Philosophy and the Christian Faith* (Downers Grove, Ill.: InterVarsity Press, 1968), pp. 108–9.

[14]Paul Pruyser, *Between Belief and Unbelief*, p. 59.

[15]Ibid., p. 60.

[16]Wallace B. Clift, *Jung and Christianity: The Challenge of Reconciliation* (New York: Crossroad, 1982), pp. 3–4.

[17]Ibid., p. 6.

[18]Ibid., p. 5–8.

[19]Gerhard Wehr, *Jung: A Biography*, trans. David M. Weeks (Boston: Shambhala, 1987), pp. 292–93.

[20]Bruce Hunsberger, "Social-Psychological Causes of Faith," *Free Inquiry*, summer 1999, p. 35.

[21]J. Budziszewski, "Escape from Nihilism," *CPOL Readings*, fall 1998, p. 45.

[22]David Dean, "Just As I Am," (2000) Institute for First Amendment Studies <www.ifas.org/wa/dean.html>.

[23]Ibid.

[24]*Chicago Tribune*, October 25, 1987, G14.

[25]Emily Dickinson, #520, in *The Poems of Emily Dickinson*, ed. R. W. Franklin (Cambridge: Harvard University Press, 1996), 1:528.

Chapter 10: Disappointment with God & with Fellow Christians

[1]Shusaku Endo, *Silence*, trans. William Johnston (New York: Taplinger, 1980), p. 55.

[2]Ibid., pp. 60–61.

[3]Ibid., pp. 68–69.

[4]Ibid., pp. 167–68.

[5]Thomas Edward Dow, *When Storms Come* (Kitchener, Ontario: Thomas Dow, 1995), pp. 52–53.

[6]Harold S. Kushner, *When Bad Things Happen to Good People* (New York: Schocken, 1981), p. 133.

[7]Nicholas Wolterstorff, *Lament for a Son* (Grand Rapids, Mich.: Eerdmans, 1987), p. 68.

[8]Ibid., pp. 76–82.

[9]Judy Kupersmith to Ruth A. Tucker, March 31, 2000.

[10]Ibid.

[11]Ibid.

[12]Frank Schaeffer, *Portofino* (New York: Macmillan, 1992), pp. 47–48.

[13]Ibid., pp. 51–53.

[14]Ibid., p. 172.

[15]Ibid., p. 219.

[16]Austin Miles, *Don't Call Me Brother: A Ringmaster's Escape from the Pentecostal Church* (Buffalo: Prometheus, 1989), pp. 295, 148, 268.

[17]Martin Marty, *A Cry of Absence: Reflections for the Winter of the Heart* (Grand Rapids, Mich.: Eerdmans, 1997), pp. xi–xii.

[18]Ibid., p. xii.

[19]Ibid., p. 1.

[20]Ibid., pp. 109–10.

[21]Ibid., p. 110.

[22]Annie Dillard, *Holy the Firm* (New York: Harper & Row, 1977), p. 60.

[23]Ibid.

[24]Ibid., p. 61.

Chapter 11: The New Life of Unbelief

[1]Judy Kupersmith to Ruth A. Tucker, March 31, 2000.

[2]Bruce Hunsberger, "Social-Psychological Causes of Faith," *Free Inquiry*, summer 1999, p. 35.

[3]Rudolf Nelson, *The Making and Unmaking of an Evangelical Mind: The Case of Edward Carnell* (New York: Cambridge University Press, 1987), p. 5.

[4]James Bruckner, "The Anguish of Losing Faith" (2000) Institute for First Amendment Studies <www.ifas.org/wa/bruckner.html>.

[5]Ibid.

[6]Ibid.

[7]Ibid.

[8]Ibid.

[9]Ibid.

[10]Ibid.

[11]Ibid.

[12]Ibid., 3/27/98.

[13]Edie Cottle, "January '98 Was a Momentous Month" (2000) Institute for First Amendment Studies <www.ifas.org/wa/cottle.html>.

[14]Ibid. What role does Satan play in the process of walking away from faith? That, I suppose, is a valid question, and some will no doubt fault me for not dealing with this issue until late in the book—and then only in a footnote. I believe in the power of evil in this world—a power that is referred to in Scripture as Satan and demonic forces. That Satan has a part in all the evil in this world and in anything that detracts from the worship of Christ, to me, seems obvious. But to be more specific than that would, for me, be no more than speculation. When someone tells me (as has actually happened) that Satan caused a three-hour delay in their flight departure out of O'Hare, I wonder who the source of that information was. If I were to associate the delay to cosmic power (as opposed to over crowded skies), I would more likely ask what God might have in this delay for me. Is it possible that the Lord might want me to reach out to some needy person or simply slow down and spend a couple of hours meditating on the psalms? Apart from Scripture, I do not know the mind of God, nor do I know the power and ways and mind of the devil.

[15]Ibid.

[16]Ibid., 7/19/98.

[17]Steve Locks, "Leaving Christianitiy" (2000) Institute for First Amendment Studies <www.ifas.org/wa/locks.html>.

[18]Ibid.

[19]Ibid.

[20]Ibid.

[21]A. Wetherell Johnson, *Created for Commitment* (Wheaton, Ill.: Tyndale House, 1982), pp. 40–43.

[22]Ibid.

Chapter 12: Missionaries of Unbelief

[1]Holly Chrisman, "I Deconverted from Christianity" (October 24, 1995), The Ex-tian Home Page <www.infidels.org/electronic/email/ex-tian/Holly Chrisman.html>.

[2]Dan Barker, *Losing Faith in Faith: From Preacher to Atheist* (Madison, Wisc.: FFRF, Inc., 1992), p. 28.

[3]Ibid., pp. 29–30.

[4]Ibid., p. 31.

[5]Ibid., pp. 31–32.

[6]Ibid., p. 44.

[7]Ibid., p. 45.

[8]Ibid., p. 46.

[9]Ibid., pp. 34, 47.

[10]Chris Ashton, "Why I Left the Faith," The Ex-tian Home Page <www.infidels.org>.

[11]Ibid.

[12]Peter De Vries, cited in D. Bruce Lockerbie, *Dismissing God: Modern Writers' Struggle Against Religion* (Grand Rapids, Mich.: Baker, 1998), p. 218.

[13]Ibid., p. 219.

[14]Ibid.

[15]Peter De Vries, *The Blood of the Lamb* (Boston: Little, Brown & Company, 1961), p. 241.

[16]Peter De Vries, *Slouching Towards Kalamazoo* (Boston: Little, Brown & Company, 1983), pp. 81–82.

[17]Ibid., p. 207.

[18]Ibid.

[19]Ibid., pp. 235-36.

[20]J. C. A. Gaskin, *Varieties of Unbelief: From Epicurus to Sartre* (New York: Macmillan, 1989), p. 195.

[21]Bertrand Russell, cited in Philip Yancey, *Disappointment with God: Three Questions No One Asks Aloud* (Grand Rapids, Mich.: Zondervan, 1988), p. 253.

[22]C. S. Lewis, *Surprised by Joy* (New York: Harcourt, Brace, 1955), p. 226.

Chapter 13: Answering Doubt & Unbelief

[1]Mark Buchanan, "The Benefit of the Doubt," *Christianity Today*, April 3, 2000, p. 65.

[2]Ibid., p. 67.

[3]James Bruckner, "The Anguish of Losing Faith" (2000) Institute for First Amendment Studies <www.ifas.org/wa/bruckner.html>.

[4]Sally and Robert Fitzgerald, *Flannery O'Connor: Mystery and Manners* (New York: Farrar Straus Giroux, 1969), p. 32.

[5]Flannery O'Connor, *The Habit of Being*, ed. Sally Fitzgerald (New York: Farrar Straus

Giroux, 1979), pp. 353–54.

[6]Ibid., pp. 133–34, 154.

[7]Ibid., pp. 307–8.

[8]Ibid., pp. 451–2.

[9]Ibid., p. 476.

[10]Gregory A. Boyd, *Letters from a Skeptic* (Wheaton, Ill.: Victor, 1994), p. 9.

[11]Ibid., pp. 119–20.

[12]Ibid., pp. 121–22.

[13]Lee Strobel, *The Case for Faith: A Journalist Investigates the Toughest Objections to Christianity* (Grand Rapids, Mich.: Zondervan, 2000), p. 150.

[14]Walker Percy, *The Second Coming* (New York: Farrar, Straus & Giroux, 1980), p. 188.

[15]Roy Berkenbosch, "Reformed Theology 101: What Being Reformed Is All About," *The Banner*, February 14, 1999, p. 17.

Chapter 14: Real Stories of Returning to Faith

[1]Kathleen Norris, *Amazing Grace: A Vocabulary of Faith* (New York: Riverhead, 1998), p. 6.

[2]Ibid., pp. 22–25.

[3]Ibid., pp. 41, 258.

[4]Ibid., pp. 41–42, 104.

[5]Ibid., p. 62.

[6]Ibid., pp. 63–64.

[7]Ibid., p. 64.

[8]Ibid., p. 66.

[9]Ibid., pp. 66–67.

[10]Ibid., pp. 202–3.

[11]Kathleen Norris, *Dakota: A Spiritual Geography* (New York: Ticknor & Fields, 1993), pp. 130-31.

[12]Ibid., p. 133.

[13]Madeleine L'Engle, *A Circle of Quiet* (San Francisco: Harper & Row, 1972), p. 76.

[14]Luci Shaw, *God in the Dark: Through Grief and Beyond* (Grand Rapids, Mich.: Zondervan, 1989), p. 265.

[15]L'Engle, *Circle of Quiet*, pp. 34, 35, 57.

[16]Ibid., p. 41.

[17]Madeleine L'Engle, *A Stone for a Pillow* (Wheaton, Ill.: Harold Shaw, 1986), p. 86.

[18]L'Engle, *Circle of Quiet*, p. 50.

[19]Cited in Donald R. Hettinga, *Presenting Madeleine L'Engle* (New York: Twayne, 1993), p. 19.

[20]Annie Dillard, *Pilgrim at Tinker Creek* (San Francisco: Harper & Row, 1974), pp. 89–90.

[21]Annie Dillard, *An American Childhood* (New York: HarperCollins, 1987), pp. 132–33, 222, 224.

[22]Ibid., pp. 233–36.

[23]Dillard, *Holy the Firm* (New York: Harper & Row, 1977), p. 61.

[24]Ibid., pp. 58-59.

[25]Ibid., pp. 56-57.

Selected Bibliography

Altizer, Thomas J. J., ed. *Toward A New Christianity: Readings in the Death of God Theology*. New York: Harcourt, Brace & 'World, 1967.

Babinski, Edward T. *Leaving the Fold: Testimonies of Former Fundamentalists*. Amherst, N.Y.: Prometheus, 1995.

Barker, Dan. *Losing Faith in Faith: From Preacher to Atheist*. Madison, Wis.: FFRF, 1992.

Bavinck, J. H. *The Church Between Temple and Mosque*. Grand Rapids, Mich.: Eerdmans, 1981.

——————. *Faith and Its Difficulties*. Translated by Wm. B. Eerdmans Sr. Grand Rapids, Mich.: Eerdmans, 1959.

Berger, Peter. *A Far Glory: The Quest for Faith in an Age of Credulity*. New York: Macmillan, 1992.

Borg, Marcus. *Meeting Jesus Again for the First Time*. San Francisco: HarperCollins, 1994.

Boyd, Gregory A. *Letters from a Skeptic*. Wheaton, Ill.: Victor, 1994.

Brown, Colin. *Philosophy and the Christian Faith*. Downers Grove, Ill.: InterVarsity Press, 1968.

Brown, Robert McAfee. *Is Faith Obsolete?* Philadelphia: Westminster Press, 1974.

Buechner, Frederick. *Telling Secrets: A Memoir*. San Francisco: HarperCollins, 1991.

Cali, Grace. *Paul Tillich First-Hand: A Memoir of the Harvard Years*. Chicago: Exploration, 1996.

Clark, Kelly James. *When Faith Is Not Enough*. Grand Rapids, Mich.: Eerdmans, 1997.

Clift, Wallace B. *Jung and Christianity: The Challenge of Reconciliation*. New York: Crossroad, 1982.

Dembski, William A. *Intelligent Design: The Bridge Between Science and Theology*. Downers Grove, Ill.: InterVarsity Press, 1999.

Dillard, Annie. *An American Childhood*. New York: HarperCollins, 1987.

——————. *Holy the Firm*. New York: Harper & Row, 1977.

——————. *Pilgrim at Tinker Creek*. San Francisco: Harper & Row, 1974.

Dostoyevsky, Fyodor. *The Brothers Karamazov*. Translated by Andrew MacAndrew. New York: Bantam, 1981.

Durant, Will. *The Story of Philosophy*. New York: Washington Square Books, 1964.

De Vries, Peter. *The Blood of the Lamb*. Boston: Little, Brown, 1961.

──────. *Slouching Towards Kalamazoo*. Boston: Little, Brown, 1983.

Dow, Thomas Edward. *When Storms Come*. Kitchener, Ontario: Thomas Dow, 1995.

Endo, Shusako. *Silence*. Translated by William Johnston. New York: Taplinger, 1980.

Evans, C. Stephen. *Faith Beyond Reason: A Kierkegaardian Account*. Grand Rapids, Mich.: Eerdmans, 1998.

Fitzgerald, Sally and Robert. *Flannery O'Connor: Mystery and Manners*. New York: Farar, Straus & Giraux, 1969.

Ford, Michael. *Wounded Prophet: A Portrait of Henri J. M. Nouwen*. New York: Double-day, 1999.

Franklin, R. W., ed. *The Poems of Emily Dickinson*. 3 vols. Cambridge, Mass.: Harvard University Press, 1996.

Gallagher, Fr. Michael Paul. *Help My Unbelief*. Chicago: Loyola University Press, 1988.

Gardner, Martin. *The Flight of Peter Fromm*. Amherst, N.Y.: Prometheus, 1994.

Gaskin, J. C. A. *Varieties of Unbelief: From Epicurus to Sartre*. New York: Macmillan, 1989.

Gaylor, Annie Laurie, ed. *Women Without Superstition, "No Gods—No Masters": The Collected Writings of Women Freethinkers of the Nineteenth and Twentieth Centuries*. Madison, Wis.: FFRF, 1997.

Habermas, Gary R. *The Thomas Factor: Using Your Doubts to Draw Closer to God*. Nashville: Broadman, 1999.

Harkness, Georgia. *The Dark Night of the Soul*. Nashville: Abingdon-Cokesbury, 1945.

Helm, Paul. *Faith and Understanding*. Grand Rapids, Mich.: Eerdmans, 1997.

Henry, Marie. *The Secret Life of Hannah Whithall Smith*. Grand Rapids, Mich.: Zondervan, 1984.

Herrick, Jim. *Against the Faith: Essays on Deists, Skeptics and Atheists*. Buffalo: Prometheus, 1985.

Hettinga, Donald R. *Presenting Madeleine L'Engle*. New York: Twayne, 1993.

Holmes, Marjorie. *Who Am I God?* New York: Bantam, 1971.

Klassen, William. *Judas: Betrayer or Friend of Jesus?* Minneapolis: Fortress, 1996.

Kushner, Harold S. *When Bad Things Happen to Good People*. New York: Schocken, 1981.

L'Engle, Madeleine. *A Circle of Quiet*. San Francisco: Harper & Row, 1972.

──────. *A Stone for a Pillow*. Wheaton, Ill.: Harold Shaw, 1986.

Lewis, C. S. *God in the Dock: Essays on Theology and Ethics*. Edited by Walter Hooper. Grand Rapids, Mich.: Eerdmans, 1970.

──────. Surprised by Joy. New York: Harcourt Brace, 1955.

Lockerbie, D. Bruce. *Dismissing God: Modern Writers' Struggle Against Religion*. Grand Rapids, Mich.: Baker, 1998.

Lundin, Roger. *Emily Dickinson and the Art of Belief*. Grand Rapids, Mich.: Eerdmans, 1998.

Marty, Martin. *A Cry of Absence: Reflections for the Winter of the Heart*. Grand Rapids, Mich.: Eerdmans, 1997.

──────. *Varieties of Unbelief*. New York: Holt, Rinehart & Winston, 1964.

Miles, Austin. *Don't Call Me Brother: A Ringmaster's Escape from the Pentecostal Church*. Buffalo: Prometheus, 1989.

Miles, Jack. *God: A Biography*. New York: Random House, 1995.

Miller, Elmer S. *Nurturing Doubt: From Mennonite Missionary to Anthropologist in the Argentine Chaco.* Urbana: University of Illinois Press, 1995.

Muller, Richard A. *The Study of Theology.* Grand Rapids, Mich.: Zondervan, 1991.

Nelson, Rudolf. *The Making and Unmaking of an Evangelical Mind: The Case of Edward Carnell.* New York: Cambridge University Press, 1987.

Norris, Kathleen. *Amazing Grace: A Vocabulary of Faith.* New York: Riverhead, 1998.

—————. *Dakota: A Spiritual Geography.* New York: Ticknor & Fields, 1993.

O'Connor, Flannery. *The Habit of Being.* Edited by Sally Fitzgerald. New York: Farrar, Straus, & Giroux, 1979.

Palmer, Parker. *The Courage to Teach.* San Francisco: Jossey-Bass, 1998.

Percy, Walker. *The Second Coming.* New York: Farrar, Straus & Giroux, 1980.

Philip, H. L. *Freud and Religious Belief.* Westport, Conn.: Greenwood, 1956.

Pruyser, Paul. *Between Belief and Unbelief.* New York: Harper & Row, 1974.

Schaeffer, Frank. *Portofino.* New York: Macmillan, 1992.

Shannon, William H. *Thomas Merton's Dark Path: The Inner Experience of a Contemplative.* New York: Farrar, Straus & Giroux, 1981.

Shaw, Luci. *God in the Dark: Through Grief and Beyond.* Grand Rapids, Mich.: Zondervan, 1989.

Smith, Huston. *Why Religion Matters: The Fate of the Human Spirit in an Age of Disbelief.* San Francisco: HarperCollins, 2001.

Strobel, Lee. *The Case for Christ: A Journalist's Personal Investigation of the Evidence for Jesus.* Grand Rapids, Mich.: Zondervan, 1998.

—————. *The Case for Faith: A Journalist Investigates the Toughest Objections to Christianity.* Grand Rapids, Mich.: Zondervan, 2000.

Strong, Augustus Hopkins. *American Poets and Their Theology.* Freeport, N.Y.: Books for Libraries Press, 1968.

Templeton, Charles. *Farewell to God: My Reasons for Rejecting the Christian Faith.* Toronto: McClelland & Stewart, 1996.

Tillich, Paul. *The Protestant Era.* London: Nisbet, 1951.

Vitz, Paul C. *Faith of the Fatherless: The Psychology of Atheism.* Dallas: Spence, 1999.

Wehr, Gerhard. *Jung: A Biography.* Translated by David M. Weeks. Boston: Shambhala, 1987.

Wolterstorff, Nicholas. *Lament for a Son.* Grand Rapids, Mich.: Eerdmans, 1987.

Yancey, Philip. *Disappointment with God: Three Questions No One Asks Aloud.* Grand Rapids, Mich.: Zondervan, 1988.

—————. *Reaching for the Invisible God: What Can We Expect to Find?* Grand Rapids, Mich.: Zondervan, 2000.

Index

Abelard, Peter, 90
Adam, 62, 82, 161, 217
Anselm, 90
apologetics, 27, 115, 117, 119-21, 124, 205, 210
Apostles' Creed, 223
Aquinas, Thomas, 59, 90
Augustine of Hippo, 59
Barker, Dan, 17, 170-71, 183-91, 194-95
Barth, Karl, 58, 122-23, 137, 141
Bavinck, J. H., 60-63, 65
Behe, Michael, 114-15
Benedictine, 212, 214. *See* monasticism
Berger, Peter, 40-42
biblical criticism, 12, 48
Bob Jones University, 34
Bonhoeffer, Dietrich, 180
Borg, Marcus, 120-21, 123-24, 127
Boyd, Gregory, 55, 120, 204-5
Bradstreet, Anne, 92
Brooks, Philips, 184-85
Brothers Karamazov, The, 134, 136
Buchanan, Mark, 196-98
Budziszewski, J., 146
Bulgakov, Sergei, 96, 133
Bultmann, Rudolf, 123, 187
Calvin, John, 22, 24, 60, 91-92, 124, 131-32, 154, 159-60, 192

Catholicism, Roman, 9, 14, 50, 68, 70-72, 74-75, 90, 100, 103, 106, 122, 139, 151, 158-60, 201-2
Chesterton, G. K., 122, 180
Cohen, Edmund, 124
Copernicus, Nicolaus, 106
dark night of the soul, 12, 67-68, 74, 76
Darwin, Charles, 107-12, 114, 138
De Vries, Peter, 191-95
Dean, David, 147-48
death of God, 99-100, 102, 125
Dembski, William, 99, 112-14
depression, 38, 46, 48, 67, 75-76, 85, 87, 91, 127, 147, 212
Dickinson, Emily, 24, 108-11, 115, 149, 211
Dillard, Annie, 164-65, 218
disappointment with God, 12, 33, 48, 79, 151, 154, 158, 162, 164, 188, 199
Dostoyevsky, Fyodor, 134-35. *See also Brothers Karamazov, The*
Eckhart, Meister, 69-70
Edwards, Jonathan, 92

Endo, Shusaku, 151
Eve, 62, 82, 161, 217
evolution, 107-8, 111-12, 115, 149
feminism, 148
Flight of Peter Fromm, The, 122. *See also* Fromm, Peter
Freud, Sigmund, 34, 134-35, 138-41, 143, 145, 149
Fromm, Peter, 122-24, 127
fundamentalism, fundamentalists, 9, 13, 20, 27, 52, 122, 124, 128, 147-48, 158, 172, 177-78, 184, 186-87, 190-91, 208, 214
Gallagher, Fr. Michael Paul, 25, 130-32
goddess worship, 149
Graham, Billy, 13, 29-30, 32-33, 39-43, 111
Holmes, Marjorie, 52-53
homosexuality, 147-48, 178
Hume, David, 92, 99, 103-5, 180
immorality, 48, 83
Ingersoll, Robert, 35, 180
intelligent design, 99, 112-14
James, William, 141-43, 180
John of the Cross, 68-69

John the Baptist, 83-87
Johnson, Wetherell, 181-82
Judas, 83-84, 87-88
Jung, Carl, 143-44, 149
Kant, Immanuel, 92, 99, 103, 105-6
Kierkegaard, Søren, 137
Kingsley, Mary, 8
Kupersmith, Judy, 156, 165, 171, 208
Kushner, Harold, 154
L'Engle, Madeleine, 115-16, 215
lesbianism, 148
Lewis, C. S., 63-64, 180, 186, 195
liberalism, 9, 122, 141
Luther, Martin 16, 29, 58-59, 91, 106
Marty, Martin, 82, 106, 125, 162-64
Marxism, 95, 96
Merton, Thomas, 70-72, 75-76, 179
Miles, Austin, 161
Miles, Jack, 57-58
Miller, Elmer, 128-30
modernism, 16, 41, 97, 149
Montgomery, Helen Barrett, 140-41
Moody Bible Institute, 147-48
Moon, Sun Myung, 85
mystics, 65, 67, 70-73, 219
Nelson, Rudolf, 173

new age, 16
Newbigin, Lesslie, 25, 52
Niebuhr, Reinhold, 123
Nietzsche, Friedrich, 99-102, 180, 206
Norris, Kathleen, 210, 213
Nouwen, Henri, 75-77
Noyes, John Humphrey, 146
O'Connor, Flannery, 27, 200-203
Openness of God, 55
Otloh of St. Emmeram, 90
Paine, Thomas, 35, 93, 127, 130, 180
Peter, the apostle, 84, 86-88, 202
Pinnock, Clark, 55, 57-59
Polkinghorne, John, 113
Polycarp, 89
Portofino, 158-60
postmodernism, 16
process theology, 57
Quakerism, 45
Reformed churches, theology, 9, 24, 52, 59-60, 143, 158, 160, 192, 204, 207
Robertson, F. W., 132-33
Russell, Bertrand, 35, 50, 180, 194-95, 211, 215
Sanders, John, 55, 57
Schaeffer, Franky, 158-60, 186
Schleiermacher, Friedrich, 99, 141, 143,

145-46
scientism, 111-12
Shaw, Luci, 77-78, 216
Slessor, Mary, 8
Smith, Hannah Whitehall, 13, 43-53
Smith, Huston, 111, 113
Smith, Robert Pearsall, 13, 43, 45-50
Southern Baptists, 52, 206
Spinoza, Baruch, 99
Spong, John Shelby, 184-85
Strobel, Lee, 39, 120
Taylor, Robert, 93
Templeton, Charles, 13, 29-31, 39, 43
Teresa of Ávila, 68
theodicy, 118, 154
Thérèse of Lisieux, 74, 75, 77
Thomas, doubting, 84, 87-88, 198
Tillich, Paul, 123-27, 187
Unification Church, 85
Voltaire, François Marie, 35, 92, 103, 194
Weil, Simone, 72-75
Wesley, John, 92
Whitefield, George, 92
Whitman, Walt, 49-50
Wolterstorff, Nicholas, 154
Xavier, Francis, 151
Youth for Christ, 32, 35, 128